Social Media in Industrial

WHY WE POST

PUBLISHED AND FORTHCOMING TITLES:

Download free: www.ucl.ac.uk/ucl-press

Why
We
Post

Social Media in Industrial China

Xinyuan Wang

First published in 2016 by
UCL Press
University College London
Gower Street
London WC1E 6BT

Available to download free: www.ucl.ac.uk/ucl-press

A CIP catalogue record for this book is available
from The British Library.

ISBN: 978–1–910634–62–2 (Hbk.)
ISBN: 978–1–910634–63–9 (Pbk.)
ISBN: 978–1–910634–64–6 (PDF)
ISBN: 978–1–910634–65–3 (epub)
ISBN: 978–1–910634–66–0 (mobi)
ISBN: 978–1–911307–30–3 (html)
DOI: 10.14324/111.9781910634646

Introduction to the series Why We Post

This book is one of a series of 11 titles. Nine are monographs devoted to specific field sites (including this one) in Brazil, Chile, China, England, India, Italy, Trinidad and Turkey – they will be published in 2016–17. The series also includes a comparative book about all our findings, published to accompany this title, and a book which contrasts the visuals that people post on Facebook in the English field site with those on our Trinidadian field site.

When we tell people that we have written nine monographs about social media around the world, all using the same chapter headings (apart from Chapter 5), they are concerned about potential repetition. However, if you decide to read several of these books (and we very much hope you do), you will see that this device has been helpful in showing the precise opposite. Each book is as individual and distinct as if it were on an entirely different topic.

This is perhaps our single most important finding. Most studies of the internet and social media are based on research methods that assume we can generalise across different groups. We look at tweets in one place and write about 'Twitter'. We conduct tests about social media and friendship in one population, and then write on this topic as if friendship means the same thing for all populations. By presenting nine books with the same chapter headings, you can judge for yourselves what kinds of generalisations are, or are not, possible.

Our intention is not to evaluate social media, either positively or negatively. Instead the purpose is educational, providing detailed evidence of what social media has become in each place and the local consequences, including local evaluations.

Each book is based on 15 months of research during which time the anthropologists lived, worked and interacted with people in the local language. Yet they differ from the dominant tradition of writing social science books. Firstly they do not engage with the academic literatures on social media. It would be highly repetitive to have the same discussions in all nine books. Instead discussions of these literatures are to be found in our comparative book, *How the World Changed Social Media*. Secondly these monographs are not comparative, which again is the primary function of this other volume. Thirdly, given the immense interest in social media from the general public, we have tried to write in an accessible and open style. This means we have adopted a mode more common in historical writing of keeping all citations and the discussion of all wider academic issues to endnotes.

We hope you enjoy the results and that you will also read our comparative book – and perhaps some of the other monographs – in addition to this one.

Acknowledgements

This book could not have been possible without the generosity, insights and friendship of many people or without the support of several organisations.

A big thank you goes to my PhD supervisor Professor Daniel Miller. He gave me immensely helpful guidance and most generous support throughout my field work and the writing of this book, encouraging me to try different approaches during my research and to apply my painting and calligraphy skills to document my ethnography. In many ways he pushed me to exploit my potential fully, enabling me to see, and be a better person. I was also fortunate to be part of a highly competent and friendly research team from which I not only received helpful feedback at each stage of the research and chapter drafts, but also gained family-like companionship and support.

Thank you also to Lara Speicher, Chris Penfold, Jaimee Biggins and Alison Major at UCL Press. The wonderful team guided me through a long process of peer review, copy-editing and marketing, and have always been very encouraging and helpful. I am also very grateful to two anonymous reviewers who read the book carefully; the book evolved considerably through this period. I also feel it's a great honour to publish this book as Open Access at UCL Press. The free knowledge online provided by Open Access allows the possibility of a significantly extended readership, which is extremely important for a book focusing on how the digital can possibly change the lives of a marginalised population.

Many wonderful individuals in China helped to facilitate this research. Special thanks go to Rui Zhong, who generously helped me with the filming in my field site, and to Jingwen Fan, who helped me carry out the interviews in Shanghai and provided me with many insightful observations and great interview material.

I also want to thank my parents, Zhengting Wang and Yun Chen, for believing in me and supporting me in all of my endeavours. A special thank you to my mum, a brave, kind, joyful and wonderful woman, who supported me in the most dedicated way, as only a mother can do. I am grateful to Marcus Fedder for his unfailing belief in me and commitment to helping me succeed and keep my work in perspective within life's amazing journey.

To all my informants, both in the factory town field site and in Shanghai, I owe sincere appreciation for their great trust and friendship, and for the generous way in which they shared their happiness, sadness and the incidents of their lives.

Finally I would like to acknowledge and thank the following institutions for financial support: The China Scholarship Council (CSC), the Wenner-Gren Foundation (Wadsworth International Fellowship) and the European Research Council grant 2011-AdG-295486 Socnet.

ACKNOWLEDGEMENTS

Contents

List of figures

List of charts

1
Introduction

In the decades since the de facto Chinese leader Deng Xiao Ping ended the cultural revolution and opened up the economy towards more capitalist forces, China has witnessed the largest ever human migration.[1] Such an unprecedented flow of labour from China's rural interior to more coastal factories and cities has resulted in vast economic growth, urbanisation and the proliferation of labour-intensive industries. In 2015 the number of Chinese peasants who had left their hometowns to work in these factories had risen to 277.47 million.[2] If Chinese rural migrants were the population of a country, it would be the fourth largest in the world.

In 2013, following an assumption that those Chinese migrant workers would be highly dependent on the boom in Chinese social media to remain in contact with the families they had left behind, I went to study social media usage in a small factory town in southeast China, a site for tens of thousands of migrant workers. However, during the subsequent 15 months of field work, mostly spent living inside one of these factories, I began to understand that the reality is very different from anything I had imagined.

First, I was surprised about the motivations for migration among the new generations, which I had assumed would be essentially economic. Second, I was largely wrong about what kind of social media use I would find among what is known in China as a 'floating population': it was not mainly about retaining links to users' places of origin. Most of all I had not anticipated my primary finding, which was that this would be a study of two migrations conducted in parallel: one from rural to urban, and another, undertaken simultaneously, from offline to online. We can call these parallel because both, in their own ways, were journeys to the same destination of an imagined modern China. Finally this book will make a surprising claim as to which of these migrations seems to have been more successful in reaching this goal.

Chinese migrant workers are evidently Chinese. However, many key stereotypes of Chinese people do not apply to this particular population. For example, many migrant families have managed to dodge China's one-child policy[3] and usually have at least two children. Education, generally believed to be highly valued in Chinese society,[4] is actually valued in a far more utilitarian way. Many, if not most, rural migrant parents as well as rural migrant youth in my field site did not see success in school as a priority. In such a situation, as Chapter 3 argues, social media plays a key role in filling gaps left by lack of education. For young migrant workers who dropped out of school early and became factory workers before adulthood, social media is a form of 'post-school' education and schooling that implies their 'coming of age'.

It is also necessary to update the most widely held perception, in and out of China, of these Chinese migrant workers in terms of their social development. Recent migrants are very different from the initial wave upon which most academic accounts are still based, and which tend to focus on economic concerns.[5] For example, poverty is no longer the only reason behind migration. The initial motivation of the rural-to-urban migration was economic necessity.[6] Low productivity in the countryside could not support the livelihoods of the Chinese peasants who constituted the majority of the country's population; working in factories and cities seemed to be the only viable solution. Nowadays, however, the economic advantages of migration have become less clear. The combination of higher living expenses and increased consumption (influenced by the general lifestyle of urban areas)[7] means that marginal improvements in migrants' incomes hardly warrant the costs of, for example, no longer being able to care for their parents. For the new generation of rural migrants, the whole trajectory of rural-to-urban migration has shifted from the 'push' factor of economic necessity towards the 'pull' factor of aspirations towards modernity. For young migrant workers, migration means 'to see the outside world'[8] and to gain autonomy from one's family.[9] In such a context, social media is less of a bridge that connects individuals with what they have left behind in villages and more of a projector illuminating an ideal modern life to which they aspire.

Tens of thousands of migrant workers live in the small town where I conducted my field work, but almost none of them see the place where they live as 'home'. The living quarters in this factory town, as we will see later in this chapter, mainly serve to provide 'infrastructure for labourers rather than offering places in which human beings can maintain social relationships and feel security and emotional belonging'.[10] So where do people actually live? What does it mean when a young factory girl says 'life outside the mobile phone is unbearable'? By mobile phone she meant her social media profile, to which she keeps constantly logged in and in which she portrays herself as a modern lady.[11] What her statement suggests is precisely that social media has become an alternative, and indeed a better, home to those migrant workers: given the offline conditions of their floating lives, many find social media to be the place where a new personal identity, with a 'higher human quality' (*you suzhi*),[12] can be created. This point is central to the ethnography that informs this volume. True, I spent most of this period of field work living in a factory, whereas most people just work there. In some ways I too lived with these factory workers, in as much as I shared the active social and imaginative lives they led online, rather than merely spent time in the same physical space.

In previous studies of Chinese rural migrants the issue of gender is one of the core topics. Almost all the studies focus on female Chinese rural migrants, suggesting that women workers are the most subordinated group within Chinese migrant populations.[13] Some of these claims and findings are still relevant today, but other things have changed. For this particular migrant group gender inequality may in some respects have reversed, leading to male rural migrants becoming the relatively disadvantaged group. This does not apply only to the job market or marriage market, but also to the social pressure and discrimination they suffer, compared to that of female migrants. Through male migrants' social media usage such gender anxiety comes to be represented and experienced.[14] It is worth noting, however, that this gender imbalance often reverts after marriage.

During the time of writing this book, the *Economist* published an article[15] about the children of Chinese migrant families left behind by their parents. This article rightly pointed out that such children were a damaged generation, suffering significantly higher states of anxiety and depression than their peers – a situation that may be connected to a lack of support following early separation from their parents. It is said that in 2010 there were 61 million children below the age of 17 left behind in rural areas; in several provinces more than half of all rural children had been left behind.[16] Such children have truly become a severe social problem in modern China. However, even this latest article still fails to cover some of the most recent developments and consequences of such problems. In the town where I conducted my research most young migrant workers had once been 'left-behind' children; they had dropped out of school at ages ranging from 14 to 17,[17] and then joined their parents to work in factories. Even as academics and journalists continue to discuss the population of 'left-behind' children, many of their subjects have already made themselves part of a new generation of migrant workers.

Most research and reports about Chinese rural migrants focuses on the 'first tier' cities, such as Beijing, Shanghai and Guangzhou.[18] However, the 2013 national survey on 'floating populations'[19] shows that 47 per cent of Chinese rural migrants work and live in small and medium-sized towns. Here migrant parents are significantly more likely to live with their children (more than 60 per cent of the new generation of rural migrants live with core family members in migration destinations). In the factory town where I worked more than 80 per cent of newborn babies came from migrant families, while migrant children also represent the majority at the local primary school.[20] This new generation faces difficulties, however, as it is not yet integrated into the local society.[21] Today's young migrants confront the same problem as their parents did, of not being able to access urban social welfare. They may feel even more frustrated by social discrimination,[22] as they are usually keener to integrate into modern city life.[23] This new generation of migrant workers has been experiencing insecurity and impermanence since childhood. As a result them seem to have learned to present themselves as unflappable or even unconcerned about their own lives. Such a highly performative attitude almost detaches them from either their own or other people's judgements. Once again it turned out that a study of social media was also a really effective strategy for understanding these young people; only through this inner but online world[24] did it seem possible to find out who they really are and what they really want from life.

Social media use among Chinese migrant workers also challenges some basic ideas that have formed the premise of several heated debates about social media worldwide. For instance, there is a constant worry that the mediation of social media has rendered our social relationships in some way less authentic. Here, however, people find social media is the only place to establish a 'purer' (*geng chun*) relationship, free from all the practical concerns of offline life.[25] Furthermore, when we are questioning the impact of social media on friendship we may not be aware that merely using the concept of 'friendship'[26] is problematic. This is particularly so when applied to people from traditional communities in which kinship and regional relationships (such as fellow villagers) are dominant; the Western notion of a separate sphere of friendship may simply not exist.

As Chapter 4 illustrates, it is on social media that Chinese migrant workers have created and experienced a real sense of 'friendship' for the first time. A similar situation occurs when we look into the issue of privacy. In the West, it has become commonplace to accuse social media of being a threat to privacy,[27] but what if the very idea and practice of privacy has hardly existed in a society? Migrant workers have their origins in village families with no provision for individualised space, a situation compounded in adulthood by current conditions of shared dormitories. Many are also linked to a traditional idea that 'anything that is hidden from others must be something shameful or bad' – in effect saying that a mere preference for privacy is a bad thing. Given such factors, one has to consider the use of social media from a totally different perspective. In the real life of migrant workers, social media has remarkably increased the experience of privacy and legitimised the right to it.

When it comes to the impact of social media on politics, the ideals of the 'cyber-utopian',[28] which regards the internet as a politically progressive force and has become a very popular argument worldwide, may also be problematic. In the specific case of China and the Chinese internet, it is also widely believed that the development of the internet and social media might actively empower a future civil society. However, the ethnography suggests an entirely different picture, based on the evidence for the daily use of social media and its political content at a grass roots level. As will be shown in Chapter 5, the evidence here is that social media has far less impact on political participation than expected and rather than empowering or encouraging political participation, its use tends to diminish any motivation for turning discontented thoughts into active political action. Rather, in many ways social media helps to monitor and channel public opinion (*yulun daoxiang*)[29] and further legitimise the Chinese party-state.

Here, then, is a litany of ways in which the results of this research differ from the expectations of both myself and others. Given the degree of these discrepancies, and the many quite surprising claims that follow, much of this book focuses on the evidence that arose from the ethnography and provides the foundation for these claims. It is also hoped that the detailed ethnographic descriptions will also provide a sense of empathy and immersion in the lives of these people. We perceive them in the irresistible tides of these social transformations, and can see what this 'floating population' felt, believed or mistrusted; what their fantasies, hopes and fears might be; how they understood situations and reacted offline and online. This book is composed from hundreds of voices and images and fragments of individuals' daily lives, but not one of them is trivial. In addition a bigger, but also very different and distinct picture of modern China appears in view when we bring these individuals together analytically.

A brief review of the book

This book is about a new population and a new media. It depicts a situation in which a very particular group of people has emerged as an adult working population alongside the rise of social media in China. The Chinese rural migrant population that did not exist three decades ago is taking on its new form, very much facilitated by the capability they find in social media. At the same time social media, a new media that did not exist two decades ago, has rapidly come into daily use for a large proportion of the population. We can only make sense of both modern China and social media if we appreciate the dynamic, dialectical context within which both are being formed.

In Chapter 1, besides an introduction to the context of this study, we take a tour around the factory town and meet the people who inhabit it. Chapter 2 gives a detailed description of the Chinese social media landscape and budget smartphone market, while Chapter 3 focuses on what people post on their personal social media profiles – thus opening a window on to individuals' aspirations and anxieties, expectations and social lives. Drawing on Chapters 2 and 3, Chapter 4 maps out social life on social media, exploring in detail the ways in which people navigate various relationships. Why, for example, are classmates, neighbours and colleagues valued less than strangers online? Why and how does the mediation of social media constitute a 'purer' interpersonal relationship? Answers to those questions can be found in Chapter 4. Meanwhile Chapter 5 focuses upon the specific impact of social media on politics and gender, both closely examined through the online and offline behaviour of different groups of local people.

Finally Chapter 6 further explores how we can make sense of the dialectical relationship between 'online' and 'offline' – from postings of deity images to bring good fortune to the QQ homeland albums which in a way 'transport' people's home villages to online; from 'recording the youth' in salon photography to practising a modern life online. An understanding of people's struggles and their negotiation between online and offline leads to one of the main arguments of this book: that dual migrations are taking place simultaneously in the daily lives of

Chinese rural migrants – one from rural to urban, the other from offline to online. Could it be the latter which in practice proves more efficient and effective than physical migration, and which empowers people to achieve their aspiration of modernity?

Chinese family and *hukou*

Before presenting the evidence and arguments, there are two key historical questions that provide the foundations for the situation encountered here. Where do these migrant workers come from? And why have they had to take up a 'floating' life?

The first question is an inquiry into a traditional agricultural society in which not only these migrants but also the vast majority of Chinese people used to live – merely half a century ago. Here we can find answers in the anthropology of a more traditional China. The scholarship is simply too rich to review here, but a few key concepts will be briefly mentioned as a starting point. In Chinese the word 'family' (*jia*) actually refers not only to kinship, but also to a group of people, an estate of property or an economy (a set of economic activities).[30] The Chinese institution of family[31] is regarded as the nucleus of society. No one who has delved into the intricacies of Chinese social relations would deny the leading role kinship plays in Chinese political[32] and economic[33] affairs; this further sets the foundation for Chinese cosmology, where ancestors were worshipped as deities by descendants.[34] Patrilineal descent, or agnate kinship,[35] in which only men can inherit family property and a child's lineage is only calculated from the father's side, constitutes the social order of both the domestic and public domains.[36]

Age, generation and gender served as the three hierarchical principles within a Chinese family: that is the old are superior to the young, the male is superior to the female, the older generation is superior to the younger.[37] The senior male members usually control family affairs, and were regarded as the maintainers, providers and protectors of the family. Parent–son relationships are the most important in a traditional family. In an extended family a married son is supposed to stand firmly by his parents' side, regardless of what he thinks is right. Filial piety requires children to 'show respect and obedience to their parents under all circumstances and a daughter-in-law is always in the wrong if she dares to talk back to her mother-in-law'.[38]

In traditional Chinese society, human relationships start with the immediate family as an in-group and then radiate to encompass the extended family, village and wider social connections.[39] With Confucianism providing the philosophical basis of Chinese family and society,[40] the country has long been seen as a typical collective or 'low-individualism' society – placing the needs, interests and objectives of in-groups at a higher priority than those of individuals.[41] Other traditional Chinese ethical concepts, such as the importance of interpersonal relations (*guanxi*)[42] and face (*mianzi*), which refers to one's own sense of dignity and reputation in a community,[43] are all closely related to these collective features of Chinese society. These emphasise the distinction between in-groups and out-groups, the importance of engaging in co-operative tasks, and a focus on avoiding conflict in the ultimate pursuit of communal harmony.

In regard to the second question, the reason why Chinese peasants had to take up a migrant life, rather than settling down in cities, lies in a policy called *hukou*. Established in the 1950s, the Chinese household registration system (*hukou*) plays an important role in migrant workers' lives. One's *hukou* status determines one's rights to welfare, employment and land, with people formerly only being permitted to work and reside at their place of *hukou* registration.[44] Because of *hukou*, mainland Chinese were divided into rural residents and urban residents. Urban residents enjoyed a range of social, economic and cultural benefits that rural residents did not receive.[45] With its strict rules against migration between rural and urban areas, *hukou* tried to limit mass migration from the land to the cities to ensure social stability.

This situation started to change in the 1980s, when industrialisation of China needed more and more cheap labour. The control over rural-to-urban migration has been gradually relaxed, enabling a vast number of rural labourers to work in cities while remaining registered as rural residents.[46] 'Floating population' (*liudong renkou*), a term in Chinese official discourse,[47] describes the migration pattern[48] of those rural migrants. Peasant workers (*nongmin gong*), a combination of 'peasant' and 'worker', is another word used in colloquial discourse to refer to the same group. As this term suggested, migrant workers are still peasants; they do not have access to the same welfare benefits as urban workers do under the allocation system of *hukou*. In such a rural–urban divide migrant workers usually find it difficult to establish roots in their temporary residential places – despite being the backbone of China's economic miracle based on labour-intensive industries.

Three decades ago, when the first wave of Chinese migrant workers left their villages,[49] they were leaving behind dreadfully poor agricultural communities and entire families that were desperate to be supported. Three decades later, the second or even the third generation has now become the main force of migrant labour,[50] and it is important not to extrapolate our understanding of the first generation and assume that it applies equally to these later generations. At this point, however, having considered these issues in the abstract, the actual ethnography encountered them through the lives of individuals such as Dong, a 21-year-old migrant worker and part of this new generation.

The story of Dong

The bad news finally arrived. At the other end of the phone call Dong's niece told him that his old grandfather (*lao ye zi*) had died.

Three days later, with his parents and two other relatives who work in the same factory, Dong was on his way back to his village in a mountain area of YunNan province to join the funeral. It was a long trip: 2 hours on a minibus, followed by 48 hours on the train, then 3.5 hours by bus, and finally an hour on foot. Before the smartphone battery ran out, Dong had a last check of his QQ (a Chinese social media platform). When the train left Zhejiang province, he deleted the *GuanYin* (the mother Buddha) deity image that he had posted on his QQ a week ago in the hope that his grandfather would recover from his stroke. '*GuanYin* didn't do me the favour,' he told me later on QQ.

Dong had mixed feelings about this old man. Left behind by his parents who had worked outside of the mountain village more than 20 years ago, Dong was raised by his grandparents. Ten years ago his grandfather suffered an attack by a snake in the field, which left him unable to do any more heavy farm work. The only job he was offered was that of a public toilet attendant in a nearby town centre. Dong thus accompanied his grandparents to the single room attached to the public toilet, and there he lived. 'My classmates called me *shiwa* [shit boy] from then on, and I hated my childhood and my schooling time … my grandparents really couldn't help me … I mean for them to make sure I was not ill or hungry or lost was the best thing they could do.' Both Dong's grandparents were illiterate and could hardly give him any advice on school problems. The experience of being left behind as a child and the bullying in school partially pushed Dong to drop out of education at the age of 16. He left his home village and became a migrant factory worker. Since then he had only visited his grandparents twice in four years.

'Everybody was coming back and saying the outside world was full of beautiful things, and I was so looking forward to a new life outside at that time...couldn't wait to escape the desperate village life and my grandparents,' Dong once recalled. After four years of hard work in various factories, he would not necessarily agree with his initial dream about working as a migrant worker (*da gong*) any more. Nonetheless, as he said, 'Even though life outside was truly not as easy as I thought, struggling outside is always better than waiting for death in the village'. Dong believes in the saying 'the real man travels the world' (*hao nan er zou si fang*). At least that is something he can boast about one day in front of his children: that their father once visited many places. Dong planned one day, when he had finally saved up enough money, to start his own business in the town centre – no longer just labouring work, but a real business. Much of what he shared on his QQ profile were stories of successful entrepreneurs who had started from scratch, some of them from an even worse situation than his own. After all, most of the factory owners for whom he worked were once peasants like him. If they could succeed, why not him? 'I just need a bit of luck and maybe some patience,' he observed.

Two days after his return to his home village, Dong updated his QQ status: 'Farewell grandfather, sorry for being so *buxiao* [unfilial].' Two weeks later Dong had still not returned to the factory. One day I got a message from him on QQ: 'I am not coming back; I am going to marry a girl in our village soon.' The marriage was arranged by fellow villagers, and after the wedding the young couple are going to work together in another factory town in southeast China. As for Dong's current job, a relative working at the same factory would help him to sort everything out. Hopefully Dong would still get a proportion of his final month's wage, but to be honest he did not expect to receive it.

I realised that the moment when I saw him off to the local bus station would be the last time I ever saw Dong. 'Oh, my poor *nv boshi* [female PhD], I think that is something you can never learn,' Feige, a forklift truck driver, remarked. 'Things happen like this all the time: there's nothing unusual in saying goodbyes. You know, I have seen so many new faces appear and disappear in factories and nobody really cares...except for you.'

The GoodPath: A transitional town

Feige is probably right. In GoodPath, a small factory town, people do come and leave, day in day out. GoodPath town for them is indeed a 'path' rather than a destination. Although others have talked of the town as a destination point, it is more accurately a transitional place connecting village and city.[51] The town itself is not an enclave in a city, but a rural place in the process of 'becoming' urban.

GoodPath has a long history as an agricultural village that dates back to the Tang Dynasty (610–907 BC). However, as a factory town it is very young. It was only in 2004 that the local government decided to develop industry. A decade of industrialisation has turned 76 per cent of the farm land in the centre area of GoodPath into 61 massive factories and 224 related companies. In 2004 agriculture contributed 89.2 per cent of GoodPath's GDP; in 2013 this figure has shrunk to 12.7 per cent.[52] Rural migrants who work in factories account for two-thirds of the resident population (totalling around 62,000). The population density of GoodPath has also jumped to 1,341 persons per km², compared to 142 per km² for China as a whole and 255 per km² for the UK.

Many rural migrants chose to come to GoodPath because of the job opportunities that are gained through the personal network of fellow villagers or relatives. Here 79 per cent of local rural migrants live with at least one family member, with only around five per cent living alone.[53] On the one hand these figures are consistent with the 2013 Chinese national census of domestic migration,[54] which shows that across China 70 per cent of rural migrants live with at least one family member. On the other hand, these numbers reject the cliché of Chinese rural migrants being totally isolated in their new locations. As a 'transitional town' GoodPath provides everything for rural migrants – except the sense of belonging. 'It (GoodPath) is just where I work... of course it's not a home. Home is where you go back once a year to celebrate Chinese New Year.' Guo Biao, 49, lived with his whole family in GoodPath; his three adult children work in two different factories. GoodPath for him is still by no means 'home', even though he has spent a good deal of time here.

Like many other Chinese 'urban villages', newly developed in the process of rapid industrialisation and urbanisation,[55] the economic and social development in GoodPath is unbalanced. The co-existing urban and rural elements manifest themselves in complicated, often conflicting ways. The changes served to disrupt the existing social order; crime rates shot up and living conditions deteriorated, with local people blaming rural migrant workers for all the troubles.[56] In GoodPath there is a very limited social bonding between local people and rural migrants. Seventy-two per cent of rural migrants reported[57] that they had no communication with local people apart from functional relationships such as 'shop owner/customer', 'landlord/tenant' and 'factory manager/factory worker'.

Such separation begins at primary school. In GoodPath's only primary school most of the students (around 85 per cent) come from migrant families. There were five classes at each grade, divided in turn into four 'outsider classes' (*waidi ban*) and one 'local class' (*bendi ban*). Better teachers were allocated to the 'local class', which only enrolled local students. A local teacher explained the reason behind the structure:

> ...(Local) parents were so worried that their children will pick up bad habits from those 'wild kids' from rural migrant families...which in many cases was true. You cannot expect children to be well-behaved if their parents do not care about their school performance and they have no discipline at home...

The social and economic transformation of GoodPath described above has been taking place gradually. However, the change in this small factory town's appearance seems to have happened overnight. During my stay in GoodPath, an advanced cinema, which can show 3D movies, popped up in the first six months. On the one side of a busy national motorway there is a freight parking area. On the other side a large shopping mall with an advertising pillar like London's Big Ben rose from the ground (Fig. 1.1). On the front facade of the mall a huge advertising hoarding depicts a foreign woman holding a box of Häagen-Dazs ice cream. A slogan beside the billboard recommends 'keeping up with the world' (*yu shijie tongbu*). Together with the heavy trucks and the long-distance minibus, the massive industrial area seems to give concrete form to the numerous abstract forces driving China's 'reform and opening-up policy' over the last three decades – especially globalisation, migration, industrialisation and commercialisation.

The following section seeks to capture a greater awareness of GoodPath, a place within which all these transitions and transformations

Fig. 1.1 The varied scenes of a freight parking area, farmland and a modern shopping mall in GoodPath

occur. 'Walking' around in the town and 'talking' with people as a researcher usually does may help you to become more familiar with the town and its people, and so understand better all the stories in this book. A map of the town centre is given (Fig 1.2) to help anchor the discussion in this particular place.

A tour of GoodPath

The first stop: The high street

A mere country road a decade ago, the high street today has more than 100 shops lining both sides. Along with the development of the factories, the local government repaved the road and sold the land on both sides to property developers to build residential buildings, four or five storeys in height, with shop fronts. Most shops deal with useful household items and men's and women's clothes and shoes, as well as hairdressers and digital devices. As you walk along the street, all of one's senses are overwhelmed: loud music, bright colours, strong scents, flavours of food, and people everywhere.

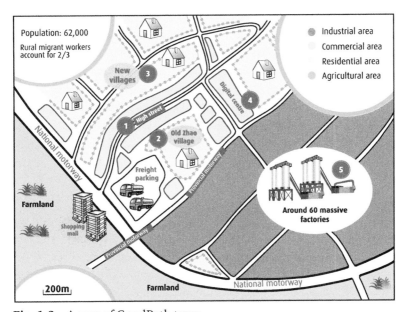

Fig. 1.2 A map of GoodPath town

Even at first glance something is striking about the people here: young people and children are in the majority, and people seem to like being in groups. Around 22 per cent[58] of the pedestrians are babies and children under the age of 15; only three per cent of them are elderly; 79 per cent are walking in groups, and 38 per cent of the adults are accompanied by children. One thing that distinguishes rural migrants from local residents is that many of them are young parents with more than one child, in apparent contradiction to the Chinese one-child family plan policy.[59] This in turn explains the 'graffiti' on the whitewashed mortar walls of lanes off the main street. This graffiti is actually mobile phone numbers offering to provide all kinds of fake authorisations. One of them is 'birth permission' (*zhun sheng zheng*). Under Chinese family planning regulations, a pregnant woman will be turned down by a hospital unless she can show a birth permission document. Nor can a baby born without 'birth permission' be given a *hukou* (household registration), creating all kinds of problems in future life. For people employed in the public sector (government administration, education, hospitals, etc.), having more than one child will result in the loss of one's job and income, a penalty imposed on unplanned birth (*chao sheng*). People who work in the private sector may not lose their jobs, but they still need to pay a huge fine[60] to obtain a 'birth permission'. In rural areas, however, people are allowed to have a second child if the first one is a girl. A decade ago, when 'one-child' policy was carried out strictly, rural mothers had to give birth in secret (*tou sheng)* to avoid the penalties imposed on unplanned births. 'Years ago they [local officials] would chase you to the end of the Earth if they knew you had a baby hidden elsewhere, but now they can't be bothered', explained Ma, a factory worker aged 29. His three young children were born in three different factory towns.

On the high street, there is a mobile phone shop called 'Wan Hua China Mobile Franchise mobile phone shop'.[61] From time to time I helped at the shop. Wan Hua, the middle-aged owner, is a typical smart, shrewd and very hard-working local man; he opens the shop at 6.30 a.m. and closes at 10.30 p.m., seven days a week, 12 months a year, except for a ten-day break at Chinese New Year. Behind piles of mobile phone boxes there is a double bed where Wan Hua and his wife sleep during the night. In front of the shop is parked a brand new Ford car. Although he has little reason to drive, the car means a lot to Wan Hua. 'It's all about face (*mianzi*), you know. If I can't even afford a car, people will think I am doing badly!' As Wan Hua said, the concept of 'face' is truly important, important for understanding some aspects of social media use later in the book. *Mianzi,* known as 'Chinese face', is a sophisticated, self-conscious feeling with regard to the opinions of others. It is a typical 'front-stage' behaviour[62] whose goal is to establish a particular favourable image in front of others.[63]

The second stop: Zhao village

Zhao village is a slum right in the heart of GoodPath, besieged by concrete residential buildings. The former busy pathway into the village is now an empty lane with scattered funeral supplies stores and blacksmith's shops (Fig. 1.3). Old people, the only local residents who continue living in this area, sit in bamboo chairs outside their front doors, looking at a world in which they no longer play a part. Nowadays their neighbours are often strangers who speak totally different dialects. After a century's wind and rain, most of the wooden buildings previously owned by local wealthy families are in poor condition; they are occupied by around 300 rural migrant households. Few toilets and no proper rubbish bins exist, with the result that everywhere has become a potential toilet or rubbish bin. The rural migrants who live here are regarded as the poorest, unable to afford a better room. Rent for rooms in these those old wooden houses is 50 RMB (US $8) per month, only one quarter of the cost of a room in concrete residential buildings.

Located in long and narrow lanes, a few illicit minibus service routes constitute the busiest areas. Minibuses run from GoodPath to around 70 counties in Guizhou, the poorest inland Chinese province from which almost half of the rural migrants in GoodPath originate. Given the fact that the central provincial coach station provides services to only two counties in Guizhou, GoodPath's transport capability clearly

Fig. 1.3   The Old Street in Zhao village, GoodPath town (traditional Chinese painting 82 × 34.5 cm; painter: Xinyuan Wang)

reflects the high mobility of its population. Along with many declining villages in Chinese factory towns, Zhao village resembles a large, withered tree. The birds that used to live on its branches have left, one by one; only old birds who cannot fly any more remain. Gradually the tree becomes a big trunk of standing wood, covered by thick moss. Yet when you look at it closely, you are amazed at the diversity of creatures still living on the tree.

The third stop: Peasant flats (*nongmin fang*) in the new villages

If Zhao village is a large, withered tree, then on the other side of the high street, in the new villages, are the clusters of trees in which most immigrant 'birds' dwell. Rural migrants account for two-thirds of the total number of GoodPath's residents. All the buildings are concrete houses, three to five storeys in height, built in the past 15 years by the local peasants, from which derives the name *nongmin fang* ('peasant flat').

> The reason for a five-floor house is mainly that my parents tried to build a taller building than our neighbours. Well it's about *mianzi*. Now thanks to those migrant workers, all vacant rooms are full.

Mr Fan's family had built one of these buildings, in which eight rural migrant families now live. Chun's family from Jiangxi province is one of them. In the corner of the room (Fig. 1.4) a pile of unpacked luggage seemed to indicate that the family is about to move out, or arrived only yesterday. Actually Chun has lived here for eight months.

A yard outside provides an extended living space. Here women cook in the open air on simple stoves; young men play cards around a short table; young mothers gossip with their female friends while breastfeeding their babies; children play at hide-and-seek behind strings on which their neighbours' underwear hangs. Many 'indoor' activities take

Fig. 1.4   Peasant flats in the new villages

place outside – not only because there is simply not enough room inside, but also because these residents, who have come from a rural area, like to maintain their habit of 'living in public'.

The fourth stop: The digital centre

Adjacent to the bustling new villages, the digital centre is another place full of life and colour (Fig. 1.5). The centre is a collection of 24 shops dealing with mobile phones, digital products and other digital services, for example digital photographic studios. Displays of newly launched mobile phones or internet payment structures are everywhere. One can find a range of smartphones varying from 300 RMB (US $45) to 4,000 RMB (US $600), as well as easy to use mobile phones for elderly citizens featuring larger buttons and louder sound (Fig. 1.6).

Chapter 2 discusses the budget smartphone market in the context of social media usage. Since early 2013 rural migrants have dramatically boosted the consumption of smartphones, especially budget smartphones. Ma Yu, a mobile phone dealer, rightly spotted the trend of smartphone use among rural migrants:

> Ninety-five per cent of budget smartphones were sold to local rural migrants. Those rural migrants know clearly what they want... they care about the memory card, the quality of the mobile phone camera, and whether it can play games, take videos, etc.

Fig 1.5   The local digital centre

Fig 1.6   Mobile phones for elderly citizens

For rural migrants, a smartphone has become the 'everyday essential' since it is their only private access to the internet and all the digital entertainment to be found there. Where demand exists, a market will supply. Cheap digital content is also available in the digital centre. For 5 RMB (less than US $1), you can get 50 music tracks, while 10 RMB will buy five full-length films. Catalogue books for music tracks, smartphone pictures and films are piled up on tables for consumteers to select their purchases. All the content is smartphone-friendly; in most cases, people bring their smartphone to the shop and download content direct from the shop owner's computer. Mr Zhu, a shopkeeper selling digital products, explained why the digital content business is profitable: 'Most of them (rural migrants) don't have a PC and they usually don't have broadband at home, so they are willing to pay a bit money to buy them here.'

The fifth stop: Factory plants

From the digital centre, cross a provincial motorway to reach the industrial area of GoodPath. Here are more than 60 factories, many less than eight years old, though still older than the newly planted trees along the roads. The small trees and roads of equal width, with road signs marked in arabic numerals, combine with the identical factories to give the whole area a bland uniformity.

These factories are massive. Each plant covers around 8,000 m², and holds 700–1,000 factory workers. Even in daytime there is no

Fig. 1.7 Scene from the assembly line in a factory plant

natural light inside the factory plants, and the air is full of incessant loud machine noise and the pungent smell of paint. Steel is one of the main raw materials. Every day hundreds of rolls of steel plate are shipped to the factory, where usually one worker works with one machine to cut the original material into various shapes. The logic of the assembly line is 'humankind as a part of the machine', and the noise and the relentless assembly line certainly deprives people of any possibility of conversation. There is only limited automation here: labour remains cheaper than a fully-automated production line. Following the pre-set machine pace, a factory worker repeats his or her action roughly 2,000 times per day.

Jing, a 19-year-old factory worker on an assembly line, told me the trick of 'not missing one punch' is to 'forget yourself'. 'If you think things, your hands will slow down and you can't follow the machine,' she explained. Yet it is important to recognise that these factory workers do have options. After working at the factory for three months Jing got fed up. She then left her job and found a new one as a shop assistant in an accessories shop on the high street.

Labour work in a factory is divided into assembly line and heavy manual labour. Women are always welcomed as factory workers, since they are regarded dexterous, attentive and obedient. Compared to manual heavy labour, assembly line work is relatively light and dominated by women. Given the mechanisation taking place in the factories, more and more heavy manual labour will be replaced by the assembly line. As a result young women can find a job easily in GoodPath, whereas young men find it more difficult to get a job, especially if they do not want to do the heavy manual labour. In the factories Jing earned 3,500 RMB (US $583) per month if she worked ten hours a day, 29 days a month. On the high street, by contrast, her month salary is 2,500RMB (around US $417).

> They (factory managers) like young women to work on the assembly line, you know; they thought we were obedient (*ting hua*) and attentive (*zi xi*). Young women are the best. Men are nothing compared to us. But it's so tiring working in the factories. I prefer to work here even though I earn less.

Jing is typical of a new generation of rural migrants. She dropped out of middle school after a big row with close friends at school. At that time all she wanted was to see the outside world, to escape. School was boring, and she felt lonely since her parents and all her relatives had left the villages to work in factories. Jing did not think twice before joining them. The older generation shared the common Chinese aspirations based on achievement through education and hard work, but Jing's generation pride themselves on 'playing it cool', and the motivation driving migration is more about a chance to see the world.[64] The new generation change jobs more often than the old generation, and are more selective about jobs.[65]

The end of the tour

We have looked around GoodPath, and what we have seen in the town centre has set the context for exploring social media usage in later chapters. As a result of this tour it should be clear why it would be quite misleading to imagine this book as simply situated in 'China'. Rather, we should start with a very open mind as to who these people might be, and not make assumptions about their values or concerns.

As we shall see, this 'new generation' of rural migrants is very different from its parents: they are motivated more by interest and have stronger aspirations to 'see the outside world'. This very particular population has emerged as working adults alongside the rise of new media and social media in China. So this book is not about how a given population takes up and appropriates this new media. It rather considers a situation in which a population that never previously existed assumes its new form very much under the influence of the capacities they find in smartphones and social media. Social media in turn can only be appreciated if we understand the very dynamic context within which it is being formed.

A final note on methodology

This book is based on a 15-month period of ethnography in GoodPath. In undetaking our tour of GoodPath you have experienced something of doing field work with me and seen how I gained data and insights – by walking around, listening to what people say, observing what people do and being a participant in their daily lives.[66] In anthropology we call this method of data collection in ethnography 'participant observation'.[67] So what is special about 'participant observation'? As the anthropologist Margaret Mead rightly pointed out, there are actually several layers of self-representations in a person's social life. 'What people *say*, what people *do* and what *they say they do* are entirely different things,' she observed. In many cases, simply doing questionnaires or interviews (that is, collecting what people *say*, or what people *say* they *do*), is quite different from observing what they actually *do*. Self-expectations, social norms and taboos may prevent people from saying what they really do and think in daily life, or sometimes people simply fail to express them-selves articulately. Thus it is essential to observe what people do in their daily lives over a relatively long period of time. Another reason why long-term field work is so important is that it enables the researcher to become 'taken for granted' in the landscape and even to become friends with his or her informants. Nobody will behave naturally if they are aware of 'being watched', so effective observation only really starts at this point. In my case, several times people came back to me after know-ing me for six months or more and admitted that stories they had told me when we had first met had not been true, because they had not really known me at the time.'

There were also some specific and local issues. At first a key prob-lem was the suspicion of factory owners that researchers can be under-cover journalists. I encountered such hostility on the first day when I was taking photographs of a factory building. The security guard dashed out and urged me to leave: 'Our boss said no journalists!' It took people no time to spot me as somebody 'unusual' – somebody who was not a rural migrant looking for a factory job.

A friend suggested that I should work on relationships (*gao guanxi*), rather than regulations to gain access to factories. 'The smaller the place is, the more important the social relations (*guanxi*) become.' Just as she said, *guanxi* opened factory doors for me. After several twists and turns of social networking, I managed to get an introduction to a factory owner by his family friend, a previous student of a family member of mine. Thanks to that, my presence was finally no longer seen as an unpredictable threat. A temporary factory ID card that allowed me to visit the factory plant without extra permission was issued, and a room in the factory where I could stay during my research was allocated to me. Before even entering the factory, I had learnt one of the most important lessons about my field site: in most cases, the local society is based on personal social relationships. I could therefore understand the strategy of migrant workers making a living in a strange place better, as so much of it depended on their personal social networks.

Being a friendly and trusted outsider turned out to be most rewarding thing. People shared their opinions freely with me without worrying that I would judge them, and confessed their secrets to me without worrying such secrets would be revealed.[68] Having said this, it was a constant struggle to try to explain to people that an anthropologist, a word they had never heard, was not a journalist who has a channel to report local problems, nor a philanthropist who has resources to help them, nor an official who has the power to improve conditions. Even though some turned their back on me after their requests for money or a job from me were turned down, in most cases relationships between me and local people were built on an emotional, rather than an instrumental basis.

Curiously, my situation as an outsider seemed to draw a parallel when it comes to the role of 'strangers' on social media in migrant workers' daily lives. As we will examine further in Chapter 4, among migrant workers, friendships with strangers established and maintained but remaining only on QQ, have become an important part of their social lives. Unlike offline relationships, which are usually constrained to fixed social roles and mixed with various practical needs, online relationships were viewed as 'purer' relationships based on feelings and emotions.

In order to cover the diversity of local people, I applied various methods (Fig. 1.8). For instance, I often had several different breakfasts on the same morning in various breakfast booths in order to chat with 'strangers' who shared the same table with me. I visited all the shops on the high street one by one to do interviews and questionnaires, and paid a regular visit to waiting halls of different banks, clinics and train or bus stations to observe and chat with people. I also helped at a local mobile phone shop, giving me access to the first-hand material of the local mobile phone market and the opportunity to get to know a lot of

Fig. 1.8 (a) Wang driving a forklift truck at a factory; (b) Wang eating one of several breakfasts that she had in one morning at local breakfast booths as part of a plan to get to know more people; (c) Wang conducting a survey of workers from a temporary bed made of protective netting on a building site. (Three small paintings from a traditional Chinese painting booklet 'Field Note', 31.5 × 384 cm; painter: Xinyuan Wang)

customers. On top of this, to avoid unnecessary suspicion, balance in different social networks had to be carefully maintained. Few factory workers knew I had a good relationship with their bosses, and factory owners and senior managers did not know that I was very close to their workers.

In terms of quantitative data, questionnaires[69] were conducted online and offline. The problem in practice was unwillingness and inability to complete a questionnaire. For most people a formal academic questionnaire was challenging and even intimidating, given the limited education they had received.[70] Thus questionnaires were usually finished under my explanation in colloquial language. In general research inquiries were integrated in casual chatting both online and offline, situations in which real thoughts were more likely to be revealed.

Naturally an ethnography about social media was also conducted through social media. First of all, thousands of postings on social media profiles are vivid, original records of people's thoughts and living experiences. For this reason Chapter 3 is devoted to a discussion and analysis of the actual postings we find on personal social media profiles. This is not just a place of observation, however: it is also one of engagement. In GoodPath social life usually took place in noisy and public environments such as restaurants or open-air markets. There are very few places which allow for relatively private, 'one-to-one' talks. Social media thus became the place I talked with people privately about personal feelings and problems. Furthermore, social media helped me to overcome the communicative problem caused by the high mobility of migrant workers. In 2014, after the Chinese New Year break, almost one-third of the factory workers I had got to know did not come back to GoodPath. A few women got married and stayed in their home villages, but most of the workers simply got a new job in a different factory town or city. In the factory where I stayed, half of the factory workers were newly recruited. In such a situation, social media became almost the only way in which I could retain contact with former factory worker friends.

In addition to the ethnography in GoodPath, in July 2014 I spent one month in Shanghai – the closest metropolis, a few hours from GoodPath by train. I went there to conduct surveys and in-depth interviews among the urban Chinese. The trip to Shanghai was actually inspired by people in GoodPath. In the late stages of my research, the powerful longing to become urban and modern among migrant workers, clearly reflected in their social media postings, prompted me to have a look at the way in which urban Chinese use social media. In many ways the use of social media among this 'control group' in Shanghai[71] presented a contrast with rural migrant usage of social media, which helped to resolve other questions – such as whether certain uses of social media are better explained in terms of the specific population or the social media platform, or both. As a last note, I also applied my artistic skills to record the field work. All of the traditional Chinese paintings included in this book and translations of the calligraphy can be found at the 'visual ethnography' website (http://www.visualethnographyxy.co.uk).

2
The social media landscape in China[1]

On 20 September 1987 the first ever email in China read: 'Across the Great Wall we can reach every corner in the world.'[2] Compared to the brick-and-mortar Great Wall, the Chinese internet 'Great Firewall' (*fanghuo qiang*)[3] is actually the more difficult for people to climb. To this day China has completely blocked the world's four most visited websites: Google, Facebook, YouTube and Twitter. Yet it is by no means a desert in the social media landscape. As well as possessing the world's biggest internet user base (649 million)[4], China also has the world's most active environment for social media. Of the online population of China 91 per cent has a social media account, compared to 67 per cent of people in the US.[5] In practice, most Chinese netizens do not really notice the absence of global internet applications because they have accustomed themselves to indigenous websites; there is no particular sense of an absent 'outside'. Far from being a desert, therefore, mainland China is a thriving rainforest which grows its own diverse and unique social media 'species'. The discussion of Chinese social media in this chapter begins with a brief introduction to Chinese internet development. It then moves on to consider the main features of Chinese social media platforms, followed by a discussion of smartphones as the main digital device from which people gain access to social media.

A brief history of Chinese ICTs' development[6]

In 1978 China embarked upon a massive economic reform. The country's leadership realised that modern China had to seize the opportunities of the 'revolution in information technology'[7] taking place in the rest of the world. Modernisation of technology was included in the national development goal of 'Four Modernisations' (*sige xiandaihua*) in

1978. In fact 'sponsor' is more like the role played by the Chinese government in the development of ICTs. Using its administrative power and allocating national resources, the state made a remarkable effort to develop China into a technological superpower.[8] Chinese policy makers have been using the internet to achieve a 'digital leapfrog' of economic development.[9]

The explosive growth of digital development has contributed significantly to the modernisation of China, which in turn has legitimated the regime of the Chinese Communist Party.[10] In 2003 China became the world's largest telephone market, and in 2008 the number of Chinese internet users became the largest in the world. China had also overtaken

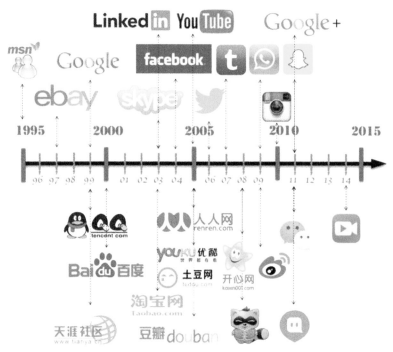

Fig. 2.1 The timeline of internet applications, both inside and outside China. Logos (left to right): [upper line] MSN (1995), eBay (1997), Google (1999), Skype (2003), LinkedIn (2003), Facebook (2004), YouTube (2004), Twitter (2005), What'sApp (2009), Instagram (2010), Google+ (2011), SnapChat (2011); [lower line] QQ (1999), Tianya BBS (1999), Baidu (2000), Taobao (2003), Renren (2005), YouKu (2005), Tudou (2005), Douban (2005), Kaixin (2008), YY (2008), Sina Weibo (2009), WeChat (2011), MoMo (2011), Meipai (2014)

the US by that date as the world's biggest supplier of information technology goods.[11] Probably because of the huge concern and interest in the single issue of Chinese internet censorship, there has been a reluctance to acknowledge the crucial role played by the central government – and also by local bureaucrats – in achieving this extraordinarily rapid shift to an efficient and widespread information technology sector.[12]

The timeline (Fig. 2.1) shows the development of the principal Chinese internet applications in comparison with their global counterparts. As can be seen, QQ started five years earlier than Facebook. Yet viewing QQ in the context of a comparative global social media study risks reducing QQ to being purely 'social media'. The first very important reminder, therefore, is that QQ is not a Chinese version of Facebook. It is also quite common to see the social media site 'Renren' described by Western media as the Chinese version of Facebook. This is misleading, however, because in terms of popularity Renren's market share is not comparable. The chart (Chart 2.1) shows the monthly active users (MAU) of different social media platforms inside and outside China. Even though Chinese social media platforms share a limited international market, QQ has 843 million MAU – more than half of Facebook's global users. Having explored the policy and company background, the following section will consider in more detail the three most popular Chinese social media platforms among people in GoodPath.

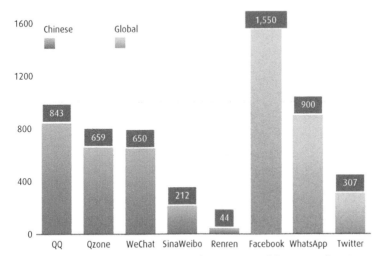

Chart 2.1[13]   Number (in millions) of active monthly users of main social media platforms

QQ: The dominant social media platform in GoodPath

In 1999 the Chinese central government launched a 'Government online project' (*zhengfu shangwang gongcheng*) which urged all levels of administration to set up their portal websites.[14] In response to the project, the local government of GoodPath purchased a computer. However, the problem was that neither local officials nor residents found any use for it, even though many villagers felt the purchase boosted morale, as one of them recalled:

> Officials claimed that the computer marked the moment that our town had entered the high-technology age. Well, to be honest, you just heard so, but didn't really think about what that meant exactly. At least, it sounded exciting... it was like our folk saying: 'Even though you have never tasted pork, at least you have seen a pig running' (*mei chiguo zhurou, zongsuan jianguo zhu pao*).

GoodPath's 'high-tech pig' lay gathering dust for almost eight years until one day people found it was too old to run. For most people in this small town, the gap between the 'national policy' and 'daily life' remained unchanged until a penguin wearing a scarf walked into their life. The penguin (Fig. 2.2) is the mascot of Chinese ICT giant *Tencent*. In 1998 HuaTeng Ma, a young software developer, set up a software company called Tencent, and his first product was 'QQ',[15] a free instant message (IM) service. Nowadays, in terms of numbers of users,

Fig. 2.2   The mascot of QQ

QQ is unquestionably the biggest social media platform in China. Besides IM, Qzone (*QQ kongjian*) is another important part of QQ's digital service. Strictly speaking Qzone,[16] the personal social networking platform on which users update statuses, write blogs and upload and share articles, photographs, music and videos with online contacts, is the social media platform usually compared with Facebook. For non-QQ users, QQ is truly different from other social media platforms in many ways. Five concepts will be used to consider the striking features of QQ: 1) high degree of anonymity; 2) high media convergence; 3) high customisation; 4) rich visuals; and 5) hierarchical structure.

A QQ account is actually a string of figures generated by the system, usually called a 'QQ number' (*QQ hao*). Users can choose any nickname they like for their 'QQ name' (*QQ ming*). Real names are very rarely used for QQ names, and usually do not even look like a traditional 'name'. In many cases people use a sentence such as 'I am crying with a smile' or 'soaring in the blue sky' as their QQ names. Exchanging one's QQ details always refers to exchanging the 'QQ number' rather than 'QQ name', as the QQ number will always remain the same. Young people frequently change their QQ names; during my research I had to make a note and 'rename' all my QQ contacts on my list so that I could recognise the users.[17] In GoodPath 98 per cent of QQ users did not use their real names as QQ names; 64 per cent did not use real photographs as QQ avatars (profile pictures). The anonymity of profiles was slightly lower, but still very high among QQ users in Shanghai, where 95 per cent of QQ users do not use real names, and 50 per cent did not use a real photograph for their QQ avatar.[18]

The main feature of the QQ 'menu bar' is a contacts list, with other add-on functions. In contrast to Facebook, which does not highlight 'contacts curation', QQ strongly guides users to sort out their contacts into different categories. The default categories of QQ contacts are 'Friends', 'Family', 'Classmate', 'Work colleague', 'Strangers' and 'Black list'; users can always rename the categories.

As one can see on the menu bar (Fig 2.3), QQ offers multiple digital services. These include group chat (QQ group), video call, social media (Qzone), microblog (Tencent Weibo), email, online game, online music, and online shopping (QQ shop).[19] Offering a whole package of digital solutions, QQ is the starting point for many people in China of their digital life: QQ email is the first email, Qzone is the first social media platform, QQ music is the first online music programme and QQ games are the first online games. Nowadays the 'convergence culture',[20] in which previously separate multiple media technologies have gradually merged

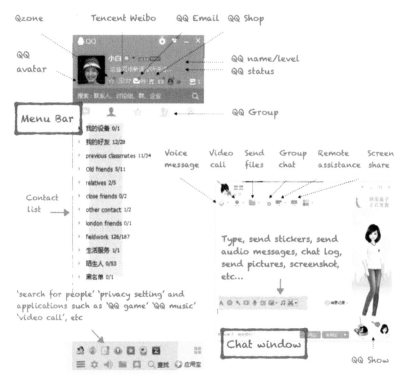

Fig. 2.3 The main body of the QQ menu bar

into one, has become the mainstream in the West. However, few have acknowledged that the trajectory of digital development in China actually started with a high-level media convergence.

The high customisation of QQ is well illustrated by the hundreds of personal webpage models, background pictures and music, and decorative elements offered on Qzone (Fig. 2.4), as well as thousands of online clothes and accessories enabling users to dress their online avatars up as they desire (Fig. 2.5). Among hundreds of Qzones I have visited during my research, none have ever been identical.

Customisation of digital space is actually commonplace throughout the Asia-Pacific region, and such a feature contributes to a far more humanised relationship between users and online spaces.[21] One illuminating example on QQ is the 'check-in' (*qian dao*) service. Unlike on Facebook, where a check-in service allows users to mark the physical locations they are currently in online, the check-in service on QQ actually refers to checking into the *online space* of QQ, no matter where the

Fig. 2.4 The decorative elements on Qzone

Fig. 2.5 Dressing up avatars on Qzone

users may be in the offline world. QQ offers different check-in stamps for users. For example, Fig. 2.6 shows the daily horoscope and Fig. 2.7 shows the 'everyday wish' stamps, offering helpful guidance: 'no procrastination', 'quit smoking', 'go to bed earlier', 'do exercise', 'do not waste food'. Xue, a 25-year-old factory officer, tried to use QQ check-in to quit smoking, acknowledging 'To some extent I think it [QQ check-in] helped...it's always more effective when you know that you're being watched'. For weeks Xue checked in on QQ every day, and his QQ friends would see a 'quit smoking' stamp from Xue's news feed, which meant that he did not smoke on that day.

The feature of 'high customisation' and 'strong visuals' are highly consequential. Chinese website design has been known for its richer colours and more complicated, cluttered layouts compared to Western websites, which value simplicity far more.[22] On QQ the situation is the same. As one of the most popular good wishes at Chinese New Year, *niannian youyu* (to have ample surplus by the end of every year) suggests,

小白
16:53

http://h5.qzone.qq.com/constellation/index?_bid=2165&_wv=5985

评论　　转发　　赞　　删除　　置顶

Fig. 2.6　Daily horoscope as 'check-in' stamps on QQ

Fig. 2.7　Daily wish as 'check-in' stamps on QQ

to have 'more than enough' is traditionally considered the lucky sign of prosperity. The principle of 'the more, the merrier', frequently found on Chinese dining tables, also contributes to the 'visual feast' available on QQ.[23] Unlike the blue and white uniform of Facebook, the Qzone interface appears much more colourful and visually rich.

Finally the QQ level system is another unique function of QQ, reflecting its 'hierarchical structure' feature. Launched in 2004, the QQ level system is based on customers' usage time – the longer the user is signed-in on QQ, the higher the QQ level that can be obtained. Different QQ levels offer users different functions and services: the higher the level, the more online privileges users enjoy, such as the ability to set up a QQ group and access more decorative elements.

> At that time [around 2001], everybody in my middle school was crazy about the QQ level, people with a higher QQ level were even more likely to have a say...I also used all the means to gain a higher level...even today I have no clue of what kind of privileges I've got or whether I've really used any of them, but at that time you just felt good about being upgraded to a higher level...maybe it's just about *mianzi* (face).

Huo, now a 26-year-old factory worker, sensed that the varied QQ levels, like all other systems of hierarchy, divide people into different classes; he thus felt the urge to gain a higher level on QQ to gain some face (*mianzi*), even though he hardly saw any instrumental value in a higher level. Huo even asked his older sister, who worked at a local internet cafe, to sign in on his QQ during the daytime when he had no access to the internet. Ten years ago Huo was just one of millions of Chinese QQ users working hard to climb the social ladder on QQ. The practice of signing in on QQ for as long as possible, purely for the purpose of upgrading to a higher level (*guaji*) became so popular among the population that the Chinese National Grid had to warn of the nationwide waste of electricity caused by QQ.[24] In 2005 Tencent had to change the QQ upgrading algorithm to address such criticism. The new algorithm counts days of active usage, rather than hours, and two hours per day is counted as an active day of usage.[25]

Besides the basic QQ level system calculated by time, users can also purchase different kinds of privileges or QQ VIP membership. Juan, a 20-year-old rural migrant who worked at a local foot massage shop, bought herself a VIP QQ membership, which cost her around 250 RMB (US $40) for a year. As such, Juan's QQ name was shown in red with a golden VIP label, and was always listed at the top of my QQ contacts list. When asked why she wanted to spend almost one-tenth of her monthly salary for a VIP membership on QQ, Juan shrugged her shoulders: 'I don't know...I just feel good being a VIP.' At the foot massage shop where she worked, the VIP guests were usually rich factory owners – the *da laoban* (big bosses) as Juan addressed them. According to her, they were treated as kings. For Juan, the VIP title on QQ is the only affordable VIP status in her life, and it truly made her feel better about herself.

At the first glance, the whole QQ level system seems simply to reflect the deep-rooted hierarchical social structure in Chinese social life; people seem intrinsically to accept the rules of the game. In practice, however, the hierarchy on QQ is fundamentally different from the social hierarchy in China. In offline life it is very difficult or almost impossible to overcome various existing inequalities and to reduce class differences, as the rural–urban divide, based on *hukou* household registration (see Chapter 1) clearly demonstrates. Deep frustration about reality was common among rural migrant workers, especially young people. The older generation of migrant workers appeared to have accepted reality after years of 'floating' life; they were primarily concerned with how to make the best of the existing situation. The new generation was more likely to challenge and refuse to accept such inequalities, constantly struggling with the gap between dream and reality. Such frustration, however, does not exist on QQ, since the rules are much simpler and more straightforward: as long as one spends either money or time, success and upgrading is almost guaranteed.

QQ – once the symbol of urban lifestyle

> I begged my brother to get a QQ for me. I thought it would be extremely difficult for our rural people to get one…you have to get your application stamped in government offices or things like that…anyway, now you may think it's silly…I felt so happy and so proud of having a QQ, even though I didn't have internet at home and I didn't know what to do with it at that time. You know, only a few people in our village have ever heard of QQ, let alone used it.

Da Guo, a 22-year-old factory worker, had his first QQ nine years ago. At that time, he was still a schoolboy, living in a poor village in inland China and knowing nothing about the internet. His older brother had already worked away in cities for two years. During Chinese New Year when his brother came back for the family reunion, Da Guo heard for the first time about the magical QQ that urbanites used. As Da Guo remarked, once upon a time QQ was regarded as the symbol of modern life, especially among people in rural areas.[26]

In the early stage of internet development in China, the eastern area had much higher rates of internet penetration than the less developed western and inland regions.[27] China's commercial internet came into existence in 1995 in urban areas such as Beijing and Shanghai,[28] and was mainly used by urban elites.[29] Even though the 'digital divide' between urban and rural has been reduced following two decades of major investment in internet and information service infrastructures in rural China, by the end of 2014 only 27.5 per cent of 649 million netizens in China belonged to the rural population.[30] Due to the digital divide and other gaps in material life, as well as the *hukou* status assigned at birth, urban lifestyles have long been considered superior,[31] and admired by the rural population.[32] In such a context QQ, perceived as a digital privilege enjoyed by the urbanites, immediately gained a lofty status among the rural population when it first appeared in their lives. Clearly among rural young people such as Da Guo, the symbolic meaning of QQ outweighed their actual use of it. To get a sense of how many people had a QQ before they had private access to the internet, a survey was conducted in September 2014 among 200 people in GoodPath and 48 people in Shanghai (Chart 2.2).

In Chart 2.2, both in Shanghai and GoodPath, the use of QQ started before the ownership of personal digital devices (PC or mobile phone). In GoodPath 63 per cent of people had QQ before the ownership of a mobile phone. QQ had been used for 5.8 years on average, with 11 years as the longest and 4 years as the shortest. It is also clear that the popularity of QQ first started among China's urban population and spread from urban to rural (the average years of use of QQ is 7.2 in Shanghai and 5.8 years in GoodPath). The digital gap between urban population and rural population in terms of ownership of digital devices seems to still exist, but when it comes to smartphones the gap has become less obvious.

Chart 2.2 Use of QQ and ownership of digital devices in GoodPath town and Shanghai

	GoodPath (small town)	Shanghai (city)
Having a QQ before having a private mobile phone	63%	48%
Ownership of Smartphone / functional mobile phone	89% / 100%	98% / 100%
Using QQ before having a personal computer	96%	67%
Ownership of PC	42%	83%
Average years of use of QQ	5.8	7.2

Despite all the disparities and differences in terms of QQ usage between rural migrants and residents of Shanghai, there is one common feature: after more than a decade of popularity among Chinese people, and despite remaining the biggest social media platform, QQ has lost its 'coolness' and its association with urban life or 'modernity'. The contrary now applies with some people even using terms such as 'old friend' or 'hometown' (*lao jia*) to describe QQ in a nostalgic tone. As Xu Hong, a 30-year-old factory officer, said, she would not give QQ as her contact details any more since on her Qzone one may discover 'an immature girl of ten years ago'. However, she did not want to delete any of the postings on her Qzone as it was always good to go back and visit her much younger self on QQ. For Xu Hong, her QQ has become her digital legacy.[33] Among young rural migrants who are active QQ users, the use of QQ *per se* has become a routine of daily life. This is precisely the reason why they spend a lot of energy on designing and beautifying their Qzones to make them more stylish and unique (*gexing*), as being unique is still considered to be modern. Meanwhile for urban young people QQ has become a land of 'hustle and bustle', which has somehow become associated with rural youth culture.

Compared to QQ, which is no longer associated with urban fashion, WeChat, a smartphone-based messaging app launched in 2011, has become the major new social media platform used by urban residents. In 2015 the penetration rate of WeChat (the percentage of people who use WeChat at least once a week) in Chinese 'first tier' cities (Beijing, Shanghai and Guangzhou) had reached 93 per cent,[34] while in small counties and fourth or fifth tier cities the figure was 26 per cent.[35] The survey conducted during field work[36] in Shanghai also illustrates the absolute dominance of WeChat: 86 per cent of people in Shanghai reported that their use of QQ had become less active since the use of WeChat. Meanwhile 95 per cent have now switched to WeChat as the main communication tool in personal relationships. Consequently when it came to the question: 'How would you react if somebody wanted to add you on QQ?' a typical answer is that of Yi, a 30-year-old white-collar worker in a Shanghai international company: 'If somebody asks for my QQ, I would be like . . . Are you kidding me? Can you be any more rustic (*tu*)?! . . . Sorry, I don't think we are on the same planet.' Yi's opinion of QQ was actually representative of the majority of interviewees of Shanghai. Of these interviewees 61 per cent, like Yi, admitted that in their eyes QQ was out of fashion (*guoshi*) or rustic (*tu*), and exchanging QQ numbers in social life[37] would appear awkward.

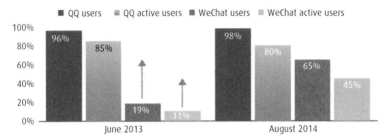

Chart 2.3 Change in QQ and WeChat use from June 2013 to August 2014 in GoodPath

GoodPath also witnessed the fast growth in popularity of WeChat among rural migrant workers (Chart 2.3). At the beginning of the research a survey[38] shows that 19 per cent of people in GoodPath town had WeChat on their smartphones, whereas 96 per cent of them used QQ. Among these only 11 per cent regarded themselves as active WeChat users,[39] whereas 85 per cent of them use QQ as their main personal social media. About a year later a similar survey[40] shows that 65 per cent of people had installed WeChat on their smartphones and the rate of WeChat active users had soared to 45 per cent, whereas the rate of QQ's active users had slightly reduced to around 80 per cent.

The figures above come from relatively small samples. Yet they do serve to showcase the different cultural capital ascribed to the use of QQ and WeChat, which has been confirmed by the long-term ethnography. To analyse the difference between QQ and WeChat further, we need to have a closer look at WeChat first.

WeChat — China's favourite new social media

Launched in 2011 by the same company that owns QQ, known in China as *WeiXin* (literally 'micro letter'), the growth of WeChat is impressive: by November 2015, the total of monthly active users of WeChat was 650 million, already 72 per cent of WhatsApp's global achievement.[41] In 2014, a survey by Global Web Index[42] shows that WeChat is the most popular messaging app in the Asia-Pacific region. In terms of basic functions (Fig. 2.8), WeChat provides text messaging, voice messaging and video calls, as well as multimedia sharing (links, photographs and videos). WeChat 'moment' (*pengyou quan*) is the personal profile, and the WeChat subscriptions/public account (*gonggong zhanghao*) is where users can subscribe information from more than 10 million accounts[43]

Fig. 2.8 The interface of WeChat (left to right): The one-to-one chat; the group chat; the moment; and the subscriptions

on the platform – ranging from media outlets and various institutions to personal blogs and more. Information on WeChat is storable and searchable. Users can save postings to their built-in WeChat files, or search for postings and conversation logs by key word on WeChat. In 2015 a WeChat user on average read 5.86 articles per day, 20 per cent of WeChat users read articles from subscription accounts, while 80 per cent of users read on WeChat personal accounts.[44] Given that in 2015 Chinese people only read on average 4.56 books per year, far less than in neighbouring east Asian countries,[45] one can conclude that WeChat has also become also a 'reading app'.

To summarise, there are seven features of WeChat. Some of them are actually very different from QQ, which in a way also explains why WeChat and QQ are favoured by different groups of people: 1) smartphone-based; 2) visually oriented; 3) strong voice message function; 4) low degree of anonymity; 5) high degree of privacy; 6) closed community; and 7) high monetisation.

Being launched at the time of the fast growth of the smartphone market in China – in contrast to QQ which started as a web-based messaging service and then was adapted for mobile – WeChat leapfrogged the PC era to the smartphone direct.[46] WeChat is designed to suit the 'smartphone lifestyle' and has become an aggregator of mobile services. Compared to the 'visual feast' on QQ, where users are allowed to design and decorate the whole page of their personal profiles, the room for customisation on WeChat is limited. The layout of WeChat profiles is fixed, and one can only change the avatar and cover photograph, which is similar to Facebook. However, WeChat gives priority to the visual in a different way. Posting on WeChat is designed to be visual-orientated. For each posting one has to upload at least one image first, before the text input area appears. As a result it is effectively impossible to post anything on WeChat without an image. On WeChat the word 'album' (*xiangce*) is used to refer to a user's personal profile, which also highlights the importance of the visual. In this perspective WeChat works a bit like Instagram, where images are regarded as the main body of the post. Even though later on WeChat added the 'pure text' function – meaning that if users select 'long press' then select 'add a new post', a pure text posting is possible – this was known by less than five per cent of people in both Shanghai and GoodPath field sites during research. WeChat did not officially prompt the pure text function. Studies have proven that visual clues are much more effective in directing attention to core information, enhancing comprehension of information and strengthening memorability.[47]

Visually orientated and mobile-based entry on WeChat also encourages users to take more photographs with their smartphones to capture 'on the go' occasions. These visuals are not only shared with others immediately, but also stored on WeChat for users' future recall. Such patterns of communication seem to boost more positive interpersonal communication, as well as offering the possibility of enhanced emotional well-being.[48] It is known that a timely response to good or nice things in daily life serves to maximise their positive effects on our lives.[49] In addition 'savouring', namely a mindful engaging in thoughts or behaviour that highlights positive emotions, heightens and enhances the positive experience of daily life.[50] Having said this, the study in GoodPath and Shanghai shows that different social groups actually made very different use of, and had very different attitudes towards, the visuals on WeChat. This will be further discussed in Chapter 3.

Besides visual orientation, voice messaging, another major function of WeChat, also enhances the platform's media richness.[51] Statistics in 2014 show that 84.5 per cent of WeChat users employ WeChat for voice messaging,[52] and in 2015 the average daily amount of WeChat voice messaging was 280 million minutes – equivalent to 540 years of phone calls.[53] In GoodPath 60 per cent of WeChat users send or receive voice messages almost daily. In Shanghai voice message is also becoming popular among the elderly, as noted by Sang, a 66-year-old retired company official. '[Leaving a] voice message is as simple as making a phone call. I never use instant messages because first I don't know Pinyin,[54] second I can't see such small words on a small screen.'

Voice messaging has enabled an older generation of Chinese, in their fifties and above, to enjoy much easier communication; text entry has always been a big barrier for users over 50 who are not good at Pinyin.[55] Having said this, WeChat users are in the main still very young, with those aged between 18 and 35 accounting for 86.2 per cent of the total.[56] Besides 'being convenient', some other nuanced implications of voice messaging have also been acknowledged, as noted here by Guli, a 21-year-old factory worker:

> I only feel comfortable about talking with my boyfriend in whatever situation; with others you will be worried about whether your voice is right or not or sending voice message is proper or not.

To Guli, voice messages are more personal and private than sending a text message. She was once annoyed by a male colleague who recorded his own singing and sent it to her as a voice message:

> ...It's so disturbing; if it's just text I can easily ignore it...but why did you send me voice? Why don't some people understand the simple fact that they can't sing?...Anyway I just think you shouldn't send voice messages at all to people who are not that close to you.

Compared to text, voice messaging – carrying the unique biophysical feature of a person – is commonly regarded as an intimate mode in personal communication. Like Guli, many saw voice messaging as primarily suitable for intimate and private contacts. Only 28 per cent of rural migrants in GoodPath town reported that they had ever sent voice messages to their managers, and this reduced to only nine per cent in Shanghai[57] who had ever used voice messages in supervisor–subordinate relationships.

In answer to the question 'Have you ever listened to your own voice messages after sending them off?',[58] 47 per cent of female and 22 per cent of male respondents in GoodPath said yes, whereas in Shanghai the figures were 70 per cent and 59 per cent respectively. The main reasons included: 1) 'I want to check whether my voice message has been recorded completely'; 2) 'I am curious about my own voice'; 3) 'I want to check whether my tone is proper or whether I express myself properly'. In China few people have had the prior experience of leaving and receiving voice messages on telephone answering machines. Compared to Europe or America, therefore, voice messags are viewed as a much more radical innovation.

Jack, a successful businessman in Shanghai, uses WeChat to train his speaking skills.

The way you talk matters. I listen to the voice messages I have sent off to my business partners all the time. It's like a voice 'mirror' so that you know what you sound like and how you can do better...

In the book *Webcam*,[59] the authors noticed that one of its important features of the webcam is that it effectively acts as a mirror, allowing many people their first ever opportunity to see themselves in conversation. It is interesting to note that a similar novel state of communication is taking place in the case of voice messaging among Chinese users: people can actually listen to themselves in daily communication for the first time. Even though people started to use voice messages for speed and convenience, they ended up with a new awareness of their voice as something that one can creatively craft.

The three features of WeChat we have observed so far are: 1) smartphone-based; 2) visually oriented; and 3) strong voice message, all relating to the pattern of interpersonal communication. The fourth feature of WeChat, 'low anonymity', serves as the starting point of our inquiry into the nature of interpersonal communication on WeChat. Compared to QQ, real names are used more frequently on WeChat. For WeChat public accounts, registration with real names is required;[60] even on WeChat personal accounts, real names are more often used than on QQ:

> The majority of my WeChat contacts are either my family or friends who knew my real name in the first place anyway, or some business partners or clients where you need to use real names to talk with them. A non-real name is not professional.

This remark by Zhao, a 32-year-old businessman in Shanghai, serves also to reflect another feature of the WeChat network: its relatively closed community. There are a few ways[61] to add new contacts on WeChat (Fig. 2.9), the most common being scanning a QR Code,[62] using mobile contacts, QQ numbers[63] or WeChat IDs. Scanning a QR code in most cases[64] requires a face to face situation, which means contacts added by QR code are usually those one has met. Either mobile phone number, QQ number or WeChat ID all suggest a very targeted contact search; it is extremely difficult for users to add random strangers by those methods.

WeChat users can nonetheless still add strangers by functions such as 'people nearby' (*fujin de ren*), which facilitates users to search for

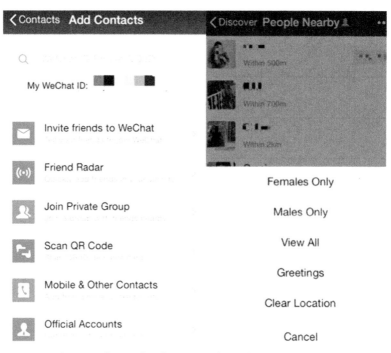

Fig 2.9 The 'people nearby' function of WeChat

strangers, listed by gender, who have allowed themselves to be located and are within one's vicinity (Fig. 2.9). Another option is 'shake' (*yao yi yao*), which allows user to shake their device to find any random people who are shaking their smartphone at the same time all around the world (Fig. 2.10), or 'message in a bottle' (*piao liu ping*). In this function, as its name suggests, you can pick up digital messages in the form of a text or short voice clip from random people, as well as toss digital messages into a 'sea' and allow others to pick them up (Fig. 2.11). Even though there is no exact demographic data of people who use WeChat to connect with strangers, in field work it has become certain that young adults (18–29) and older adults (30+) remain in general less likely than teens to use those WeChat functions to connect with strangers. They may have tried once or twice and then stopped using them, whereas teens both in Shanghai and GoodPath were more attracted to those game-like functions. The exception is that male adults, from age 18–50, seemed to be as keen on 'people nearby' and 'shake' as teens, in order to pursue potential romance and/or sex.

Generally speaking, across China WeChat is mainly used by urban adults with a relatively stable social network, stable income and

Fig. 2.10 The 'shake' function of WeChat

Fig. 2.11 The 'message in a bottle' function of WeChat

relatively high education.[65] For those people, WeChat represents a closed community that mainly consists of offline network (family, friends and colleagues at work), with little room for online strangers. Also, since the urban user's online identity overlaps strongly with their offline identity, real names are widely accepted and applied. However, the situation is very different for rural migrants, who constantly feel frustration in their 'floating' offline life. They therefore have a stronger desire for higher anonymity online, in order to lose or deny their unsatisfactory social identity offline. A survey in the study[66] shows that 71 per cent of WeChat users in Shanghai applied real names or easily recognisable nick names or initial letters for their WeChat profiles. Eighty-two per cent of them used real portrait photographs (photos of themselves or their children) as WeChat avatars. Of the rural migrant users in GoodPath, however, only three per cent show their real names on WeChat, while the rate of real photos is as low as 12 per cent. Even though we label WeChat as 'low anonymity' in general, therefore, the situation can be very different in different social groups.

Designed mainly for urban users, the privacy setting on WeChat is stricter than on QQ and Facebook. For example, on QQ visiting one's Qzone profile is in most cases[67] visible not only to the profile owner, but also to all of the profile owner's QQ contacts. This basically means that social media 'stalking' on QQ is difficult. On Facebook, by contrast, viewing someone's profile trying not be noticed is not only possible, but also popular.[68]

Compared to the situation on WeChat, however, the visibility of one's social network on Facebook[69] is still much higher. On WeChat users have no access to their WeChat friends' contacts list. On top of this, in many cases users have no access to the 'likes' and 'comments' left on their friends' profile pages. For example, if A and B are both friends with C, but A and B are not friends on WeChat, then A cannot see B's comments or likes to C's posts. Moreover, one can only share postings from WeChat 'public' accounts. That is to say, sharing a friend's post by just clicking on 'share', which is very common on Facebook, is not possible on WeChat. For Hu, a 33-year-old journalist from Shanghai, such filtering on WeChat is helpful. 'I like the design, neat and simple; social relationships are complicated and it can avoid a lot of trouble if irrelevant contacts are separated rather than mixed up.' It allows her much more freedom and flexibility to deal with different social networks:

> Sometimes banters between me and my close friends on comment
> can be very improper in other's eyes ... If all my friends' comments

could be seen by all my WeChat contacts, I am afraid my reputation would be totally ruined, haha!

Whereas, nothing is perfect, sometimes Hu also wished that the comments and likes can be seen by all, '…but funnily enough, things are different if you post some good news, then you actually want everybody to see that you are "liked" by many and you got such and such praises on comments'.

Like Hu, Hao Wen, a university graduate in his twenties has also spotted the consequence of the 'common friend only' (*gongtong haoyou kejian*) setting on WeChat. However for him, rather than feeling regret that he cannot make highly praised posts visible to all the contacts, he actually makes his less popular postings appear to be very popular:

> The point is you don't know exactly how many people liked or commented on my posts since you have no idea how many are not our common friends…then that's something I can work on. For example, I comment on my own posting saying 'Thank you to all of you and I am really touched'. Now this comment can be seen by all, and people would believe that there are actually many people who have commented on or liked this posting; they couldn't see any just because those who commented or liked were not common friends…I guess it's also about *mianzi* (face); you just don't want to lose face in front of your friends.

It is difficult to judge how many WeChat users actually applied the same trick as Hao Wen did to produce a more popular and positive self-image online. Interestingly what Hao Wen revealed was an anxiety about one's public image in a relatively closed and strong-tie based online community.

'"Face" represents an individual's claimed sense of positive image in the context of social interaction.'[70] In this instance social media is the context of social interaction, with concerns or even anxiety about one's positive image on social media being commonly shared among people in the research. Without doubt Hao Wen successfully solved the problem by taking advantage of the setting of online display, and made the disadvantage of WeChat's function in certain situations into a valued trick.

The features of 'low anonymity', 'high privacy' and 'closed community' on WeChat are embraced by many urban citizens, but they are not necessarily viewed as advantages among rural migrants in GoodPath. In fact the opposite is true: more than two-thirds of migrant workers, especially younger people, showed a clear preference for QQ over WeChat. Some of them gave as a reason that on QQ the social connection is more open. As we will discover in Chapter 4, visitors of Qzone are encouraged or even urged to engage with more interactions, which help to contribute to a 'hot and noisy' (renao) ambience of Qzone. Furthermore, strangers on QQ have become an important part of social life online[71] for rural migrants whose real names are cautiously avoided, given the discrepancy between people's online and offline social identities.

'High monetisation' is the feature of WeChat to emerge most recently. The field work has witnessed a successful monetisation of WeChat, beginning at Chinese New Year 2014. On 28 January 2014 WeChat launched a new function called 'WeChat red envelope' (hong-bao), which allowed users to send 'digital red envelopes' of money to WeChat contacts electronically. 'The red envelope' (which contains real money) has a long tradition in China as a festival and ceremony gift (for example a gift for Chinese New Year or a wedding), with the implication of bringing good luck and best wishes in addition to the monetary value. The new function on WeChat allows Chinese people to move this tradition online, and to make it more fun: the sender can either send a 'fixed amount' digital red envelope to certain contacts or alternatively decide how much to hand out in total to how many people and then leave everything else to the system, which randomly chooses how the total is divided. For instance, A decided to hand out 20 RMB to five WeChat contacts. The money could be divided into five digital red envelopes by the system randomly as 2.4, 3.6, 2.3, 1.5, and 0.2 RMB. Then the first five WeChat contacts of A who clicked the link got envelopes. Being the first one does not guarantee the most money, however: he or she may unfortunately end up with the envelope containing the least. The gambling-like red envelope grabbing soon went viral. From Chinese New Year's Eve to 4 p.m. on the first day of the Chinese New Year (31 January 2014), more than 5 million users tried out the feature to deliver in excess of 75 million red envelopes. Every minute an average of 9,412 virtual red envelopes were received during this period.[72]

Given the fact that users had to link their bank account(s) to their WeChat accounts before they could hand out or withdraw[73] money from red envelopes, the red envelope phenomenon significantly fuelled the monetisation of WeChat. This in turn paved the way for mobile payments via WeChat. Via a WeChat 'wallet', the WeChat payment account[74] (Fig. 2.12), users can make instant payments for online as well as in-store

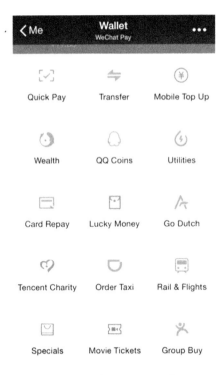

Fig. 2.12 WeChat pay interface

purchases. In 2015 at least one in five active WeChat users were set up for WeChat payment.[75] Besides business institutions, all the WeChat public accounts can also sell products or services on WeChat. WeChat payment verified service accounts (retailers) on its platform. Through WeChat payment, service accounts are able to provide direct in-app payment service to users. Customers are allowed either to pay for items or services on web pages inside the app or to pay in store by scanning the digital ID (WeChat QR codes) of products provided by offline retailers. In 2015 WeChat launched the 'City Services' project,[76] further expanding the scope of services to pay utility bills, book a doctor's appointment, get bank statements, send money to friends, obtain geo-targeted coupons, etc. Through such practices WeChat has become an aggregator of the most frequently used and popular services available on mobile devices. We can conclude that WeChat has gone far beyond a social media tool. It has the potential to become a highly hybrid mobile and social commerce platform, with built-in payment accounts (e-wallet), LBS (location-based services) and much more.

The high monetisation of WeChat leads us to a wider exploration of e-commerce in China.[77] China is leading the way in this field with high mobile purchase rates (69 per cent of Chinese consumers made a purchase through their smartphone, as opposed to 46 per cent of consumers in the US) and a more active participation in social media.[78] In GoodPath, around ten per cent of people[79] actively engaged with e-commerce, for example setting up one's own online shop or selling goods on one's personal WeChat profiles. Most of them have full-time jobs and do WeChat business part-time; others do it more professionally, since they sell the same products in their physical stores. Around 60 per cent of people engaged at least once with mobile payment functions or other forms of online commercial events, with an even higher rate among young people of 95 per cent.

Generally speaking, special/local goods (local specialities) or products endorsed by friends sold by friends sell best. Dee in GoodPath represents a successful example of doing business on WeChat. Her best-selling product is free-range chicken eggs form her parents' farm.[80] Towards the end of 2013 the outbreak of bird flu seriously affected the chicken farm's business because all the regular buyers stopped purchasing. Hundreds of organic chicken eggs became unmarketable products overnight. This became one of the most difficult moments in Dee's life as she watched the family business slide into a desperate situation. Inspired by the commercial posts on WeChat that she encountered every day, Dee decided to turn to it. She posted a photograph of a basket of eggs and wrote:

> My dear friends, if you want to buy healthy, organic eggs, please let me know. My parents' chicken farm offers 100 per cent healthy and organic free-range chicken eggs at the most reasonable price! And also please spread the word!

On the same day she got five orders from her friends and all the eggs were sold within two weeks. A friend of Dee's, Yun, who ordered 50 eggs on WeChat, commented 'I think it is a good deal, I helped her out, but it's not that she owes me a big favour (*renqing*) since I also benefited a lot from the good price of the quality eggs'. During the next two months of the egg crisis, I continued to trace the interaction between Dee and Yun on WeChat, observing that Dee's 'like' and comments on Yun's new postings had become much more frequent since the egg crisis. 'I think I owe her a favour (*renqing*), so maybe because of that I paid more attention to her updates on WeChat since then…and I do think we have a better relationship now,' Dee explained.

At first glance, Dee's egg sale on WeChat is just one instance of 'word-of-mouth marketing', of which I encountered plenty in field work. This also seems to echo a study which shows that in China 66 per cent of Chinese consumers relied on recommendations from friends and family, compared to 38 per cent in the US.[81] However, in Dee's case there is something more to consider. On the one hand, as we mentioned in Chapter 1, in the collective society of China social relations (*guanxi*), the derivative of kinship or 'in-group' personal relationships, has its fundamental impact on a whole range of social interactions from business activities to public relations.[82] On the other hand, it is important to acknowledge that business activities which manifest themselves, for example, in a form of traditional red envelopes – the gift money which was given with the expectation of return[83] – is always an integral or even necessary part of personal relationships in China.[84]

In the anthropology of China, there is a rich literature on the 'gift economy'. The major argument is that in the cycle of giving, receiving and the reciprocity of gift exchange, social relationships are established and maintained.[85] In Dee's case, the gift exchange does not take place in the form of a physical gift, but by way of a favour (*renqing*), which also follows the principle of reciprocity.[86] *Renqing* literally means 'human feelings', and refers to the feelings inherent in personal relationships. In practice *renqing* also provides a moral sense of obligation (such feeling as 'I owe you') towards others, which motivates further gift exchange.[87] In Dee's case, therefore, her return 'gift' was actually more attention and more positive interaction with her friend on WeChat. In *guanxi,* 'any act of helpfulness or generosity, no matter whether given or received, begins to draw one into the network of reciprocal exchanges'.[88] In the end, as Dee remarked, the relationship between herself and her friend had become closer and more positive through the cycle of 'gift exchange'.

Thus, unlike Western societies, where business is supposed to take place in a professional context without personal touch and element, doing business and establishing personal relationships in China are usually the same approach, with slightly different fronts. In this sense doing business on social media in China seems to match with the very feature of *guanxi*. The success of the monetisation of WeChat, to a large extent, is a result of Chinese personal relationships, which intrinsically include business elements; such forms of success cannot necessarily be copied by other societies.[89] Furthermore, in the case of WeChat red envelopes, we see a challenge to our very understanding of the social meaning of money. In the West money is traditionally regarded as an impersonal medium; it is only supposed to apply in business where social connections are mainly functional. In *The Philosophy of Money* Georg Simmel contended that money can never become an 'adequate mediator of personal relationships' as it 'distances and estranges the gift from the giver much more definitely'.[90] In China, by contrast, money has long been used to express concern and love in social relations. It has long been selected as a 'perfect' gift because it can be used to buy whatever the recipient desires, eliminating the unnecessary risk of choosing a wrong gift or the wastefulness of speculating on the recipient's needs.[91]

In retrospect, some features of WeChat actually emerged in the process of use given the 'technology affordances'.[92] In practice these features are interlocked, and work together as a new form of sociality online. A further discussion of how social relationships become reshaped or reinforced in the use of QQ and WeChat will continue in the rest of book. But now let's move to Weibo, another buzz word surrounding Chinese social media.

What is Weibo?

For many Westerners, Weibo (microblogging) is the equivalent of Twitter. In China there are several Weibo platforms, such as Tencent Weibo and Sohu Weibo. Because of the popularity of Sina Weibo, however, with 212 million monthly active users,[93] 'Weibo' is often used generically to refer to Sina Weibo. Many features of Weibo appear familiar to Twitter users,[94] such as the 140 character limit, use of '@' to mention people and addition of '#' to keyword the postings. Additionally Chinese users were able to embed multimedia content in Weibo more than 18 months before Twitter users could do so in the US.

Weibo is a celebrity hub. Chinese celebrities depend on Weibo as a way to connect with their fans and drive their popularity. However, the statistics in GoodPath show that the usage of Weibo among rural migrants is extremely low. Even though many have heard of Weibo, less than one per cent[95] actually used Weibo to post or follow others. Among the one per cent Weibo users, Tencent Weibo, rather than Sina

Weibo, was the main site – mainly because Tencent QQ 'bind' its users to embedded Weibo services. Gui You, a factory official in his forties, has Tencent Weibo which synchronises updates automatically with his QQ status updates:

> When I updated a status on QQ, the 'Weibo' would do the same thing automatically. I have no idea about Weibo, but I can't be bothered to figure it out.

Gui You's confusion about Weibo is widely shared among people in GoodPath. Few know what it is really about or what it is good for. Duo Tian, a 26-year-old factory worker, explained why she abandoned her Sina Weibo account after using it for a couple of weeks. 'I tried, but I really don't like it…it's too complicated, and you have no friends there.' It is true that the specific grammar in Weibo, such as the @ and # function, are a bit confusing for beginners. However, the main reason seems to lie in the fact that Weibo is more like a public publishing platform rather than a personal 'chat' platform between friends. People find it more difficult to establish personal connections on the platform, and so prefer to remain with the platform that most of their contacts use.

Compared to WeChat, Weibo addresses a far bigger audience. Big cities are Weibo's main market,[96] since the urban population shows a stronger information-seeking motivation, driven by a need for richer, more diverse information. The limited market of Weibo in towns and villages further discourages people from using Weibo as a personal communication tool.

Having said that, the use of Weibo among China's urban population has also witnessed a decline. It is not only my field work in Shanghai that has shown that people are using Weibo less[97] because of the increasing use of WeChat. The WeChat public account has taken the place of Weibo for the purpose of news reading and information searching. National statistics show that the number of Weibo users in 2013 declined by 27 million compared to the number of users at the end of 2012. The level of activity also declined, with around 80 per cent of users hardly ever logged in.[98]

There are several reasons that the Chinese urban population has become less interested in Weibo. First is the decline in the quality of Weibo information, the result of an overflow of advertisements. In contrast to WeChat and QQ, strangers have the right to leave comments on any Weibo profile, which leaves a loophole for the posting of commercial advertisements[99] by the millions of 'online water army' (*shuijun*) who get paid for such work. This has significantly diluted the user's experience of Weibo. Secondly, since 2013 the Chinese government has started to 'clean' up the internet, targeting Weibo.[100] Officials have intensified attacks on the spread of online rumours, and Weibo users can be jailed for up to three years for posting false information that is forwarded 500 times or viewed 5,000 times.[101] As a result, a large number of online public intellectuals have had to give up their accounts. Some of them began to shift towards WeChat,[102] as a WeChat public account works much less publicly than on Weibo. Information on WeChat spreads more slowly than on Weibo, but because of the 'slow burn' feature, which appears less intimidating to the regime, WeChat content seems to undergo less strict censorship.[103]

This chapter has introduced the main social media platforms. Given the low rate of usage of Weibo among people in this study, the discussion of Weibo here will be relatively brief. It is also true that there are other Chinese social media platforms, but given the limited space they will not be introduced one by one, particularly as they are not used by the majority of people in the study. However, a few of them will be introduced later in the book when discussing a specific individual's use of social media. The next section will focus upon the very digital devices on which most of the engagement with social media in China now takes place.

Social media and smartphones

By 2014 the number of Chinese mobile internet users had reached 527 million, making mobile phones the most common device for access to the internet.[104] For people who cannot afford a PC,[105] a smartphone has become their first private access to the internet. Budget smartphones dominate the smartphone market in GoodPath, the average price being around 500 RMB (US $80). The average monthly cost is around 100 RMB (US $16). A smartphone is definitely the number one internet device.

It has been young rural migrants who have driven the local budget smartphone market. The majority (80 per cent) of rural migrants aged between 17 and 35 already own a smartphone, and 70 per cent of those in current use are their owners' first. One-third of people reported that they wanted to have a smartphone by a 'good brand' (*hao paizi*) in a couple of years' time, when they will have saved up enough money. A 'good brand' smartphone (such as iPhone and Samsung) is regarded as a symbol of social status.

According to the local mobile phone dealers, *shanzhai* mobile phones used to be very popular, mainly because of their huge price advantages (usually the price is between one-fifth and one-tenth of the 'real brand'). A *shanzhai* mobile phone refers to a fake, low-priced mobile phone: *shanzhai* in Chinese refers to the mountain camps or mountain villages under the control of regional warlords or bandits, far away from governmental control.[106] Several unique features of *shanzhai* mobiles attract users. For instance, the ringtone of most *shanzhai* phones is extremely loud and some of them even have a funky and sparkling 'incoming calls flashlight'. This is regarded by customers as not only 'convenient' (as most rural migrants work in noisy factories), but also fashionable. The function of 'Dual SIM card dual standby' (*shuangka shuangdai*), which allows two different SIM cards in one mobile phone, is also welcome as people usually choose separate phone packages for keeping in touch with local people and those back in their original villages.

Since the end of 2012, however, the *shanzhai* mobile phones have started to shift in terms of sales strategy. Previously they just copied famous brand names. Now some *shanzhai* mobile phone manufacturers have set up their own branded phones, and newly designed budget smartphone brands such as 'XiaoMi' (Mi-One) have established their market position.[107] Major Chinese telecom companies have also started to invest in the market for smartphones with a price lower than US $150 (*qianyuan ji*)[108] and launched a few packages for contract mobile phones (*heyue ji*) together with Chinese local mobile phone manufacturers such as HuaWei. With a guaranteed consumption (*baodi xiaofei*) of US $10 to $15 dollars per month, one can get a smartphone for around US $50 or even for 'free'. These inexpensive smartphones quickly captured the low-end smartphone market, offering not only a similar price advantage but also better quality and after-sales service than their *shanzhai* competitors (Chart 2.4).[109] As a result the *shanzhai* era of Chinese low-end mobile phone market has already passed.

QQ was the first digital platform in China that successfully practised 'media convergence', and smartphones have considerably accelerated the process. Smartphones have not only been woven into the patterns of people's daily lives, but also function as the 'mega media'

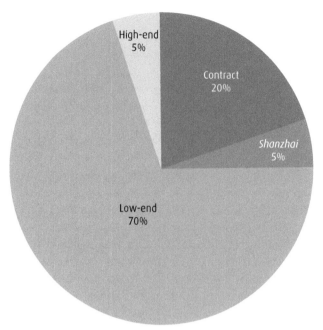

Chart 2.4 Distribution of different kinds of mobile phone devices among 200 rural migrants in GoodPath

that allow people to navigate various social networks, enjoy forms of entertainment and participate in consumer culture. Cara Wallis notes:

> For those who study convergence among more privileged users, there is a tendency to downplay its technological aspect, or the way one device can increasingly handle numerous media functions. However, millions of people in the world must make do with a single delivery technology for most of their digital media use, and almost always it is a mobile phone.[110]

As quoted, even before the smartphone had become available among this 'information have-less' group,[111] mobile phones had already played an essential role in the lives of low income people. Now the smartphone has become the first music player, video player and camera, as well as the first private access to online reading, online payment and online social networking (Fig. 2.13). The popularity of budget smartphones has therefore largely closed the gap of the digital divide in China.

Fig. 2.13 A rural migrant family watch television via a smartphone over dinner. (Chinese traditional painting, 68.5 × 41.5 cm; painter: Xinyuan Wang)

Conclusion

So what can be learned from Chinese social media such as QQ and WeChat and the wider technologies of the smartphone? The real significance of this chapter is only apparent if it is not read as a chapter about Chinese rural migrants and social media, or even a chapter about Chinese social media, but rather as part of a comparative ethnographic study on the very meaning and nature of social media.

The starting point has been the radically different historical trajectories of these developments between China and the West. In the West, people have a tendency to assume they know what social media naturally 'is', because there has been a slow incremental development based on clear precedents. In the developed West the smartphone has gradually been appropriated as a new digital device, the natural successor to the personal camera, mobile phone and PC. Social media has also been quite a specific development in personal communications, forming a niche within more general IT development. By contrast the Chinese social media landscape has been formed as a result of a dynamic movement. It has been cut apart from the global environment outside China, pushed by a very deliberate policy of the party-state, carried forward by a vast domestic market demand, and accelerated by the booming growth of smartphones. In due course this was the demand that collided with the traditional pattern of social relations and technological innovation. This dynamism continues to grow apace, with new forces continually arising such as dating and commerce. We need to start by acknowledging the sheer, incredible scale of this. Now hundreds of millions of people, who only a short time ago had no experience of anything digital, suddenly find themselves in possession of instruments that are as powerful as their Western equivalents and, as we have seen, often used for an even greater range of purposes.

3
Visual material on social media

Seventy-nine per cent[1] of people have taken more photographs since they started to use social media; 64 per cent believe that a visual post is more convincing on social media than a text-only post, and 85 per cent prefer visual posts to text-only posts.

Compared to former times when for most ordinary people it was only possible to circulate a few visual images, the contemporary world is very much a phenomenon 'seen online'.[2] Because of the use of social media and the popularity of smartphones, our relationship to visual images has reached a level of ubiquity that is historically unprecedented.[3] Moreover, unlike mass media, visual material on social media is produced and circulated in a 'two-way' interaction, becoming an essential part of interpersonal communication. This chapter will discuss what people actually post on social media[4] and see how the visual is culturally constructed – what is made to be seen and what is made to be unseen.[5] In some cases the 'face value' of the visual can be misleading or confusing, and needs to be interpreted. Although visual images are the focus of this chapter, the analysis of visual material on social media occurs throughout this volume. Some genres of visual images are mentioned here only briefly and will receive further analysis in other chapters.

Much of this chapter consists of a brief survey of what I have identified as the 15 main genres of images posted by rural migrants. This is in order to identify some key patterns to this practice when viewed as a whole. This is clarified when the dominant genres of rural migrants are compared in the conclusion with a survey of middle-class people from Shanghai. What we find is that, although there is a continuity between visual postings and traditional photography, there is also a series of key new genres on social media added by rural migrants.

These new genres on social media are actually crucial to understand these factory workers. Relevant issues include the compression of being 'young' into a very short time, and the way in which social media compensates for this by providing a place where people can identify with youth themes. While analogue photography recorded life as it was lived, social media can be used for the opposite purpose of envisaging a life to which people aspire, articulating this far more effectively in visual terms than they could in words or text. Once again we see how social media has gained immense significance as 'another place' in which migrants come to live: one that takes them further towards their intended destination than mere offline life can do.

Genres of visual material on social media

An inspection of the huge amount of visual postings on rural migrants' social media profiles suggested 15 main genres: 'relationships', 'selfies', 'trivia' 'compulsorily shared', 'chicken soup for the soul', 'humour', 'fantasy', 'children', 'travel', 'events', 'archive', 'political', 'food', 'anti-mainstream' (*feizhuliu*) and 'commercial'. In some cases, the genres overlap with one another and can easily be subjected to further division. The main point is not to classify the different visual genres 'scientifically', but rather to help us appreciate and clarify the range of these postings.

1 'Relationships'

This is 'social' media and the majority of the visual material deals in some manner or other with relationships. However, the genre of 'relationships' here refers only to certain kinds of directly depicted relationships, such as kinship (Fig. 3.1), romantic relationships (Fig. 3.2) or friendship (Fig. 3.3). The majority of images about kinship refer to the relationship between young parents and babies, partly due to the fact that in this study the main contributors of the visual postings are young people.

Friendship between females is usually expressed in a very straightforward way. It may include photographs of women hugging or walking hand-in-hand, and in many cases takes the form of group selfies (Fig. 3.4). While 32 per cent of females had photos of their best friends on their social media, only 3.5 per cent of males did the same. The demonstration of male bonding seems to be different – for instance, through

Fig. 3.1 Typical images of kinship on social media

Fig. 3.2 A typical image showing a romantic relationship on social media

Fig. 3.3 A typical photograph of friendship on social media

Fig. 3.4 Typical group selfies of women

Fig. 3.5 A typical image of intimacy on the social media profiles of young men

playing video games together, as we will see in Chapter 4, and postings of related deity images, which we will further discuss in Chapter 6.

In terms of romantic relationships, the visual representation for young men seems to be slightly more drawn to sexual intimacy; rather than posting any image of themselves, the common practice is to collect photographs from the internet (Fig. 3.5). For women, on the other hand, a typical image seems to be more about emotional intimacy (Fig. 3.6). As Chart 3.1 shows,[6] 98 per cent of young women and 85 per cent of young men posted images from the 'relationships' genre. More than half of middle-aged people also have such postings, whereas elderly people seem to be least inclined to post on this theme. At all ages, women showed more interest in posting 'relationship' images.

2 'Selfies'

The 'selfie', defined as 'a photographic self-portrait; esp. one taken with a smartphone or webcam and shared via social media',[7] has become a universal phenomenon. Among rural migrants selfies also have become an instant visual communication of where they are, what they are doing,

Fig. 3.6 A typical image of emotional intimacy on the social media profiles of young women

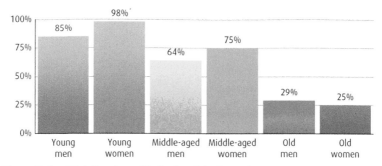

Chart 3.1 Distribution of 'relationships' postings

who they think they are, and who they think is watching. There are a number of sub-genres of selfies, and interpretations of different genres vary. A typical or classic selfie is usually shot from a high angle, with a full focus on the face. It is common for young women to have a great number of this type of selfie, capturing different facial expressions, accessories or make-up (Fig. 3.7), whereas for young men a typical form is a 'hair selfie', focusing on their stylish haircuts (Fig. 3.8). The fact that the average height (around 167 cm) of male rural migrants from inland provinces is below the national average may explain the cult of hairstyles that make them appear between 2 and 5 cm taller. The other reason would be the desire to show a rebellious gesture; such hairstyles

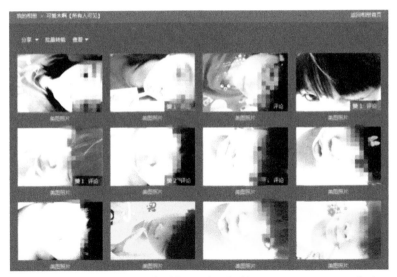

Fig. 3.7 A typical range of selfies uploaded by young women to their social media profiles

Fig. 3.8 'Hair selfies' by young men

seem to accord with the anti-mainstream (*feizhuliu*)[8] aesthetic of youth culture.

'Mirror selfies', i.e. those taken through a mirror, come across as another popular selfie genre. The mirror selfie is convenient to take, but also allows a wider view which helps to unfold some other details, for example dresses or shoes (Fig. 3.9). It may be used to show some part of the body to best advantage (Fig. 3.10), or even the very digital device with which the selfie was taken. As discussed in Chapter 2,

Fig. 3.9   A typical 'mirror selfie' illustrating one's dress or shoes

Fig. 3.10   A typical 'mirror selfie' helping to show part of the body to best advantage

iPhones are regarded as symbols of higher socio-economic status among low income people such as rural migrants, thus revealing the ownership of an iPhone is regarded as a plus on a selfie. Of all the mirror selfies posted by rural migrants, the majority (around 90 per cent) were taken by iPhones. However, such figures do not match with the relative low ownership of iPhones among rural migrants, as shown in Chapter 2. There are thus two possibilities: that non-iPhone users choose not to take mirror selfies, or that the people featured on their selfies may not necessarily own the iPhone. For example, the young factory worker Huatian took a mirror selfie using the iPhone of one of his friends (Fig. 3.11) and posted it on Qzone. On this selfie he was wearing a fake Adidas T-shirt and Doc Martins, acquired at the local night market. As he said, 'I think you just want to show the best of you on a selfie'. Comments on this selfie, as he expected, focused on the nice material world shown in the photograph; one of the comments read, 'Life is not too bad . . . Lucky you!'

Fig. 3.11   A 'mirror selfie' taken by a young factory worker to portray himself as somebody enjoying a good life

However, not all the selfies seek to portray glamorous aspects of oneself. 'Pyjama selfies', which people take in their bedrooms in their most casual look, are examples of a different trend. As the text on Fig. 3.12 reads 'Can't fall asleep, too tired', these 'pyjama selfies' were usually posted at the end of the day before people went to bed, or sometimes when they could not get to sleep. Even though most rural migrants do not have their own private space, given the limited living accommodation, a 'pyjama selfie' seems to be the first time people intentionally invite the public to view some of the most private moments of their lives.

The results are regarded with some scepticism. 'I think she is faking it; even though it looks like no make-up, I bet she photoshopped it to make sure her skin looked perfect...It is actually a carefully posed selfie to show how cute she is...look at the duck face and the collarbone,' commented a young female participant, who did not know the subject of Fig. 3.14. On the other hand, in a separate interview, the subject of Fig. 3.13 herself remarked, 'I just feel like taking a selfie, no specific purpose'. With or without any specific purpose, the very action of posting a pyjama selfie is always a deliberate act by the person posting.

A pyjama selfie usually attracts more 'likes' or comments, partially because it looks different from people's usual daytime appearance and

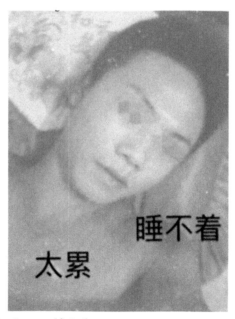

Fig. 3.12 A 'pyjama selfie' of a young man

Fig. 3.13   A 'pyjama selfie' of a young woman

helps the senders to get closer to their online contacts. As the male factory worker featured in Fig. 3.12 observed, for women a 'pyjama selfie'
may mean removing physical make-up, but for men it can be the moment
when they finally take off the 'mask' of social expectation of being a man:
'I let you see the real me which you can never see during the daytime.
At work I won't show a weak part of me as a man.' Even though people
may interpret pyjama selfies in different ways, to unfold a private and
different aspect of oneself voluntarily is usually regarded as a friendly
gesture on social media, where self-exposure can lead to mutual trust.
In this sense a pyjama selfie is an example of how a selfie is a skilful
self-representation that can connect to, and communicate with, others.[9]
In terms of the awareness of relationships, the 'group selfie' takes a step
further, directly portraying the closeness of the relationship (as mentioned in the section on 'relationships' postings above). Compared to
other kinds of group photographs, group selfies require physical prox-
imity in order to include a group of people in a photo frame, which in
a way also legitimises more intimate and informal body contact. Such
body language, triggered by group selfies, enhances the sense of con-
nectedness, which is further reinforced when group selfies are posted
on social media.

In retrospect, self-love or narcissism is rarely the only motivation behind selfies.[10] In many cases, rather than recording themselves, people are in fact recording their social network via selfies. For many, a selfie is not 'complete' until it has been uploaded to social media and viewed by others. Thus it makes little sense to single out any individual selfie without acknowledging the context of the anticipated audience on social media. A selfie is actually a new form of social interaction facilitated by social media; it reflects how people see themselves in a network. As shown on Chart 3.2, so far the genre of 'selfies' is still the exclusive preserve of young people among rural migrants. However, it is highly likely that the situation will change in the near future, given the evidently increasing popularity of smartphones among older people and the increasing social acceptance of selfies in China – especially now China's President Xi has also started to post selfies.[11]

3 'Trivia'

The genre of 'trivia' refers to photographs of insignificant housework or household items (Fig. 3.14). It usually takes place when people feel bored, and it seems that the very action of taking a photo and posting it on social media is the less tedious activity that enlivens the daily routine.

As Chart 3.3 shows, in 'trivia' gender and age play important roles. For some middle-aged women trivia made up most of their original visual postings on social media. Men are less keen on posting trivia. Older people rarely posted trivia as they tended to view social media postings as significant personal statements, whereas many younger

Fig. 3.14 Typical trivia postings

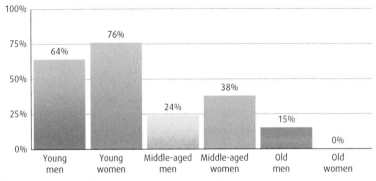

Chart 3.2   Distribution of postings of selfies

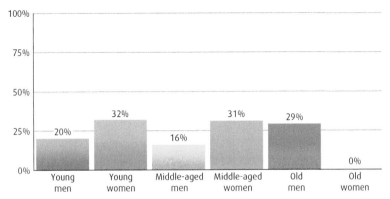

Chart 3.3   Distribution of 'trivia' postings

people have no problem in posting daily trivia on social media as they see it as a personal diary.

4 'Compulsorily shared'

The reason this genre has been labelled 'compulsorily shared' is summed up by one participant's response to the post's sharing request: 'you feel you have to share it, otherwise you would worry that there will be something wrong.' The majority of 'compulsorily shared' posts are deeply related to beliefs in the efficacy of the images of deities (Fig. 3.15), lucky animals (Fig. 3.16) or even strange beings (*yishou*) (Fig. 3.17), all of which derive from Chinese folk religion. In some cases the texts accompanying these images make the compulsion to share even stronger; the text on Fig. 3.17 reads 'If you don't share it, your parents will have a disaster in 7 days'.

Fig. 3.15 A typical image of a deity shared on social media

Fig. 3.16 A typical image of lucky animals shared on social media

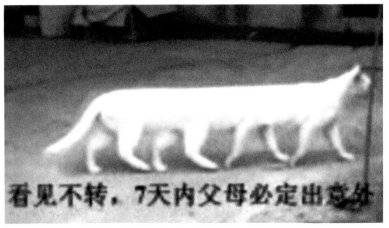

Fig. 3.17　A typical image of strange beings shared on social media

A further discussion of the practice of Chinese folk religion on social media is discussed in Chapter 6. One sub-genre, however, consists of regional images. For instance, the text embedded on Fig. 3.18 says: 'If you come from JiangXi, you have to share this post!' JiangXi is an inland province of China, from which many rural migrants come. The dirty face of the rural boy in Fig. 3.18 strongly contrasts with the large, cool sunglasses and cigarette. As a factory migrant worker who shared it commented: 'Our peasants are poor, but we can also have an attitude (*zhuai*).' On top of the image, the text blurb declares JiangXi to be the best place in China:

> The high buildings in Beijing are nothing compared to huts in JiangXi; the fast cars in Shanghai are nothing compared to the bikes in JiangXi; JiangXi has the most beautiful women in China, and men in JiangXi are all very handsome and rich.

Such posts have become 'memes'.[12] Rural migrants from other provinces also share similar postings about their hometowns. In the face of severe social discrimination and a strong rural–urban divide, the pervasive lack of self-confidence and sense of belonging among rural migrants is somehow expressed in an extremely proud tone in these postings. And many people feel a compulsion to share such postings to make a proud public statement. The reason for sharing such posts also lies in some pragmatic concerns. As we will see in Chapter 5, social connections between people from the same hometown is the fundamental social

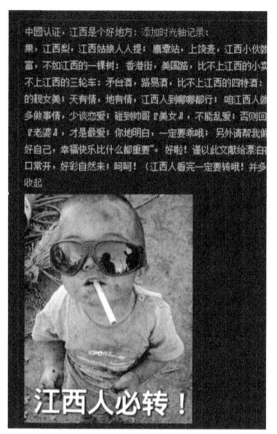

中國認证，江西是个好地方：添加时光轴记录：
果，江西梨，江西姑娘人人提；鹰潭站，上饶妻，江西小伙
富，不如江西的一棵树；香港街，美国路，比不上江西的小吃
不上江西的三轮车；矛台酒，路易酒，比不上江西的四特酒；
的靓女美！天有情，地有情，江西人到哪哪都行；咱江西人就
多做事情，少谈恋爱；碰到帅哥『美女』，不能乱爱；否则回
『老婆』，才是最爱；你地明白，一定要乖哦；另外请帮我做
好自己，幸福快乐比什么都重要。好啦！谨以此文献给漂泊
口常开，好彩自然来！呵呵！（江西人看完一定要转哦！并多
收起

江西人必转！

Fig. 3.18 A typical 'compulsorily shared' posting among rural migrants with a focus on regional connections

network on which rural migrants rely to get a job, find a place to live and get access to other forms of support.[13] Thus a collective identity based on the same hometown (*tongxiang*) not only serves as a sense of belonging for individuals, it also plays a key role in the collective allocation of social resources in rural migrants' economic lives. Given all the reasons above, images from the 'compulsorily shared' genre are pervasive on the social media profiles of rural migrants (Chart 3.4).

5 'Chicken soup for the soul'

Images from the 'Chicken soup for soul' genre are usually the illustrations of articles on the same theme. When people shared this kind of article, they also shared the images embedded within them.

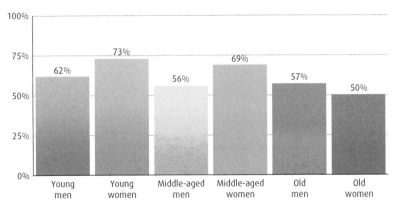

Chart 3.4   Distribution of 'compulsorily shared' postings

Originally *Chicken Soup for the Soul* referred to a book series from the US, consisting of inspirational true stories about how ordinary people managed to have happy and successful lives. The book was translated into Chinese around a decade ago and became a major bestseller. Nowadays people use the expression 'chicken soup for the soul' (*xin ling ji tang*) to describe shared articles on social media offering career and lifestyle advice. It is very common for those articles to contain photographs of celebrities. Ma Yun,[14] for instance, a successful businessman who started from scratch, frequently appeared as a great source of advice. Ma is viewed as a living legend, especially as he failed the university entrance examination twice and ended up at a third-class university. This relatively unimpressive educational background resonated with rural migrants, many of whom have a poor educational background, making people accept him more easily in this role. Titles of such articles run along the lines of 'You are poor because you are not ambitious enough' or 'How to seize the most important opportunities in your life'. There is no direct quotation from Ma Yun or similar celebrities in those articles, but they all read as if suggestions came directly from the celebrities, and people who share them truly believe this is so.

Many rural migrants, especially young men, believe that if one follows the advice they will also become rich and successful men. Such conviction is reinforced by the fact that many factory owners in GoodPath also started from scratch. The majority of the factory owners also come from villages; they were born with a rural *hukou* and did not have higher education, not dissimilar from the situation that factory migrant workers are in. In the eyes of many rural migrants, the reason

Fig. 3.19 A meme about a touching love story of a pair of lizards

this group of people rose to become the nouveau riche (*tu hao*)[15] is not because they are more hard-working or smarter; it is rather because they had the luck to be born in coastal villages rather than inland rural areas, and were blessed by the opportunities offered by economic development in China.

Women on the other hand, especially young women, turn more towards *Reader's Digest*-style articles which, together with sweet and cute images, deal with wise attitudes towards relationships and life. Titles of such posts are along the lines of '30 pieces of advice for young women', 'What is real love?' and 'Men, if your woman no longer needs your protection, she no longer loves you'. Fig. 3.19 shows a male lizard grilling his tail for his girlfriend. The text reads, 'Don't worry, it said that my tail will grow again'. Here the sacrifice of oneself to please a partner is presented as a touching sign of true love. On Fig. 3.20, the text reads: 'When you have to take a break and think about whether you are still in love with somebody, that means the love has already gone.'

Among all the memes which tend to give people advice for life, one specific topic, the 'passing traveller' (*guoke*), seems to stand out. The text (Fig. 3.21) reads: 'If you are not happy, you should let it go...someone appeared at some point and brought you a big surprise, which made you believe he or she was your god in life; however, you are wrong, some people are doomed to be just passing travellers in each other's lives.' All the 'passing traveller' memes deliver the message

Fig. 3.20 A popular meme about the nature of true love

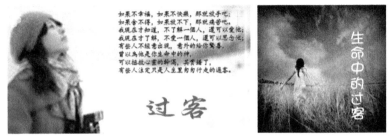

Fig. 3.21 Two typical 'passing traveller' memes

that one should not take current encounters too seriously since life itself is unsettled and nobody can really control it. It is not hard to see the attraction of 'passing traveller' memes given what we know of the transient lives of rural migrants. All in all, the 'chicken soup for the soul' genre stands out as a major feature in postings among rural migrants (Chart 3.5).

6 'Humour'

Most images in the 'humour' genre seem to be straightforward, with some obvious focal points for laughter. The text on Fig. 3.22, for example, reads: 'Young man, you have grasped the rule of the

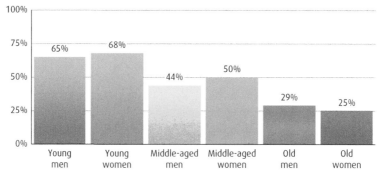

Chart 3.5 Distribution of 'chicken soup for the soul' postings

world: swiping credit cards.' In addition there are many amusing photographs related to children or animals (Fig. 3.23). The gender difference in humour postings is clear, with men all appearing to enjoy humour postings more than women (Chart 3.6). Middle-aged men seem to be the biggest 'jokers', which bears some consistency to people's offline social life: making good jokes at the dinner table is seen as a blessed talent, especially among middle-aged men. Such capability often contributes to the 'hot and noisy' (*renao*) ambience of social life that we will discuss further in Chapter 4.

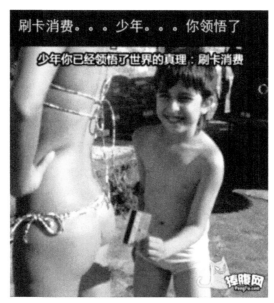

Fig. 3.22 A humorous posting shared by a male factory worker

Fig. 3.23 A typical humorous posting related to animals

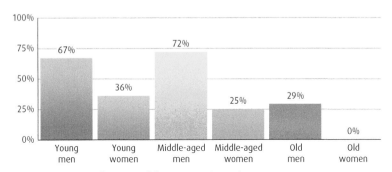

Chart 3.6 Distribution of 'humorous' postings

7 'Fantasy'

The 'fantasy' genre refers to beautiful and polished photographs of luxury lifestyles or prestigious goods, none of which seem to have anything in common with rural migrants' offline lives in GoodPath. Those images showcase the ideal lives for which both young women (Fig. 3.24) and young men (Fig. 3.25) are longing. Chapter 6 will further discuss the

Fig. 3.24 Images showcasing the ideal lives of young rural migrant women

Fig. 3.25 Images showcasing the ideal lives of young rural migrant men

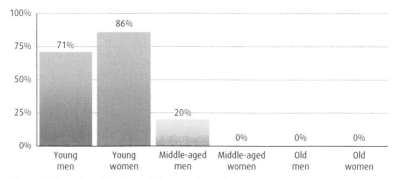

Chart 3.7 Distribution of 'fantasy' postings

reasons behind the popularity of this genre. As apparent in Chart 3.7, the genre of 'fantasy' exists mainly among young people.

8 'Children'

Most photographs of children are taken in a 'natural' way, not posed, and rarely have any art filter or decoration. In our north China field site, it was found that parents express their best wishes for their children

Fig. 3.26 Typical postings of children

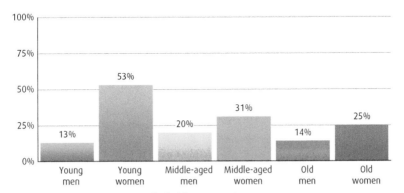

Chart 3.8 Distribution of 'children' postings

through professionally shot studio images.[16] However, such studio photographs of children are very rare on rural migrants' social media profiles. Photographs of children (Chart 3.8) are one of most popular topics among women, and the 'children' genre is a major feature[17] on social media.

9 'Travel'

Photographs in the 'Travel' genre were usually taken when people were travelling, whether for work or on holiday. It is common to see images of train tickets or landscapes encountered on the way, posted to mark the journey. Even though rural migrants are characterised by high mobility, such 'mobility' mainly refers to the concept of 'unsettled residence'.[18] In terms of work and living patterns, the flexibility and mobility they enjoyed in daily life were actually very limited. Most of them spent long hours labouring in factories or other workplaces, and could not afford to spend money and time travelling around for leisure.

Having made this point, one nonetheless has to observe that there is growing interest in the idea of tourism among rural migrants. Many migrant workers started to experience tourism after they left their villages, and those trips, arranged either by more experienced colleagues or the factory workers' guild (*gong hui*), were usually very short, but they still introduced 'tourism' as a feature of modern lifestyles for the first time.[19]

Dawei, a 20-year-old factory worker, is a typical example. He took many photos on his new smartphone during his first trip, and posted all of them on his Qzone (Fig. 3.27). Last Chinese New Year, when Dawei returned to his village, he showed the photographs to some of his relatives and fellow villagers. 'In my home village, no one has ever done tourism. People don't even have the idea (*mei zhe ge gai nian*),' he explained. Dawei's relatives and fellow villagers who had stayed behind in the villages were inspired by Dawei's tourist photographs, and a few weeks later they took a group trip to a nearby mountain. The local mountain area was actually a very famous sightseeing attraction in China, yet the peasants from neighbouring villages had never been there before.

'Travel' genre postings on social media have introduced the modern idea of tourism, and their impact on people's offline travelling behaviour is evident. Here we see how visual material on social media is not only the record of thoughts and daily lives. It is also an efficient way to transmit ideas that may have a significant impact on people's offline activities. In Dawei's case, the ideas of modern lifestyles that

Fig. 3.27 Unedited travel photographs on social media

he picked up during his migration were spread by him to the remaining villagers via social media. The way in which cultural practices diffused from rural migrants to rural populations also suggests that rural migrants' contributions to their home villages cannot be valued only from an economic perspective. As well as financial remittance, there is another, simultaneous remittance – social remittance.[20] Through this so-called social remittance, urban culture can increase its impact on the rural via interpersonal interaction between rural migrants and the remaining village residents.[21]

There is another feature of those travel photos: such a large number of photographs are not usually selective. For instance, Dawei uploaded 248 photos about a day trip to his Qzone. There is always more than one photo about the same person, object and similar scenery (see the differently coloured circles on Fig. 3.27). What Dawei did is very common among rural migrants, and the major reason for it lies in technology. Most rural migrants do not have a personal computer or other digital device for storing all their photographs, in addition to which the smartphone's memory space is limited, so QQ online albums actually serve as a hard disk. Even though none of them have ever heard of 'cloud technology', their QQ albums have actually been used as a 'cloud' long before this became a global technological trend. Generally speaking, young men appeared most active in posting travel photos (Chart 3.9). 'Those photos show that you are a man with a lot of travelling and experience,' explained Zhi Qiang, a 24-year-old factory worker. As he said, the idea that 'travelling makes a man' is deeply rooted. Travelling as a youth is viewed as the road to growing into a real man.[22]

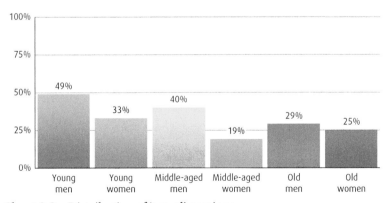

Chart 3.9 Distribution of 'travel' postings

10 'Events'

Weddings, performance, public activities (Fig. 3.28)...all events that stand out from the routine of daily life are appropriate subjects for the 'events' genre. Like travel photographs, visual material surrounding events also tends to include a large number of repetitive images.

Fig. 3.28 Typical postings of events

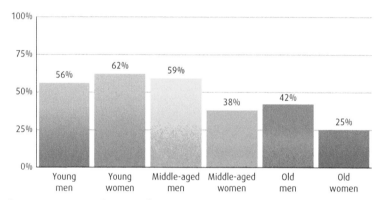

Chart 3.10 Distribution of 'events' postings

11 'Archive'

Postings in the 'archive' genre contain how-to information, ranging from how to cook delicious soup and tips for using essential balm to emergency first aid for children rescued from water (Fig. 3.29). The reason people share these postings is that they want to store the useful information on their QQ profiles, just like a digital archive. For many people such shared articles have provided them with useful knowledge, and

是，你造吗，清凉油的好处真的是太多了，老祖宗留下的真的是好东西，看看这篇文章，告诉家人不要暴殄天物。

实际上一年来我看到即将溺水的孩子，就是上一排中间的图：眼睛睁着，嘴巴半闭，

Fig. 3.29 Typical 'archive' postings

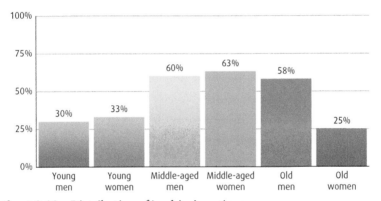

Chart 3.11 Distribution of 'archive' postings

some have already applied information learned from social media in their daily lives. For rural migrants without a higher level of education, these 'archive' postings actually offer an effective learning experience: the genre is an important form of adult education.

12 'Political'

The most popular topics of the 'political' genre include criticism of corruption, social discrimination, injustice and poverty (Fig. 3.30). All of these issues evoke high levels of sympathy among rural migrants, since they perceive themselves as direct victims. The most popular international political issue was the China–Japan relationship (Fig. 3.31),

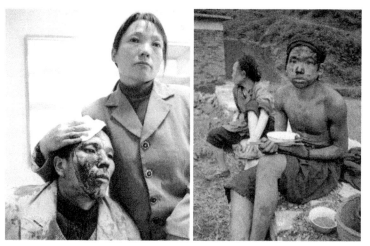

Fig. 3.30 Typical political postings relating to criticism of corruption, social discrimination, injustice and poverty. The text beneath the photograph in the article reads (left): 'Her husband was beaten by the factory owner when he asked for unpaid wages. That's the living situation of our Chinese rural migrants.' The text beneath the photograph in the article reads (right): 'When people in big cities enjoy luxury life in China, this is what rural life looks like in backward inland China!'

Fig. 3.31 Typical political postings with strong elements of patriotism and nationalism. Text reads (left): 'Diaoyu (Senkaku) islands belong to China – share it and let the world see it'. Text reads (right): 'Chairman Xi tells the world that China is going to teach Japan a lesson. Share it!'

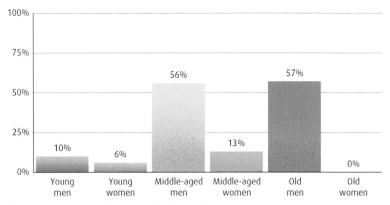

Chart 3.12   Distribution of 'political' postings

invested with strong emotions of patriotism and nationalism. Among factory workers, suffering from all sorts of domestic problems on a daily basis, anti-Japan postings are still far more popular than any other political postings related to domestic issues. Suffice it to say that nationalist sentiment against Japan is an instrument that the Chinese Communist Party uses to ally public support, to bolster the population's faith in the party-state and to hold the country together during its rapid and turbulent transformation.[23] As shown on Chart 3.12, the political genre is definitely male-dominated and generally speaking rural migrants, especially the younger generation, have an extremely low rate of participation in this social media genre.

13 'Food'

The genre of 'food' refers both to images of food alone or to 'people + food', which shows the food being collectively consumed as a social event. 'You are what you eat', as people say: food is such an important part of Chinese perceived cultural experience.[24] The use of food to express sophisticated social norms is highly developed in China.[25] As Kao Tzu, an ancient Chinese philosopher, observed, 'the appetite for food and sex is human nature' (*Shi Se Xing Ye*). Also, in a traditional society, division of a stove is symbolic of family division.[26] A marriage without eating together is not considered legitimate, while the birth of boys and adoption of heirs are both events marked and celebrated by eating together.[27] Given the high social significance of food and 'eating together', it is not difficult to understand the popularity of food photographs on social media to highlight the social connection.

Fig. 3.32 Typical postings of food

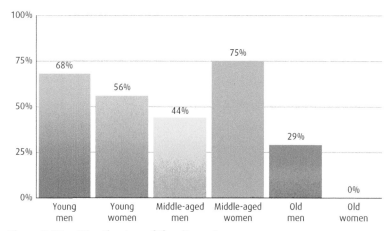

Chart 3.13 Distribution of 'food' postings

As Chart 3.13 shows, middle-aged women and young men contribute the highest number of postings in the 'food' genre. The images of food shared by males were in most cases about dining events, which usually include a group of people and food.

Contemporary China has witnessed the emergence of a motley group of youth subcultures or countercultures since the beginning of the economic reforms.[28] The concept of *Feizhuliu* (hereafter *FZL*), meaning anti-mainstream or non-mainstream, has become very popular among the Chinese post-1990s generation,[29] and *FZL* culture has its full expression on the social media postings of rural youth. There are two subgenres of *FZL*, one rebellious and cool (Fig. 3.33), the other extremely cute (Fig. 3.34). On 'rebellious' images there are figures of evil gangsters, always depicted in popular Hong Kong films,[30] or some brave and rebellious statements (on Fig. 3.33 the text reads: 'crush, fly'). Young men seem to be keener on sharing 'gangster' images, whereas other rebellious images and memes are equally popular among young men and women. Cute and sweet images seem to be more popular among

Fig. 3.33   Typical rebellious anti-mainstream postings

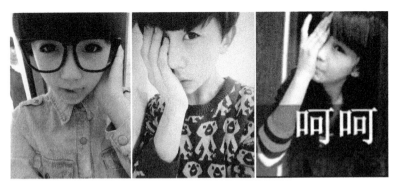

Fig. 3.34   Typical cute and sweet anti-mainstream postings

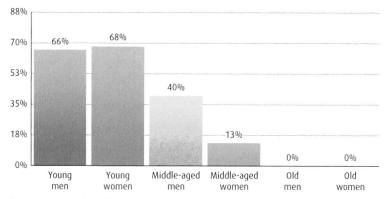

Chart 3.14   Distribution of '*FZL*' postings

young women, although you can often see men sharing some extremely cute and sweet images. Chapter 5 will explore these issues of gender as reflected by the posting of cute images. As shown on Chart 3.14, postings in the 'anti-mainstream' or *FZL* genre seem to be confined to young people and middle-aged men. In Chapter 5 we will take a closer look at the issue of gender identities behind these *FZL* images.

15 'Commercial'

Postings in the 'commercial' genre started to become popular among all ages following the monetisation of social media (Chart 3.15) – especially WeChat, as discussed in Chapter 2. Fig. 3.35 is a typical post in which

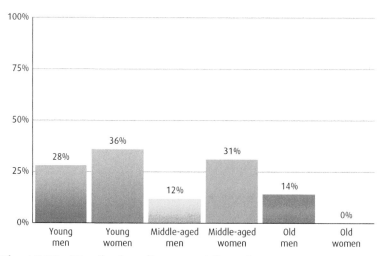

Chart 3.15   Distribution of 'commercial' postings

the user sells stuff on his or her profile. Another common commercial activity, *Jizan* (collecting 'likes') involves users collecting 'likes' from their online friends to win a coupon (Fig. 3.36). On this screenshot, the text on the top reads 'I kneel down for more "likes"'; the image and link below form part of the advertisement of a local photography studio.

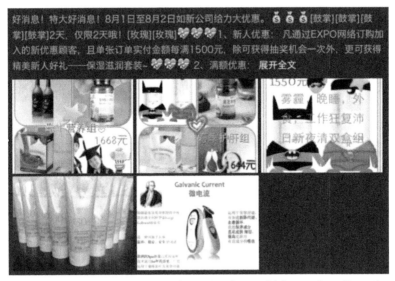

Fig. 3.35 A typical commercial posting from which people sell goods on their profiles

 雨丝摄影十三周年庆跨年狂欢会----转发赞52个以上就可免...

27 December 2013 07:12

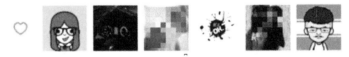

Fig. 3.36 A typical commercial posting from which people collect 'likes'

What is special about the visual postings of rural migrants?

'We are becoming a visually mediated society. For many, understanding of the world is being accomplished, not through words, but by reading images.'[31] So far we have discussed all 15 genres of social media visual postings. Some of the images require more contextual knowledge to be interpreted fully, and we will continue the discussion in the rest of the book, especially in Chapters 5 and 6. Even before further discussion, however, we seem to have reached a good point to consider what is special about the images posted by rural migrants on their social media profiles. Are these a result of Chinese people's general visual preferences, or do they reflect the choices of this specific social group? A comparison between the visual postings of rural migrants and those living in Shanghai (Chart 3.16)[32] offers us a perspective from which to consider this question.

As shown on Chart 3.16, 'relationships', 'selfies' and 'children' are the three visual genres popular among both rural migrants and the

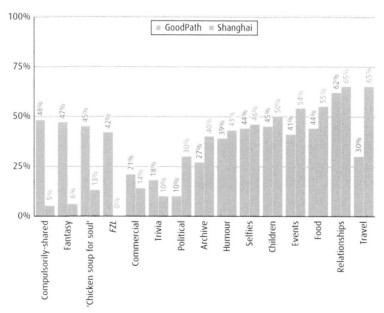

Chart 3.16 Distribution of 15 visual genres among rural migrants of GoodPath and residents of Shanghai

urban population. The urban population showed more interest in post-ing visual material on the genres of 'travel', 'political', 'archive', 'events' and 'food', partly reflecting the difference of socio-economic status and lifestyle between Chinese rural migrants and the urban Chinese. However, the most outstanding discrepancies occur in the genres of 'compulsorily shared', 'fantasy', 'chicken soup for the soul' and 'anti-mainstream' (*FZL*), where rural migrants have definitely shown more passion.

These four genres can very well serve as the starting point for us to explore the features of visual postings among rural migrants. Firstly, a strikingly common point between these four is that none of them records domestic offline life, and none is a type of social memory com-parable with the former use of analogue photography.[33] The majority of images in these four genres is memes and images collected from the internet, rather than original photographs that people took themselves. All the images of postings in the 'compulsorily shared' genre are related to folk religion or hometown-related memes: those in the 'fantasy' genre, meanwhile, present a modern, materialistic world, dramatically different from rural migrants' offline life. Similarly, the 'chicken soup for the soul' visual genre provides a whole set of aspirational life mod-els with artistic images or images of celebrities. And for rural youth the 'anti-mainstream' (*FZL*) genre provides the specific visual language to express rebellious gestures or gestures that are not really acceptable in offline situations. The desire for a modern life is efficiently expressed by the popularity of these four visual genres. In Chapter 6 we will explore further how the beautified life on social media helps rural migrants to think through changes in their own existences and to live different daily lives.

Secondly, among rural migrants, the three least posted visual genres are 'political', 'trivia' and 'commercial'. Given all the argument in Chapter 2 about the booming of social commerce in China, it may appear strange that the 'commercial' genre is still among the last three. Here, however, 'commercial' refers to postings of doing business, selling goods or posting commercial advertisements on one's personal social media profiles. To put things in perspective, therefore, the absolute fig-ure of 21 per cent is already very impressive compared to the situation on Facebook, where it is very rare to see postings on personal accounts for the direct purpose of making money. As for 'trivia', the result is not unex-pected. However, probably the most surprising fact is that among all the 15 genres, the concept of 'political' – much discussed as a key element that can facilitate political participation – turns out in practice to be the least posted by rural migrants. Yet this may be the very population that need social media most, as they are least likely to express their political opinions in any other media. What has happened? Is this because of the internet censorship in China? Or were people simply indifferent about politics, or saw no point in political postings? Chapter 5 will address all these questions through a closer look into the engagement with politics, both online and offline, among different groups in GoodPath and a discussion of the social media's impact on political participation.

Thirdly, it turns out that age is a key factor in terms of posting activity. Young rural migrants, both female and male, are far more active in posting images, especially aspirational images about modern lifestyles, on social media, whereas older people, especially women, were the least active. One can easily argue that is because young people are supposed to have more dreams about life, and that such youthful passion will gradually disappear over time. However, there is something more about the special situation of young people among rural migrants.

The coming of age of young rural migrants on social media

The phase of youth is a period of transition between one's childhood and adult life. However, for young Chinese rural migrants this phase is shortened by around five years compared to their peers in cities. The period from age 15 to the early twenties has become the time when young people from rural communities leave villages and enter the workplace for the first time, where they gain financial independence. By contrast, most urban young people remain at school at this age, and are still financially dependent.

Achieving financial independence at such an early age effectively catapults young rural migrants into adulthood. With regard to maturity, what those young rural migrants miss is not just formal education, but the longer time in schools and colleges that usually provides a relatively flexible and safe environment for a more gradual coming of age.[34] At school young people usually spend a great deal of time with their classmates and school friends, and through this interaction their personalities and social skills are developed and their world views are shaped. The missed or significantly shortened time in education hinders the personal development and social lives of young rural migrants.

Once they embark upon rural-to-urban migration they hardly have any quality time with peers, given the high mobility they experience and the limited places to spend time after work. It is in such a context that we can further explore the role played by social media in young rural migrants' lives.

The importance of social media for China's young rural migrants lies in the fact that it offers a place in which they can meet peers, and where they have the freedom from their families and fixed social norms to imagine something different. Like young people around the world, the ideals of individualism and autonomy find expression in a slightly rebellious gesture.[35] These gestures, reflected from the 'fantasy' or *FZL* genres of images, have become a set of new norms agreed by young people on social media. This gives young people the security that they are sufficiently rebellious and have a similar modern consumer taste, all of which can easily be recognised and approved by their contemporaries. In this sense, activity on social media has become an essential part of social life. It bears some similarity to the experience of school, allowing social media to provide a place for young rural migrants where they can be 'educated' by themselves or by their peers into adulthood.

In some previous studies of Chinese rural youth, researchers noticed that youth culture in rural China was not really rebellious or counterculture;[36] it was rather an attempt to follow the mainstream culture of urbanity by conforming to key characteristics of modernity, including being fashionable, materialistic and individualistic.[37] However, the fact is that in the eyes of older relatives and villagers in rural communities, the pursuit of being urban is already 'countercultural' enough in the face of traditional, established rural culture. Furthermore, most previous studies of young people were carried out in rural areas, but the culture of young rural migrants in townships and cities is different. Just imagine one of the most common scenes in GoodPath: young factory workers in their early twenties, wearing the uniforms they described as 'ugly as shit', working on repetitive and uniform tasks on assembly lines for 10 hours a day, 29 days a month...and when they finally get back to their dormitories they log on to QQ profiles and upload some really cool images of young people wearing the fanciest and most bizarre costumes or exaggerated make-up and hairstyles. The anti-mainstream (*FZL*) visual we saw online cannot really tell what happened offline; only when we put the online and offline aspects together can we fully appreciate the message delivered by the *FZL* or fantasy visual.

On social media, rural youth can take a break from the uniformity imposed by heavy industry that has occupied most of their offline time. On social media these young people get inspired by all sorts of fantastic images, freeing their imaginations to go as far as they can. They may aspire to fast cars or to have a wedding like a princess, to be slightly funky or to create slightly edgy selfies. Above all, such imagination and aspiration can easily be conceived and visualised by images rather than text. The relatively low levels of education received by young rural migrants no longer prevent them from expressing themselves vividly and accurately. For example, Xiangjun, a 20-year-old factory worker, always shares 'chicken soup for the soul' memes with only one word: 'wo' [I]. Xiangjun explained that he felt these images had simply expressed everything he want to say, so he just needed to add a word 'I' to indicate 'that's exactly what I think'. When people feel they are not especially articulate in text and speaking, the visual can be particularly empowering. In a social media context this means they can articulate their feelings by simply sharing a meme edited by others.

The visual on social media – a new language

The observation that visual images on social media help young people to express themselves better actually extends to the entire population of rural migrants. In many cases it is not just a question of improving the ability to express oneself: some of what we find is unprecedented offline. To see this more clearly we can start from one particular tragedy. In 1993, 87 young female rural migrants lost their lives in a large fire in a toy factory in south China. A researcher managed to get access to 77 personal letters that the victims had received from friends and relatives, as well as to the letters they were about to send.[38] Those letters revealed for the first time the hidden inner world of Chinese migrant workers. The main topics mentioned in those private letters were 1) wages; 2) work conditions; 3) problems related to physical well-being; and 4) loneliness and isolation. Money is the biggest concern, and a few workers mentioned they felt lonely in cities. Curiously, two decades later, the common topics of phone calls and other offline conversations among rural migrants remain much the same. The most common subjects in today's phone calls were 'how much one has earned or saved so far', 'whether one can find a better paid job', 'whether the children can get into the local schools' or 'whether one can help a relative or a fellow villager to find a job'. Generally speaking, how best to get by remains the dominant concern within these phone calls, just as they were in letters and personal phone calls at that time. Even in these communications, personal feelings are subsumed by pragmatic concerns. Topics such as thoughts about life or personal aspirations seem to be 'unspeakable'. Ke Li, a factory worker, put it in this way: 'It is not something you will talk about on a phone call or in front of people you know – it's just weird, you only talk about what needs to be done or what's wrong, rather than those daydreams.'

By contrast Chi Hui, a 24-year-old factory girl, used 'giving idealistic speech' (*jiang dadaoli*) to describe the memes about romance that she constantly shared on her Qzone.

> Well, you won't call your friends and give them those idealistic speeches (*jiang da dao li*), people must think you are insane…When you share those online that's normal, because everybody does so.

As Chi Hui observed, social media has become the 'normal' and 'proper' place in which people can talk about their (day)dreams, their aspirations and what they think about life, rather than what they want to have for tomorrow's dinner. The easily shared and ubiquitous visual material on social media certainly facilitates such new forms of communication. Besides this, the one-to-many nature of social media postings also encourages people to be more focused on their own feelings, rather than addressing specific daily issues to particular individuals. Furthermore, communication on social media is usually asynchronous, which enables people to manage their self-presentations more strategically, without time pressure. On Ke Li's Qzone there are many shared postings about how to become a successful businessman. He also regularly posts photographs of luxury night clubs which he collects from the internet, both representing the kinds of personal aspiration that would not have been expressed in phone calls.

This chapter started with a description of the 15 genres of visual images that rural migrants commonly post on their social media, followed by an analysis of the motivation behind them. These highly diverse and sometimes unexpected images are like a treasure trove to outsiders trying to understand the feelings and aspirations of a marginalised but massive population – one whose voices can hardly be heard in mainstream media, and which has kept its feelings and thoughts to itself over the past three decades. The chapter then proceeded to examine the difference between the visual languages shared by rural

Fig. 3.37 The colourful online world of rural migrants. (A partial image of a traditional Chinese painting booklet 'Field Note', 31.5 × 384 cm; painter: Xinyuan Wang)

migrants and those of the urban population in Shanghai. Only through such comparisons does a unique 'visual grammar' appear. Rather than being a digital memory which records offline life, the evidence suggests that images on social media can illustrate complementary aspects of life. Before social media we used to see photography as a historical effort to represent or duplicate life.[39] However, the situation here can be the opposite. Certainly in visual genres such as 'children', 'food', 'events', and 'travel' we see continuity between traditional photos and visual postings online. However, in other cases visual postings in the genres of 'chicken soup for the soul', *FZL* and 'fantasy' detach people from their offline situation and construct a whole new world online. People talked about what is happening on their social media in their offline life – in a manner that suggested that it was their online lives which for them represented a colourful and interesting world constructed around aspirational images. So online space has now become the world that people truly enjoy, dream about and want to replicate in their offline lives (Fig 3.37).

4
Social media and social relationships

The dynamism of Chinese social media is truly impressive. Even more impressive, however, is the speed of response of Chinese social media users. They pick up almost instantly on each subtle gesture and movement allowed by social media, and skilfully apply these to navigate their relationships with families, friends, romantic partners and even with strangers online. A whole set of social norms have emerged regarding the use of social media, which people soon take for granted: social media thus comes to feel an essential part of their daily lives, as if it had always been with them. In this chapter we will explore different kinds of social relationships in the context of social media usage. The evidence in this chapter suggests that social media has not only become an integral part of everyday life, a place where people live alongside their offline life. It also provides the potential for people to experience relationships that are not fully developed, or do not even exist, in prior offline situations. In this chapter we will explore different kinds of social relationships, which are also called 'sociality' in anthropology,[1] in the context of social media usage.

'Thank you for keeping me on your contact list'

This is a general understanding of rural migrants' social media contacts. Since the autumn of 2014 people in GoodPath have been bombarded by a particular type of text message from their WeChat contacts. A typical one reads:

> My dear friend, it's getting cold, please keep yourself warm as I do care about you. btw, this a group message. Copy this, and send it as group message to all your contacts so that you will see who have removed you from their contact lists since the system will tell. Try it; you will have a clear picture of your social relationships, and it's

also convenient for you to clean up those who had removed you. If you receive this message, then thank you for keeping me on your contact list.'

Starting with a sweet, caring line, followed by some practical advice about cleaning up contacts, such text messages have become so popular among people in GoodPath that almost everyone has experienced them. Some found them annoying, feeling that the subtext of the message seemed to be 'I don't really care about you, I only care about whether you care about me'. Many followed the suggestion, trying to figure out who had removed them. Some people who did so actually found a few contacts they were happy to discard. Others even discovered to their shock that those who had just borrowed money from them had already deleted the contact before they had returned the money; or that former colleagues who had recently moved to another town had already dropped them; or that their ex-partner, with whom they still wanted to remain friends, had actually severed the connection unilaterally.

The popularity of such group messages seems to indicate a pervasive insecurity and uncertainty about personal relationships, which can be explained partly by the life patterns of rural migrants. In the process of migration, this 'floating' population has experienced a large number of transient encounters and frequently had to say goodbye to others. During the research rural migrants, especially middle-aged ones such as 43-year-old Lao Zhou, talked from time to time about the interdependent rural communities they had come from:[2]

> When I was very young, in my village, if one household had difficulty in harvest, the whole village lent a hand. And when my grandfather died, male adults in the neighbourhood all came to carry the coffin … In a way you have to, everybody is watching you. If this time you don't help others, next time nobody will come to help you.

I happened to observe him on another day around dinner time, when the muggy evening brought a sudden shower: despite what he had told me, when Lao Zhou rushed to collect his clothes hanging outside in the collective yard he only collected his own. His neighbours' washing was left to get wet in the rain. I asked why. He replied:

> Neighbours? No, I don't think they are, who knows who they are? Almost every month people move in and move out. I can't be

bothered to recognise all of them. Of course, in my previous village I would have collected my neighbour's clothes, but here things are different. I am not mean, I just try to be realistic.

Knowing how fleeting a co-residence can be, rural migrants seemed to have little expectation of developing any long-term relationship with people who happened to work on the same assembly line, or happened to rent a room next door. Social connections, such as colleagues or neighbours, can be very close in the short term, but in the long run they were considered fragile and unstable, especially when one of the parties migrated to other places. Lao Zhou's experience from a 'super-stable' social structure in a village society, in which 'everybody is watching you', to an unstable and loose connection in a floating life – 'who knows who they are?' – is common among migrant workers in GoodPath. Such living experience set the tone for people's attitudes towards offline social life.

These differences help to explain the relationship pattern found on social media. Based on the analysis of 105 migrant workers' QQ profiles, Chart 4.1 shows that non-kinship relationships are dominant on rural migrants' social media. The majority of social connections on social media come from migration. Here people have more chances to interact with various kinds of people, such as 'colleagues', 'other friends' and 'online strangers'. The labels of different social relationships followed the colloquial terms and categories used by participants in this survey. For example, many people would add 'other' to 'friends' to indicate those friends were not their classmates, nor fellow villagers, nor colleagues. Nor are the categories are mutually exclusive: most classmates are fellow villagers, and some of the colleagues to whom people became connected on QQ were relatives or fellow villagers.

In comparison with the control group in Shanghai,[3] several of these figures for rural migrants on the chart stand out. One notable feature is the relatively small 'classmates' group. Classmate ties are usually extremely important in Chinese society;[4] the age-class grouping in school facilitates the formation of friendships and cliques, and the significance of the classmate friendship becomes greater over time.[5] In Shanghai, more than 36 per cent of social media contacts are education-related (classmates, school friends), whereas the concepts of 'classmates' and 'school friends' are very ambiguous among rural migrants, many of whom dropped out of school early. Furthermore, more than 80 per cent of participants in Shanghai had never added strangers on social media, let alone made friends with them. By contrast 'online strangers',

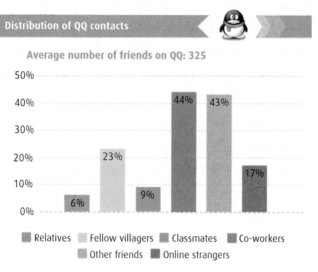

Chart 4.1   Distribution of QQ contacts among rural migrants in GoodPath

referring to contacts with no offline social connection at all, stand out as an important part of social media contacts among rural migrants.

In practice, being connected is one thing: keeping in touch is another. In fact mere figures of the distribution of various contacts do not tell even half the story. The word 'zombie' (*jiangshi*) was frequently used by many young people to refer to those online contacts with whom one hardly had any form of interaction (online chatting, commenting or sharing). Some people choose to keep those 'zombies' as contacts due to the fact that a large number of connections on social media is regarded as an achievement. Many previous colleagues and fellow villagers have become 'zombies' on QQ.

Not that this is necessarily a problem. Lu Li, a 25-year-old waitress at a local restaurant, has become more and more reluctant to keep in touch with her best childhood friend on QQ. Yet when she left the village six years ago both of them had opened QQ accounts in order to keep in contact:

> To be honest I feel the only thing we could talk about was child-hood memories and nothing else. I am not interested in her life in the village and she couldn't appreciate my sense of fashion or imagine the ups-and-downs in my life here...We no longer live in the same world, you know...but no harm in keeping her on my QQ. You look better online with more friends than less, don't you?

The experience of 'working outside' (*da gong*) has broadened the horizons of migrant workers, and so an invisible division has started to separate people who have remained in villages from those who have already experienced 'the outside world'. Even though physical distance is no longer a real obstacle, given the communication technology now available, rural migrants fail to keep many of their previous social connections: a non-physical barrier has developed between the experiences and mindsets of these two groups that is perhaps even more difficult to bridge. Many of these differences from Shanghai make sense once it is understood that, as noted in Chapter 1, the 'push' factor of economic necessity that once determined the trajectory of rural-to-urban migration has now been supplanted by the 'pull' factor of aspiration towards modernity. This also needs to be taken into account in explaining the nature and experience of social media connections considered in the next section.

The 'hot and noisy' principle

The introduction to this book discussed the importance of interpersonal relations (*guanxi*) and face (*mianzi*) in exploring Chinese social relationships. Both *guanxi* and *mianzi* emphasise the importance of the harmony (*hexie*) of social groups, which works as a powerful mediation between the individual and the society. More specifically, another principle is widely applied to achieve a harmonious ambience of social life. This principle can be literally translated as 'hot and noisy'.

From time to time people would say 'come and leave your footprints on my profile' (*lai wo kong jian caicai!*) to their friends, inviting them to visit their QQ profiles[6] (Qzone). On Qzone not only the user, but also the user's other QQ contacts can check who has paid a visit. Having said this, one is supposed to 'leave footprints' (that is to leave comments on others' profiles) in order to show the evidence of caring for one another. For example, two girls who work together on the same assembly line would still come to leave footprints on each other's Qzone after work, even though they have seen each other 10 hours a day, 29 days a month at work. Usually 'footprints' resemble a long string of banter between friends on one's QQ profile. 'Don't you think with more people coming here and more footprints left, it will appear more *renao*?' a female factory worker asked.

'Re' in *renao* means hot, and *nao* means noisy. Putting the two characters together, *renao*, creates a frequently used Chinese word, referring to a lively, bustling and exciting ambience of social connection. Traditionally *renao* was regarded as a positive and ideal status of Chinese social life, and was highly sought after.[7] For instance, in the celebrations of Chinese New Year, 'hot and noisy' is essential as the festival mood.[8] The expression 'join the hot and noisy' (*cou renao*) is commonly used to describe the attendance of any kind of meeting with others. As shown in chapters 1 and 2, social life in GoodPath is more dependent on any gathering of people, rather than people fitting themselves into a space specifically designated for that purpose. Any activity in public which is 'hot and noisy' thus automatically becomes a social event.

In GoodPath, one of the most *renao* events is the Chinese opera show. Every two months a traditional Chinese opera troupe from a nearby village would perform a show on a makeshift stage in the parking area. Hundreds of people always gathered around the stage, even though not everyone was interested in opera. Noise off the stage was just as loud as the singing on the stage. When the show was over, more than half of the audience remained in their seats, chatting with each other. It seemed that for many people *renao,* rather than the opera, was the real reason why they had come to the show. The parallel between the opera audience and social media users shows that the expectation of an ideal ambience of social life has migrated from offline to online. Social media has become the main place where peers hang out to join the *renao.*

And in some situations, it is difficult to tell the fine boundary between online and offline when it comes to a 'hot and noisy' ambience. In GoodPath, internet cafes are very popular among young men. Each internet cafe has around 100 computers. At night, around 90 per cent of the machines are in use, with male users accounting for around 85 per cent. Almost all these male users are playing massive multi-player online games. Many young men come to the internet cafe in groups and play games with their friends together. The internet cafe was always extremely noisy. As Wuli, a 21-year-old factory worker, explained:

> Playing a game alone is definitely not the same. If I win playing alone, no one can share the excitement with me! With friends I can give a shout, letting everybody in the room know that I've won – it feels so good!...And you know, you feel the brotherhood when you go to the internet cafe together and kill enemies together!

Wuli visited the internet cafe almost every day after work with a group of his fellow villagers who worked in factories. When the group was playing games together, they talked so loudly that everybody in the room could hear. Conversations that could be heard were not necessarily about gaming: they might involve boasting about one's new girlfriend or a new purchase of an iPhone. 'The human being is a part of the machine', as a factory manager said. For factory workers such as Wuli, who received little attention during working hours, the loud noise they made in the internet cafe seemed to be one of the few moments they obtained any attention, and they relished it. Furthermore, in Chapter 3 we saw that compared to women, men are less likely to portray bonding through posting group photos on their social media. Here we can see that this is not because there is less bonding, but rather that male bonding is expressed in an alternative way: through this more physical and performative companionship.

From leaving footprints on Qzones to playing online games in a 'hot and noisy' internet cafe, the principle of *renao* was followed both offline and online. As a result, the boundary between online and offline has become very blurred. Following this general discussion of 'sociality' on social media, this chapter will focus more closely on social media usage in different categories of significant social relationships.

Couples and wider family relationships on social media

When I first saw Lan, she was producing linings for pet carriers in a dark workshop. It was a small, underground workshop, converted from a residential room and hidden deep in a narrow lane. On becoming aware of my presence, Lan immediately bowed her head even lower, and hushed the two children playing around the sewing machine to be quiet (Fig. 4.1).

It took a while to make friends with Lan, her son, aged almost five, and her daughter, aged three. Like many young rural migrants, 24-year-old Lan had dropped out of school and left her village early in search of a better life. Five years previously she had married a truck driver from a neighbouring village. A year ago the couple had moved to GoodPath, working together in a factory. Then, in order to support each other and their young children better, Lan's husband took a better paid job in Shanghai, a position to which he was introduced by a fellow villager. However, the living costs for the whole family in Shanghai were prohibitive. So as a compromise Lan's husband worked in Shanghai, staying at the collective dormitory, and Lan remained behind, taking care of their children in GoodPath. She had to quit her assembly line job at a factory and take a lower-paid job

Fig. 4.1 Lan and her two children. (A partial image of a traditional Chinese painting 'Locked album', 145 × 75 cm; painter: Xinyuan Wang)

at this illicit sewing sweatshop, run by a local peasant. More flexibility was allowed at the workshop, and she could take her children there to save on daytime nursery fees. In Lan, one can see the typical kind of traditional, virtuous Chinese woman who is devoted to her family. Her Qzone possessed a few 'locked' albums, not open to visitors. 'Only my husband and I know the password', she explained. 'I only uploaded photos of our children to the albums so that he can check them over there.'

Lan's husband is a quiet man. I only met him once when he came back to visit his family. Being asked about his children's photographs, he remained silent for a while, then replied:

> I was too busy during daytime. At night, on the bed, when I couldn't fall asleep and worried about things, I would take out my smartphone and have a look at them . . . then I felt much better.

Then he became silent again.

A QQ album has become the essential connection between this young couple, bringing immense comfort to people who had no choice but to live separately.[9] Yet being physically apart was not always regarded in a negative light by a family. In some cases, it came across as a great relief, as Yan Hong, the 37-year-old owner of a local nail salon, describes:

> When he was at home he never did any housework. I needed to take care of our daughter, him and the business of the shop. You know, I was not very lucky to marry such a lazy man!.... But now things have become more bearable. I no longer need to work as a maid, and I even feel that he cares for us more on WeChat and QQ. Before he had never taken the initiative to ask about our daughter's performance at school. But now he asks me about her from time to time.

Yan Hong believed that her marriage had become more 'bearable': with the help of social media, her once unpleasant, housework-loaded married life had been transformed into a more supportive and considerate one. Compared to rural migrant families, hers is definitely much better off. Yan Hong's husband is a businessman who works in a city in north China, thus rarely staying at home. Every day the couple talk by WeChat voice messages. Once a week they have a half-hour QQ video call, during which their 10-year-old daughter, who lives with Yan Hong, joins the conversation and says hello to her father. Yan Hong seemed to be happy with her WeChat strategy:

> ...It [WeChat voice message] is similar to a phone call, but better...because you don't need to arrange a time for a conversation. Before, when I called him, he always sounded in the middle of something and impatient...which always pissed me off. But by voice message, it's still as if we are talking, but in a more relaxed way...I leave voice messages for him whenever I want, and he comes back to me when he is free.

The use of voice messaging on WeChat varied remarkably among different people. For many young people, especially those in the early stages of romance, WeChat voice messages could be sent and received so rapidly that it functioned as a synchronous mode of communication. It did not have to be, however, as in Yan Hong's case. She found that the acceptable time delay between WeChat messages has allowed her more control over previously problematic communication with her husband.

Furthermore, the 'stored' conversation on WeChat has brought some unexpected benefits. Yan had a few problems with her mother-in-law because the old lady was over-indulgent with her granddaughter;

she always became very protective of the girl when Yan Hong tried to establish discipline at home:

> I complained about my mother-in-law on WeChat, and my husband replied that, 'grandparents always spoil kids, so don't let her get involved too much, do what you feel you need to do'...The next day, she [the mother-in-law] gave me a bollocking again when I was scolding my daughter for not finishing her homework. So I said, 'ok, I can't argue with you, then let your son argue with you!' So I replayed that piece of voice message from my husband to her. She was totally shocked because my husband had never really supported me in front of his mother.

Yan Hong's husband had never considered that a fragment of the conversation between him and his wife would be taken from its original context and used as an argument by his wife against his mother – something he always tried to avoid. A similar situation also happened in other families. Jokes between family junior members on voice messages were replayed to senior family members, for example, causing embarrassment, or secrets were disclosed to non-family members by voice messages. Technologically it is possible to record a phone call, but before WeChat voice message, voice recording was very rare; most daily phone conversations had not been recorded automatically as happened on WeChat. In this sense WeChat voice message made people's daily phone conversations replicable for the first time. As a result these reconstructions of daily conversations, facilitated by the use of voice messages, have now become a part of both family life and wider social life.

Given the much higher penetration rate of smartphones and social media among older people in urban China, the one-month of research undertaken in Shanghai (July 2014) unfolded some new patterns of social media usage in kinship. These had not yet happened in GoodPath. For instance, surveillance on social media by senior family members has become a problem among people in Shanghai:

> Oh my, you just don't know how annoying it has become since my mum became a WeChat friend. I uploaded something after midnight; she left a comment, nagging me to go to bed earlier. I uploaded some photos with my friends having fun in a club; she called me the next day, nagging about why I couldn't have a proper girlfriend...In the end, I had to block her from those 'sensitive' postings.

Huang, a 28-year-old company official, decided to conduct self-censorship against his mother's ubiquitous surveillance. Compared to most men who try not to include their parents on social media, women seem to cope better with the experience of having family members there. Jing Yu Qi, a 32-year-old tourist guide, discovered that WeChat could be a nice buffer mechanism between her and senior family members:

> It's true that sometimes they were a bit nosy about my personal issues, but that's always the case, with or without WeChat. And on WeChat I can ignore their enquiries or reply later when I am in a good mood. In 'face to face' you can't do that; as the junior you can't say no to their face or ignore them…For me, WeChat is like a 'cushion'.

Such usage actually has many points of similarity to Yan Hong's WeChat strategy regarding her husband.

WeChat groups have also become popular among families in Shanghai, connecting several nuclear families together efficiently. For example, there is a WeChat group called 'Grandpa, what will we have for dinner?' on Fan's WeChat. A media worker in Shanghai, she explained that the name of the WeChat group came from the family tradition that every fortnight the big family, including four nuclear families, would try to have a family dinner at her grandfather's place:

> …In the beginning, the WeChat group was mainly functional, because it's quite convenient to check who will come for dinner on it rather than calling each family one by one…I forget when it was that one of my uncles started to post some photos on the group, and others were inspired to post various things such as family news or jokes too…now we basically catch up with each other almost every day in the group. And the funny thing is over family dinner, face to face, we continue chatting about the topics from our WeChat group.

For Fan, the WeChat family group has become the virtual family dinner. Some also found the interaction with senior family members on WeChat group allowed them to see a different aspect of their relatives. Ding Yi Han, a freelance artist in her late thirties living in Shanghai, described how WeChat transformed her relationship with senior family members:

> I have never seen him smile like a child, you know: the traditional, typical father never smiles like that. But since we had a family

WeChat group, he has somehow learnt to use WeChat stickers, and all of a sudden I found he was no longer the serious father I knew before. He has become so funny and even childish. It's not only my father; my grandfather was also taught to use WeChat this year. He too has become a lovely person, I mean before he was just the 'grandfather', you know what I mean?...I think that's best thing WeChat has ever brought to me, and to the whole family.'

WeChat stickers (Fig. 4.2) are a popular feature of WeChat. Hundreds of sets of stickers like these are available. In traditional Chinese patriarchal society senior male family members are supposed to be serious,[10] yet because of those cute stickers junior family members have started to discover the 'human' side of their fathers as well as their grandfathers. Meanwhile, for the older generation, WeChat has also opened a window on youth culture.

There are two definite trends of social transformation taking place beneath the observations of social media use in kinship discussed here. One is the massive rural-to-urban migration, and the inevitable rupture of kinship that occurs in the process; the other is the increasing popularity of social media and smartphones among low income people and the older population. In Lan's story we see a typical family pattern of rural migrants in diaspora, a situation in which the use of social media helped to overcome long physical distances and maintain a family together; features such as the 'locked album' with a password shared among family members made 'remote' parenting possible. Yan Hong's story, by contrast, reflects rather different usage. Here the new facility provided by WeChat (voice messaging) has been applied to break the

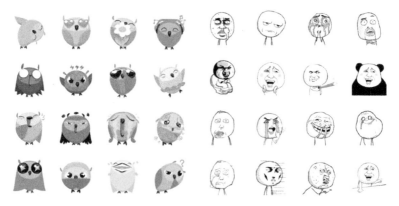

Fig. 4.2 Samples of WeChat stickers

pre-existing routine and hierarchy of family life. This may be taken further in the light of the findings from Shanghai that revealed that some new aspects of kinship were 'discovered' through social media use. From online albums to voice messaging to stickers, social media changes the practice of family relationships by providing many new possibilities for communication.

During the period of research (2013/2014), the use of social media in GoodPath was still largely confined to the younger generation (aged under 35). The majority of social connection online was still among contemporaries, and very few people connected with any senior relatives on QQ. Communication between parents and their adult children, or between senior family members in a big family, remained essentially a matter of phone calls. Thus the discussion here about social media use in family relationships among rural migrants only speaks to situations between young couples, or among junior relatives in a large family. However, the use of social media in romantic relationships is now pervasive among young people.

Romantic relationships on social media

Every day after work, a group of young female factory workers leaves the factory plant together, hand in hand. All of them are unmarried young women, and gossip about relationships is always the most popular topic. Girls chatter avidly on the 10-minute walk from factory to dormitories; everybody is trying to contribute something to the daily 'gossip time':

> 'Hey, did you hear that he just asked for her QQ number? I was surprised that he wanted to add her on QQ!'
> 'Really? I didn't know he was keen on her. Oh no – it is really bad news for his ex-girlfriend. A few days ago I just saw her new QQ status ... sounds like she really regrets the break-up. Look, look ...'

The girl then took out her smartphone, showing her friends the evidence she had spotted on QQ.

The very action of men and women adding each other on QQ can easily be interpreted as romance, since, in the words of one girl, 'QQ is not used for talking business or other things; QQ is for you to fall in love (*tan lian ai*)'. It has become almost a consensus among young people that one of the major functions of social media is to develop and maintain romantic relationships. Xiao Lin, a 20-year-old factory worker, sent me QQ messages explaining how QQ helped him to become a better lover:

> I am much more bold and romantic on QQ...you just wouldn't say those sweet words face to face...And I used lots of cute stickers when we were chatting on QQ, which made her find me really funny.

Many young migrant workers, like Xiao Lin, think they can be a better lover on social media. Vivid stickers and emojis enrich people's expression; an element of time delay allows more scope for strategic communication. Behind the screens of their smartphones, people feel more empowered and confident. Rather than a diminished form of intimate interaction, romantic relationships on social media have become an efficient modality combining elements of voice, image and text, as well as emoji and stickers. There is another reason why social media is regarded a place for romantic love: a public display of love offline is usually frowned upon in GoodPath. Walking hand in hand was the most intimate interaction that one could spot on the street. When Xiao Yu, a 21-year-old hairdresser's apprentice, posted photos of herself kissing her boyfriend on QQ, she perceived QQ to be a romantic and liberating place where one can feel free to display intimacy as the 'public' was different:

> In big cities people won't make a fuss [about kissing in public]. But here some traditional people would dislike it...but the good thing is they are not on my QQ!

Xiao Yu's kiss photographs elicited many comments. Rather than feeling embarrassed, she felt that was exactly what she was looking for: '...When you posted something like that, you just knew what people would comment. If I am not sure, then I won't post it,' Xiao Yu explained. To the question 'do you think about what kind of reaction you will receive when you post something on social media?', the majority of participants, both in GoodPath and in Shanghai, said yes. Moreover in many cases the imagined audience and presupposed reaction justify the posting. A few days later, Xiao Yu finally uttered the real reason why she posted the kiss photos – to warn another girl to stay away from her boyfriend as she assumed the girl had been stalking her.[11] 'It's so annoying, she is still flirting with him (Xiao Yu's boyfriend) on his Qzone. Is she blind? I am pretty sure she saw the kiss photo on my Qzone.'

In romantic relationships, surveillance on social media can lead to jealousy in various ways. For instance, a delayed reply to a WeChat message can make the romantic partner feel unimportant, especially when he or she can see on other social media platforms that their partner is online. Situations such as that described by Cai, a 22-year-old waitress in a restaurant, are very common: 'I sent him a message half hour ago; he didn't reply, but ten minutes ago, he updated his QQ status...that made me feel upset.' She was always online throughout the day when working at the restaurant; the multiple social media platforms her boyfriend used allowed her to connect with him constantly, but such an environment also made it more difficult for her boyfriend to hide anything from her. Many young people share similar insecurities about their romantic relationships, As Zhu, a factory worker aged 20, complained: 'She [his girlfriend] never mentioned our relationship on her QQ. My gut feeling is she is not that committed, or maybe she is hiding something from me?'

Because social media profiles are continuously subjected to scrutiny to a greater extent than most offline spaces, for many young people such as Zhu a romantic relationship gained its 'legitimacy' by a public announcement on social media. However, in practice, the attempt to make a public announcement may backfire. Lujia, a factory worker, set up a QQ group of 78 contacts in order to win the trust of his new girlfriend. He explained:

> My girlfriend said she was not sure about my love, unless I showed it in public (*gong kai*); Once I set up the QQ group and show my love for her she will believe me.

On this QQ group, every few hours Lujia wrote something along the lines of '...darling you are the most beautiful woman in my life and I love you so much'. Clearly not everybody thought Lujia's declaration of love quite as sweet as his partner did, and most people soon quit the group. As one former member complained, 'he thought QQ was his own place to do whatever he wanted...But why should I read screenfuls of such goosebump-arousing nonsense?' What was evident in Lujia's case was that 'audiences' felt extremely disturbed and offended. Unlike posting something on one's own social media profile, Lujia's QQ group messaging, which constantly tried to grab people's attention to witness something of little relevance for them, was way too aggressive and inappropriate.

However, in most cases some subtle strategies regarding the public display of love on QQ had been applied. It was very common to see a couple talk to each other in a way that others would not be able to understand without knowing the context of the dialogue. For example, a conversation between a young couple on Qzone that could be seen by all the online contacts was:

> 'Don't forget you promised me that you wouldn't tell her about that.'
> 'Yes I promised, and I didn't tell her about that at all, quite the opposite, I told her that you said those three words on my birthday, and she was so delightfully surprised. I told you she liked you.'

Even though substantial information from the above correspondence was very limited, everyone who read the dialogue got the message that these two people were close to each other and that their relationship was exclusive. That is exactly the reason why, rather than this taking place on the seemingly more convenient and private basis of one-to-one chatting, the couple chose to talk secretly 'in public'. Such 'coded' intimate talk on QQ between lovers skilfully displayed love in public without disturbing others too much.

The self-exposure of personal relationships on social media is not always about positive emotions. Having arguments on social media, for example, is regarded as a fatal hit to a romantic relationship. Huang Ling, a 19-year-old factory worker, explained the problem:

> Each time, when we had some friction, he would update his QQ status immediately with things like 'please introduce girls to me, I need a girlfriend, blah blah…I really hated him for that!

Two weeks after their break-up, Huang Ling was still complaining about her ex's outrageous QQ usage, and every female friend of hers expressed the same resentment. As one of her close female friends remarked, 'How could he say so regardless of the place and the situation (*chang he*)?! He just wanted her to lose face'. Ling applied some 'media sanctions' to cope with the break-up's aftermath. First of all she locked her Qzone, which means nobody could view it except herself.

> I need some space you know. I don't want people to gossip about my break-up. Even though they do it out of kindness, I still find it so annoying.

Fig. 4.3　A photo of 'carved flesh' on Huang Ling's WeChat

Huang Ling's elder cousin even called her very late at night to ask her what had happened when he saw her 'unusual' QQ status update. She felt embarrassed to explain the reason to her friends and relatives, and therefore locked the only channel (Qzone) from which most of her friends got news about her. After four days Huang Ling reopened her Qzone, having already deleted all her previous QQ status updates. Meanwhile Huang Ling's updates on WeChat were very remarkable, even dramatic. During the four 'non-QQ' days she uploaded a large number of emotional remarks on WeChat. One day she even uploaded a photo of her arm, carved by herself with a steel ruler (Fig. 4.3). The two 'bloody' Chinese characters she carved on her skin were hate (*hen*) and love (*ai*). It seems that only carving her own skin would fully express her strong feelings about the frustrating break-up. She told me:

> Because some of my family members are on Qzone, I don't want to scare my relatives and other friends. Whereas the circle of friends on WeChat is much smaller; most of them are just colleagues at

the factory, so it won't cause me too much trouble. And he [the ex-boyfriend] will see the photo either way as he is also my WeChat friend.

If we view Huang Ling's story together with the accounts of Xiao Yu's careless display of a kiss photo on Qzone and Lujia's less successful public display of love on QQ group, a more comprehensible picture emerges. First of all, we need to recognise that social media provides many possibilities; it enables people to practise romantic relationships online with much greater freedom than in offline situations. Social media has also become an essential arena in which romantic relationships take place in daily life. However, a more liberating place online does not equal fewer social norms. New norms about what is appropriate or inappropriate on social media dealing with romantic relationships emerged almost immediately. For instance, the release of private problems between couples on social media usually brought immense embarrassment, serving to trigger even worse consequences than in an offline situation. Sociologist Erving Goffman[12] used the word 'frame' to explain how people's behaviour is cued by elements that constitute the context of action. In the frame of social media, people were not only aware of the private/public nature of social media, but also intentionally played around with it to express the exclusiveness and intimacy of relationships – even though not everyone was successful at first.

Also, from the frequently applied and highly valued public displays of love on social media, we see how on social media the perceived public gaze is just as strong as in the offline situation. Online, young rural migrants may be free from the disapproval and judgement of senior relatives and fellow villagers, yet their peers' opinions or those of even strangers were highly valued, and can also cause concern. Regardless of what kind of social rules one follows, as long as there are 'others' the risk of 'losing face' always exists, and sometimes the uncertainty of who is watching online exacerbates the anxiety.

Another point that emerged from the varied use of social media in romantic relationships is that, in order to make sense of sociality on social media, a whole range of available communication tools must be taken into account. As suggested by the concept of 'polymedia',[13] it makes no sense to study only one particular media platform in isolation – the meaning and use of any one of them is relative to the others. As is clearly shown in Huang Ling's situation, her choice of WeChat only made sense in comparison with the role that QQ and mobile phones played in her social life. Furthermore, in a polymedia environment, once one has either the smartphone or a personal computer, the decision which media to use is no longer much affected by either access or cost; instead it becomes a social and moral choices. For instance, in Lujia's case, his choice of using QQ group messaging to declare his love for his girlfriend had been regarded as very inappropriate. The approach of polymedia, as well as the arguments put forward about new social norms on social media, are not confined to the analysis of romantic relationships on social media. We will now see how they apply equally to the analysis of all kinds of relationships on social media.

Friendship on social media

A common belief about social media friends in GoodPath, especially among young people, was basically 'the more the better'. During a survey, when asked how many social media friends one had, many people answered proudly: 'Countless, at least hundreds of them!' Some would further add comments such as 'to make more friends is what social media is for', or 'to work outside is to see the world and make more friends'. In most cases, having a great number of social media friends is regarded as convincing evidence of one's personal charm and modern taste. Bing Bing, a 23-year-old waitress in a local restaurant, articulated the opinion shared by many rural young people: that having many friends is an essential part of the experience of being a modern citizen.

> If you remain in a small village you will never know the importance of friendship. But being outside, the world is different; people in cities all have many chances to meet new friends and they have many friends, and friends will have fun and sadness together, help each other...I mean real friends will be like that.

Having said that, in field work it was not difficult to notice that in offline situations, people still tried not to be introduced or referred to others as just 'friend' (*peng you*). In most cases, they used expressions such as 'my fellow villagers' (*lao xiang*) or 'my fellow workers' (*gong you*). Some 'extra' identity was always added to the person. 'Introducing someone as a "friend" does not provide any information about the background between the party and yourself',[14] and Chinese society traditionally sees non-kinship ties as less important and less formal. Another research piece on a comparison of networking between Chinese and American populations seems to reinforce the observation in GoodPath. It shows that in China on average 6.6 per cent of the people named were described as friends, whereas in the US the figure is 67.8 per cent.[15] Nor are the Chinese alone in this. In many other societies the concept of 'friendship' as a form of social relationship only started to gain importance during the processes of industrialisation and modernisation, which allowed (or forced) people to meet and work with others outside of one's kin-ties and regional social networks that were confined to certain locations.[16] The experience of friendship seemed to have changed because of the use of social media. Evidence in this chapter shows that for migrant workers social media is not only the place where they explore and experience friendship, it is also the place where they start to value friendship in a different way.

The story of Feige, a 37-year-old forklift truck driver, presents a typical example to illustrate the argument. Feige once had three best friends, whom he called 'my good brothers' (*hao xiong di*). The four men used to work in the same section of a factory. The connection between people from the same hometown is always highly emphasised among rural migrants when it comes to social networks; it is practiced as a golden rule in the 'jungle survival' environment of factories. Fellow villagers are supposed to help each other and cover for each other, and thus form various groups in factories. In terms of recruiting new workers, section managers (*duan zhang*) – those at the bottom of the management hierarchy – have a say. In practice, section managers always try to recruit new workers from among their fellow villagers, so that their status in the factory will be reinforced. Bullying is common in factories, with victims always being those who have neither relatives nor fellow villagers at their workplace. For this reason Feige and the other three workers, who came from different provinces, 'naturally' became the victims. To cut a long story short, after enduring bullying for a couple of months, these four colleagues finally exploded and provoked a fist fight with the dominant group of over 20 workers. In the end, these four were badly injured and dismissed by the factory. 'Even though we lost the fight, we won the friendship', as Feige said.

It was in this context that Feige, for the first time, managed to establish some strong emotional attachment to his colleagues. The situation he experienced is common among factory migrant workers. For most people in a situation where nepotism dominates, it is very difficult to establish a stable friendship with colleagues who do not come from the same family clan or village, unless some dramatic event takes place in which friendship has a chance of being valued. Moreover, even if this happens, maintaining such friendship in the floating lives of rural migrants is usually very high maintenance.

Unfortunately, Feige's precious friendship did not end well. After being fired from the factory, the four men embarked on different journeys. In the beginning, though living in different places, they managed to keep contact with each other via QQ and phone calls, but as time went by such connections gradually diminished. Five years later one of the friends was killed following an explosion in the fireworks factory where he worked. The late friend's widow called the remaining three men frequently, asking for financial help, and this became the last straw that ended these friendships. 'Sometimes you really have no choice: life forces you to become more realistic and you lose your friends,' Feige said. From then on he has never managed to have such good friends as those three from his previous workplace. However, he does not regard himself as somebody who lacks friendship.

On Feige's QQ, there are more than 15 QQ groups, among which Feige actively participated in three. Members of those QQ groups are mostly factory workers with a similar rural background. Feige had never met those QQ friends in person, but they seemed to know much more about him than his colleagues who spent a lot of time with him every day did. '[Online] we are very open-minded, and you say whatever you want to say. I told my QQ friends a lot of things,' Feige explained. One reason that Feige has never worried that his QQ friends might release his secrets is that all the QQ groups he joined were anonymous. Nobody in the group knows anyone else's real name, offline address or other personal details. Usually people tell each other what they do, however, without giving any further details.

Feige is very popular among his friends on QQ. People found him funny and smart, and always asked for his opinions on social events and news, making him an opinion former in various groups. Gradually Feige's emotional attachment to his QQ groups grew to the extent that he could not bear being apart from them for even a short time:

> When I had to charge my mobile phone and went without it for a while, I felt restless and anxious, as if a very important part of me had been left behind ... and when I finally went back, I couldn't wait to check my QQ.

The friendship online has been valued highly by Feige, and that is not rare among rural migrants. Particularly in the specific situation of 'floating' life, friends online seem to be the only ones who will never change places; in a way QQ itself has becomes a loyal friend, always there and never failing people. However, this does not explain the reason why

Feige failed to maintain his previous offline friendships online. In order to answer this question, we need to take a step back and consider the expectations of friendship. Here Feige's comment on his online friends seemed to provide a new perspective:

> They [online friends] like me and talk with me because they really like me, not because I am rich so that they can borrow money from me, or I am powerful so that they can get a job from me. Here everything is much purer, without power and money involved…The friendship is much purer (*geng chun*) on QQ.

Feige regarded the friendship between his QQ friends whom he had never met in offline situations as 'purer' (*geng chun*) than offline relationships, as there are no pragmatic concerns involved online. Furthermore, for migrant workers such as Feige, who are often frustrated by their social status, social media provides new possibilities of sociality free from social hierarchy and discrimination.

Curiously, people who enjoy a high socio-economic status seem to have the same problems with their offline friends. Ms Cheng, a local factory owner, avoided her school reunion event and the chance to meet her former school friends. The reason for that was that the last time she went to a school reunion she subsequently received at least six phone calls from her erstwhile classmates, all asking for financial and other forms of help. As she sadly observed:

> I feel nowadays society is very pragmatic. I am sometime very confused and frustrated. They said the relationship between previous classmates was the purest one because there is no benefit or interest involved. But in my case it was no longer true.

Ms Cheng was not alone. Many factory owners or local officials, the local rich and powerful people, have the same problem: people befriend them for pragmatic purposes. A retired local official commented how, following his retirement the previous year, he had suddenly found that 'many friends who used to be nice to you kind of disappeared…no phone call, no text message, let alone visiting you during festivals…because for them I am useless now'.

On WeChat Ms Cheng frequently visited a WeChat group where mothers share the experience of raising children. She could talk about her struggles in dealing with her two teenage children there. It emerged that only on WeChat, with WeChat friends, did Ms Cheng feel free to release her stress and gain a great deal of support:

> At home everybody is busy with the factory stuff... but here [the WeChat group of mothers] I am a mother: just a mother, not a factory owner. I show my weakness and get a lot of support and comfort... I don't know exactly who they are, but I know they are all mothers and we share our problems with each other.

Chinese migrant workers and factory owners probably lie at the two extremes of the wealth spectrum in this industrial China field site, yet both appear willing to befriend and communicate with strangers online. In the study of social media, arguments as to whether real friendship is possible in a virtual environment, or whether social relationships will lose their authenticity in the face of social media, are constant.[17] This is mainly because of the assumption that one of the inevitable consequences of increased technological mediation in social relationships is the loss of authenticity. However, such arguments assume a foundational Western discourse, one entirely inappropriate to a situation in China that is experiencing the opposite trajectory. In this Chinese field site, friendships on social media that are mediated by digital technology were perceived to be more authentic than offline relationships – which in many cases are highly mediated (or 'polluted' as people say) by factors such as wealth and social status. Outside of such contested discourses, the premise of anthropology is that offline life has always been entirely mediated by all sorts of social norms; there is no such thing as an unmediated relationship, so there is no such opposition to authenticity.

These observations help to make more sense of the observation made at the beginning of this chapter through Chart 4.1. On rural migrants' QQ there are 43 per cent of 'other friends' and 17 per cent of 'online strangers', which altogether means that almost two-thirds of contacts have almost nothing to do with one's kinship, regional affiliation or school connections – the three kinds of relationship highly valued in Chinese society. And the general term for these contacts is 'friend': a kind of relationship that was less emphasised, or barely even existed in practice, in the hierarchy of sociality of the previous traditional society. The situation in GoodPath poses a sharp contrast to the huge debate in the West over the nature of friendship on platforms such as Facebook.[18] For the latter, the focus has been on whether friendship will lose its authenticity on social media. For the former, however, 'friendship' itself as a modern concept barely existed in a traditional society, given the dominance of kinship and regional relations. Here it is on social media that people have the possibility of exploring and practising these new relationships fully. Viewed from the perspective of China, therefore, the approach of studying friendship on social media in the West seems to be parochial.

Friendship online has become an efficient supplement to one's social life, and such sociality facilitates the process of becoming modern among rural migrants. Reasons why rural migrants felt it was more difficult to make friends offline than on social media included the reduction in their time at school and the transient, floating nature of their lives, as well as the practical use of social networks (*guanxi*) to survive. The final aspect of online sociality to be discussed in this chapter, that of privacy, follows from this – in as much as once again the online and offline situation are very different, and that once again social media is perceived as offering an important experience in becoming modern for rural migrants.

Yin si (privacy) on social media

In the discussion of romantic relationships on social media above, it was found that Lujia's public display of love on QQ group did not go down very well. This was in part because his QQ friends felt that his behaviour violated their private space on QQ. Yet given the offline experience of living in GoodPath, such an emphasis on 'privacy' stands out as something unusual.

> Of course, you know people can see you, well it's their business, I am doing my own stuff, normal things, nothing wrong, and why should I care that much . . . If you care, which means you are doing something wrong, something under the table, so I don't care.

The daily life of Mr Ma, a 43-year-old shopkeeper, literally takes place on the street. His wife cooks three meals a day on a cylindrical briquette stove on the pedestrian walkway. The couple go to sleep on the bed inside their shop after they close the grocery in the evening. In the daytime everybody passes by their shop and can see exactly what they are doing. Most people in GoodPath would agree with Mr Ma's views, and it is quite common to believe that if people want to avoid the gaze of others there must be something weird going on.

Strictly speaking, there is no Chinese word for privacy. The Chinese word *yinsi* is widely used when it comes to the topic, but it actually means 'something secret which should be hidden from others', formed from the combination of two characters: *yin* (meaning hide) and *si* (meaning secret, with the connotations of 'illegal').[19] Linguistically *yinsi* in Chinese is not neutral but negative, according to the collective culture, which highly values the right of the collective.[20] Privacy refers to something much broader than secrecy, and the etymology of the English word 'privacy' is suggestive. The basic Latin form means 'being single' with the implied context 'being not the solitary human being, but rather the individual facing the potential claims of other persons'.[21] People keep something private for all kinds of reasons, but most of the time keeping private is an act of choosing boundaries and staying comfortably within them. In a collective society such as China, however, there are social pressures to consider 'nothing private and to label refusal to disclose private information as always being shameful and secretive'.[22] In GoodPath one can clearly feel such social pressure upon individuals, conscious that 'anything one tries to hide from family members must be something wrong'. The line between 'privacy' and 'secrecy' in people's real lives is also very thin. Within a big family there is no door (doors are always open) between rooms. Staying at home with your room door closed is regarded as something weird, and people walk into each other's places without knocking. The situation among rural migrant families is not dissimilar from that described in late imperial Chinese society, where 'privacy was not a legal right but a flexible privilege, the boundary of which varied according to one's social status in specific contexts'.[23]

It is difficult to generalise about China in terms of the issue of privacy. Current scholarship has been focused on the transformation of the notion of privacy in contemporary China, demonstrating emerging emphasis on individual rights to privacy and data privacy, as well as young people's increasing demands for Western-style individual privacy.[24] However, most studies only related to elites, middle-class and urban populations, thus appearing less relevant to a specific discussion of privacy among Chinese rural migrants. Here ethnographies of ordinary rural migrants and their experience of life would have more significance. Furthermore, even though research found that more recently in Chinese villages individuals' claims for private space had become evident in the major shift of household model from extended family to conjugal family (where couples can keep their independence and privacy from senior family members),[25] such a trend was not found among rural migrant families. This was largely because, unlike in villages where spacious houses are possible, rural migrant families simply could not afford enough living space to make this a reality.[26] From this perspective, rural migrants are actually living in an even worse situation than those who remained in the villages. The latter may not necessarily have a strong awareness of privacy in terms of individual autonomy and liberty, but at least they may enjoy some private living space.

In this context, we can further examine the role played by social media and smartphones in rural migrants' private lives. As previously noted, following Huang Ling's break-up, she chose different social media platforms to avoid scrutiny from senior family members. The public/private nature of social media was not only recognised, but also applied and manipulated to address various issues in social relationships. However, not everybody was as good at handling the situation as well as Huang Ling did. Many learned from mistakes.

Hudong, for example, a salesman in his early thirties, came from a rural migrant family. For various reasons he did not have a close relationship with his uncle, who lives in a nearby town. However, as a close relative he was supposed to join the family dinner at his uncle's place. In order to avoid the event he told a white lie that he needed to work extra hours. Everything went well until Hudong's niece, who is a WeChat contact of his, accidentally showed photos at the family dinner of him having dinner with his friends. Unsurprisingly, Hudong's uncle was furious and a family crisis developed. The first thing Hudong did after the 'WeChat leak' was to block his niece on WeChat. He then sorted his WeChat contacts into several categories so that he could tailor each posting's visibility by privacy setting on WeChat.

Huang Ling and Hudong both made some effort at protecting their privacy on social media. By comparison, for many other young rural migrants: social media in and of itself means privacy. Such a view is held by CiCi, a 17-year-old hairdresser's apprentice:

> I am totally free on my QQ. People who can see my profile are my friends and would agree with what I do online: as for those pedantic idiots, they can't view my QQ . . . That's my privacy, isn't it?

The first time CiCi heard the word 'privacy' was in a television opera a few years ago. The word sounded very fashionable and modern to her. Now, on CiCi's QQ profile, visitors are greeted by this welcome page (Fig. 4.4). The whole page is pink – even the model's nails and texts are

Fig. 4.4 The welcome page of CiCi's QQ profile

this, CiCi's favorite colour. Besides the model's 'cute' face and 'cool and rebellious' hand gesture, the text reads:

> I am not a tender and sweet girl. I am careless and casual; I swear from time to time; I hate unnatural people; I hate those women who pretend to be 'knowing the world' in front of women and 'knowing nothing' in front of men…you can play with everything, but don't play with my feelings, whether friendship or love; you are just not good enough to play with my feelings.

In the collective dormitory where CiCi lives she has almost no private space. Four young women sleep together in two king-size beds, set in a basic room with no other furniture. Everyone's personal belongings can be seen at a glance. Yet for CiCi even that is heaven: when she worked in a factory, a single room held eight female workers. As she recalled:

> At night, everyone was talking with their boyfriends on phone, as noisy as the food market…there seemed to be no secrets at all because you could always hear and see each other.

In order to have some privacy CiCi started to text more on QQ, rather than speak on the phone to her then boyfriend. Like CiCi, the majority of migrant workers in GoodPath have never owned a private space that is undisclosed to anyone else's view. In such a context social media actually offers a place where people carve out their own private space. On social media they can 'shut the door', as Huang Ling did after her break-up, or refuse unexpected visitors, as Hudong did on WeChat to avoid conflict between relatives. Or, like CiCi, they can enjoy the freedom of QQ where there are neither roommates who overhear and see everything, nor elder adults to make disapproving comments.

When looking into the specific issue of the privacy experience in China, among people who grew up in a collective society where keeping private space was usually stigmatised, it is safe to say that instead of being a threat to privacy, social media and smartphones actually facilitate an increase in experience of it. Having said that, the experience of privacy is very contextualised. Such an increase of privacy on social media is relative in comparison with a collective tradition: social media does increase privacy, but has not yet reached the levels of some Western countries.

The essence of privacy is not about whether there is a public gaze or not, but more about whether individuals feel they have control of personal issues and are comfortable in a given situation. The concepts of public and private are always relative. When people choose to record their thoughts and stories on social media they recognise that these will encounter the public gaze. However, given the relative absence of senior participants, this online public is perceived to be significantly different from the offline public. Gossip offline may easily lead to harmful consequences, whereas online chat – with like-minded peers as well as friendly strangers who are not connected to anyone significant and therefore do not pose a threat – gives people the opportunity to let their inhibitions down to talk openly without too much fear.[27] In addition, sharing secrets always makes for a strong 'we-feeling' among those in-groups who know the secret.[28] Thus one can often witness people voluntarily exposing private thoughts to people online.

Conclusion

This chapter started with a relatively abstract chart used to characterise the complex pattern of social life online. For rural migrants the relationship to their classmates and kin from their villages has become somewhat attenuated. By contrast they seem to show more interest in developing new relationships with people online, and even with strangers. By the end of this chapter, the chart is hopefully no longer as abstract. A central concern of social life in China is the process of *zuoren,* which literally means 'becoming a person' or 'to make oneself a person'.[29] The implication of *zuoren* is that a Chinese individual is not born as a full person: only through the process of self-cultivation and socialisation can a person gradually become a moral individual. However, the key to understanding this term is to appreciate that in China this process of becoming a 'full' person is highly socialised rather than just an individual pursuit.[30] The relationships between kin, romantic partner, friends, classmates and colleagues all contribute to the very process of 'becoming a person'. *Zuoren* has never been an individualising concept in Chinese people's lives. On the contrary *zuoren,* as a colloquial term, is frequently used in relation to social life. In GoodPath one can always hear somebody praising a person as someone who 'knows how to *zuoren*' (*hui zuoren*), indicating that this person is good at dealing with social relationships. Accordingly a major criticism applied to someone who is awkward in social life or has difficulties in following social norms is the phrase 'doesn't know how to *zuoren*' – literally meaning someone who has not learned how to become a person. From this perspective, the discussions in this chapter represent an effort to understand the role that social media plays in the process of Chinese individuals becoming full human beings. On social media people collectively negotiate what personal relationships are and what they want them to be.

Through looking in detail at individual stories we can understand not only why the pattern shown on chart 4.1 makes sense for particular people, but also that it is hugely important. Personal relationships are often the main factor that determines people's sense of happiness, confidence and ability to get by in the modern world. In addition to telling us about a medium, communication on social media is one of the best places to see the desires and concerns of modern China, and the preoccupation with particular moments in its history. In contrast to the traditional descriptions of Chinese kinship and sociality, we can see that the radical effect of social media is best understood not simply as cause but rather as an alignment with other radical changes experienced in the lives of these rural migrants to a factory town. These include the emergence of an unprecedented concept of friendship and the creation of a relatively autonomous place not only for privacy but also for the public declaration of intimacy – as well as markedly different relationships to kinship and to place.

This was perhaps a particularly good time to be studying the relationship between social media use and sociality in modern China. The population of this field site are not only Chinese rural migrants who have travelled from rural to urban areas; they are also 'digital immigrants'[31] – a unique generation who grew up in the analogue era, but joined the technological revolution from analogue to digital. So in order to understand the transformations taking place on social media, we have first to recognise the radical difference represented by historical rural China, as well as the extreme situation of being rural migrants. The 'hot and noisy' principle discussed at the beginning of this chapter and the 'discovery' of privacy on social media highlighted at the end appear to bookmark the two ends of the social life explored and experienced on social media by rural migrants. Here the continuity of rural social life met and mixed with the new practice of modern life.

The full spectrum of sociality on social media, in return, helps us to understand further what social media is. Prior to social media, the main ways in which people communicate are either through broadcasting or one-to-one conversation. On social media, however, the two ends meet in situations that we have called 'scalable sociality'.[32] Here there are two scales, one from the most private to the most public, and the other from the smallest to the largest group. For example, as we have seen, Hudong's change of his WeChat privacy setting was to scale down his WeChat posting from full public broadcasting to more limited broadcasting; Lujia's public display of love, in contrast, led him to scale up his private and small group message to a more public statement conveyed to a larger size of group. Meanwhile Yan Hong's strategy of using WeChat voice messaging is intended to 'transplant' information from one private group to another; her slight adjustment of the group size from two persons (the couple) to three persons (the couple and her mother-in-law) made a significant change to her relationship with her mother-in-law. Similarly, by locking the QQ album, Lan's couple created a most private and exclusive space in the middle of public broadcasting on QQ. All these case studies show how social media as scalable sociality allows people to gain much better control of their social life.

5
Social media, politics and gender

The previous chapter focused upon social relationships seen through the lens of social media. Throughout that chapter, however, it was clear how far such relationships may also involve issues of power that have to be negotiated and are often exposed through being posted online, for example in the relationships of parents to children, in-laws and other family members. The focus in this chapter is directed more clearly towards this issue of power, exploring two of the most important regimes within which issues of power predominate. The first part will concentrate on the political sphere, which as will become clear may start with questions about state power but is actually mostly about power relationships between those present on the field site. This is followed by a consideration of gender, which will emerge as one of the most dynamic fields of power in contemporary life: both migration to factories and migration to online have had an impact on this.

These two fields of 'gender' and 'politics' both stood out from the mass of field work, but in quite contrasting ways. In the case of gender, it was because of its ubiquitous presence on social media; in the case of politics because of its conspicuous absence. For most people whose knowledge of China comes mainly from news reporting in the West this will come as no surprise, and it may be assumed that there is quite a simple explanation. Political content would be subject to censorship, whereas most gender issues would not. As we have seen for almost every topic covered in this book, however, an ethnographic account provides very different and often unexpected insights into the nature of Chinese social media. Often this means starting by questioning what terms such as 'politics' mean in this very different context. Similarly we shall see that once again there are quite specific issues regarding this particular 'floating' population. Gender relations may not only be different from other parts of China, but an ethnography can reveal how they may have radically changed even in comparison to a previous decade. This is really the primary aim of this chapter.

The two topics also work together as will become evident, since exploration of the political field quickly descends from issues of formal politics to the sphere of more personal relations that could be termed micro-politics – a term that applies equally well to the issues of gender as found through the role of social media in peoples' daily lives.[1]

Topics such as gender and politics also stand out because we have many preconceptions around them, and often want evidence to fit with a particular stance or concern. However, the task of ethnography is to try and resist the temptation to make evidence fit such preconceptions or interests. Instead we will first try to examine in some detail how both gender and politics actually circulate on social media, and then to explain these in terms of the wider ethnographic evidence – the actual concerns and relationships of this particular group of people.

Part A: Social media and politics

Politics is one of the least common genres of posting on social media among rural migrants, as shown in Chapter 3. On the other hand, a proliferation of studies claim digital media to be a potentially powerful tool for spreading democracy, encouraging political participation, carrying forward social justice and empowering civil society.[2] So what does the political silence on social media among ordinary Chinese tell us?

To date studies on Chinese politics in the digital age have tended to concentrate on Chinese online censorship[3] and on political participation online among political elites and activists.[4] Rarely has equal attention been given to the majority of the population – the ordinary people (especially non-political activists), including a massive working-class population. 'What is ordinary people's attitude to politics?' and 'How do ordinary Chinese people experience, perceive and talk about politics offline and online?' are still questions requiring answers.

The discussion will start with an examination of Chinese online censorship. From there discussion proceeds through four case studies, intended to show how factory owners, local middle-class citizens, ordinary rural migrants and rural migrants with a high level of education all occupy their respective place in the political spectrum. The discussion will focus on the political attitudes and consequential social media behaviour of these four different local social groups. By considering these different situations and perspectives, we reach a better position to discuss the role social media plays in ordinary Chinese people's political lives, and to explore the relationship between political engagement on social media and the governance of the Chinese party-state.

Internet censorship in China

In the 2014 report of World Press Freedom Index,[5] China (PRC) was categorised as a country with a 'very serious' situation of press freedom, the worst ranking on the scale. From nationwide and multi-level media monitoring systems to the Great Firewalls, from Google's withdrawal from mainland China to the jailing of dissident journalists, bloggers and activists, it has been widely known that the Chinese party-state has long kept a very pervasive and tight rein on both traditional and new media.[6]

Generally speaking, censorship in China is implemented in a 'three-layer-filtering' system that includes at least three types of approaches simultaneously: Great Firewall, keyword blocking and manual censoring (Fig. 5.1).

The first filter is so-called the 'Great Firewall', which blocks off certain websites and social media services (such as Facebook, Twitter and YouTube) from mainland China. The second filter is 'keyword blocking', which automatically prevents people from publishing content containing banned keywords or phrases online. Given the nature of the Chinese language, however (different characters can have the same pronunciation, and many characters look similar), people can easily replace those banned characters with alternatives, either possessing similar sound (homophones) or similar shape (homographs).[7] The third filter is thus the last line of defence, in which 'improper' information that slipped through the cracks of the previous two filters will be censored manually. Given the huge amount of information online, the labour invested in 'manual censoring' is remarkable: it includes 20,000–50,000 internet police (*wang jing*) and internet monitors (*wang guan*) nationwide, around 250,000–300,000 '50-cent party members'[8] (*wu mao dang*), and up to 1,000 in-house censors hired by each individual website for the sake of 'self-censorship'.[9]

Having said this, as a recent piece of research from Harvard on Chinese censorship pointed out, criticism of authority will not necessarily be censored: the real goal of censorship is to reduce the possibility of collective action by clipping social ties, regardless of the nature of the collective movement is (whether against, in support of or completely neutral about the authority in question).[10] That is to say, it is possible for individuals to

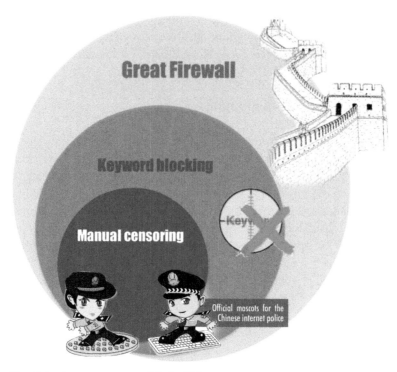

Fig. 5.1 Internet censorship in China

express their political opinions freely as long as such free speech will not lead to any potential collective action. From this view, Chinese people may be said to be 'individually free but collectively in chains'.[11]

This Harvard research is a large-scale quantitative analysis of Chinese censorship. However, the data informing this research was all collected from public media platforms to which researchers have easy access, such as Weibo and other BBS online forums. As for private media platforms, neither QQ nor WeChat, the two dominant social media platforms, were covered by this research. The reason, as Chapter 2 noted, is because the privacy settings on these two social media platforms are much stricter than on public digital media platforms. It is impossible to gain access to content on personal social media profiles unless the researchers themselves become online 'friends' of millions of individuals, which is also impossible. Given that both public digital media platforms and personal social media profiles are subject to the same censorship mechanism, the Harvard research throws light on our understanding of the censorship of personal QQ and WeChat. In the light of such a report the responsibility of the ethnography, with its access to hundreds of personal social media profiles of ordinary Chinese people, is to provide a more detailed and nuanced picture that simply cannot be achieved from merely quantitative analysis.

The living experience of politics – offline and online

The section above is clearly significant in addressing one of the most common questions, namely 'What do ordinary Chinese people think about internet censorship and how do they deal with it?' Yet the problem is that both question and answer tie the issue of politics almost entirely to the question of censorship. What if the majority of ordinary Chinese people are not particularly engaged with issues of censorship, nor feel that they have any particular experience of internet censorship on their social media profiles? The section that follows is very different because it is derived not from questions posed by outsiders, but is rather an attempt to engage with the practices encountered through the ethnography. This leads to a much broader interpretation of politics, in which issues of censorship are not particularly prevalent.

'Be in love with the government, but don't marry it'

Family-run businesses constitute the mainstream business model in GoodPath. More than 90 per cent of factory owners were formerly local peasants, and more than one-third of them have no education above middle school. Factory owners often attribute their success to the opportunities of 'doing development/industrialisation' (*gao kai fa*) led by the state party and local government, and regarded themselves as the group of people who 'got rich first' (*xian fu qi lai de*).[12] During this time China started to introduce the market economy and struggled to throw off the shackles of Maoist egalitarianism.[13] Mr Lee, the factory owner in GoodPath, who was born in a neighbouring village and became a billionaire in his early forties by opening three massive factories, once said gratefully: 'It's thanks to Deng: otherwise I would be just a peasant, farming all day long.'

It is commonplace that local factory owners see the policies established by Deng, which were friendly to private enterprise, as the main reason why they escaped from rural life to become those who 'got rich first'. As stakeholders, factory owners usually hold a very cautious political attitude; as Mr Lee said: 'You'd better just focus on business, don't touch politics at all.' However, this concept of 'don't touch politics' is really about not having an overt political stance; it in no way detracts from the practical problems that make constant dealing with the government a necessity. Keeping a good relationship with local government was essential for factories. In practice, this meant keeping a good personal relationship (*guanxi*) with local government officials, as social structure in China 'rests largely on fluid, personal-centred social networks, rather than on fixed social institutions'.[14]

There was very limited political content on factory owners' social media profiles. One of very few politics-related postings on a factory owner's WeChat read: 'Be in love with the government, but don't marry it.' Mr Zhu, a factory owner visiting from a nearby town and the source of this post on WeChat, further explained:

> We [factory owners] should always show love for them [local officials] so that they won't make trouble for our factories, but we should be cautious about making a commitment to any specific official, just in case things change.

By showing the love, Mr Zhu meant maintaining a *guanxi* with local officials. *Guanxi* can be used as instrumental tool to gain potential benefits, but not all the social connections will lead to a *guanxi,* since this needs maintenance and investment.[15] The common practice was to engage with local officials through various leisure activities, for which it would be necessary to pay. Previously, the most common one would be to have elaborate dinners together. Since the middle of 2013, however, people in GoodPath had also become sensitive to the strong impact of the nationwide 'combating corruption' campaign,[16] so dining in public with officials was avoided. As Mr Zhu explained:

> These officials had become very cautious about public appearances, since if anybody takes photographs of them having a meal with us in restaurants and uploads them to the internet, they will be in trouble. But, you know, there is always an alternative way of keeping good *guanxi* with them.

It is true that there are alternative ways of keeping a *guanxi* with officials. The way Mr Zhu dealt with a local official is through WeChat. Mr Zhu's niece was the high school classmate of the daughter of the deputy director of the local police authority. During the Chinese New Year in 2014, the WeChat red envelope game[17] was popular among students in his niece's class. Knowing that, Mr Zhu transferred money to his niece's bank account and asked her to send several WeChat red envelopes containing 2,000 RMB in cash in total (around US $340) online to the deputy director's daughter. '2,000 RMB is nothing to me, just a small gift. But it is enough to make a teenager very happy, and parents always want to see their children happy, you know,' Mr Zhu explained.

Even though 2,000 RMB is almost a month's salary for a factory worker, this amount of money is definitely 'a small gift' in the owner's eyes compared to potential penalties his factory would face if it had problems with the police. In this case, *guanxi* ties up the exchange between money and power and is officially regarded as bribery.[18] However, ordinary Chinese people do not necessarily regard it as such, since 'gift exchange' is so essential and pervasive in the daily practice of *guanxi*.[19] As we will see in Chapter 6, such a concept of doing *guanxi* through gift exchange has also been widely applied to the relationship between people and deities. More importantly, here social media is definitely not the place to express political opinions. Instead, it is an efficient tool to maintain a good *guanxi* with government officials.

Besides keeping *guanxi* with the government, the way in which factory owners managed their factories showed some genuine understanding of the national policy of avoiding the threat of collective actions to 'maintain stability' (*weiwen*).[20] The recruitment principle of local factory workers is to 'avoid recruiting factory workers from the same village or from the same family' because it is much easier to manage factory workers who are not connected. Incidents in the past had involved a whole group of factory workers quitting their jobs together; the factory consequently lost the labour for a whole assembly line overnight and was unable to deliver orders on time.

This principle was always difficult to follow, however, as relatives and fellow villagers provide the essential network in rural migrants' job-hunting. Ensuring that factory workers are not connected is thus always a big headache for employers. As one explained:

I asked my people in charge of recruiting new workers to observe them [rural migrants] first. If they are lively (*huo po*), we are not going to take them. People who are sociable are not suitable material for factory work; they can easily be distracted, get bored about things, become discontented about things, and in the worst case they will arouse dissatisfaction (*tiao shi*) in others.

This suggests that the local governance of factory workers by their employers is closely aligned to the very same principle of Chinese internet censorship. Both aim to remove the potential for collective action. It has been commonly anticipated that as China experiences increasing economic growth, private entrepreneurs will begin to claim their political rights and thus promote the process of democratisation.[21] However, the findings among factory owners do not support this optimistic view. Chinese entrepreneurs turn out to be the least politically active, generally supporting the party-state[22] and wanting to keep the status quo.[23] Factory owners represent the very few local residents who actually own the majority of local wealth. Beneath that level exists a much wider spectrum of local residents, who, despite not managing to become super rich still see themselves as living relatively prosperous (*xiaokang*) lives. The political attitude of this local middle class, explored in the next section, represents the mainstream of local residents in GoodPath.

Politics as a football game

Mr Huang is a typical local middle-class resident, now in his late forties. He was born and grew up in GoodPath and now owns a grocery shop. In his shop, under the transparent table mat of the cashier's desk, Mr Huang kept his newspaper clippings. One of them is an entire newspaper of photographs of the top leadership of Chinese Communist Party. To Mr Huang's surprise, his cat always chooses to sit right on the portrait photo of Chairman Xi. He wryly observes that '40 years ago, I would probably have been put in jail just because somebody saw my cat sitting on the face of the great leader'. At the height of the Cultural Revolution, a colleague of his uncle was prosecuted, charged with despising the great leader, Chairman Mao, as he had used a newspaper featuring an image of Mao to make insoles. Mr Huang ended his insoles story with a robust, confident statement: 'So we are both lucky you know, that we live in such a peaceful and reasonable age, and China is so powerful in the world.' Clearly he was content with the status quo and full of national pride.

On his Qzone, Mr Huang's favourite political topics were the rise of China and some historical anecdotes of political struggles – reflecting his oft-repeated view that 'men should care more about big affairs of state (*guojia dashi*) and leave those insignificant household trivia to women'. However, none of his political interests were in the sphere of local politics. The unwritten rule shared by people was that local political issues should appear only in offline situations rather than on social media. On social media, Mr Huang is a typical example of 'passive political participation'. To be able to talk about politics, including making innocent jokes about politicians, seems to be an important and necessary social skill for local middle-aged men, helping them to appear smart and masculine in front of their peers. For this purpose, social media was mainly used to 'watch' politics, in the way that football fans watch a match, rather than to 'do' politics. Similarly, when people watch a football match very few would question the basic rules of the game. On the contrary: the premise of fully enjoying the game is a sophisticated knowledge of all the rules and the ability to follow them. Like Mr Huang, many local middle-class men have a reasonable knowledge of the rules of 'playing' politics in China, but it is highly unlikely that they would challenge them. The parallel between following sport and politics is even closer, since both have become important components of contemporary Chinese ideas of masculinity. Local middle-aged men use social media to make fun of politics and to make innocent jokes; they gossip about politicians with their male friends in quite a similar fashion to the way in which they joke and talk about watching football.[24]

Both factory owners and the local middle class support the status quo, and their social media behaviour seems to be consistent with this attitude. In the next section, the situation is found to be different among rural migrants. The very concept of 'rural migrant' is itself a direct product of political developments in post-Communist China. This population is also one of the most vulnerable social groups, facing all kinds of social problems in the face of the rural–urban divide and pervasive social discrimination.[25] However, on their social media profiles there were very few references to politics, especially local political issue of immediate concern.

'I have no interests in politics, but being a Communist Party member is so useful'

After several sleepless nights Makang, a factory migrant worker in his thirties, decided to stay at the factory for another six months even though his disabled father and three-year-old son, who had remained behind, desperately needed him to come back. The main reason for his decision was a 'probationary Communist Party member' certificate which he had not yet received from the factory party branch. If he chose to quit his job at that moment, all his previous efforts would be in vain: the village party branch would not recognise the political screening undertaken at the factory party branch unless he had already obtained a 'probationary Communist Party member' certificate.

To join the Chinese Communist Party involves an extremely rigorous and long screening process lasting at least three years. Applicants first need to attend study sessions, make a sustained effort to join party activities, submit self-assessment reports regularly and subject themselves to monitoring by the party branch on a daily basis (each applicant is assigned two Party liaison members, who monitor and assess the applicant's political loyalty, work performance and social relationships). Two years of monitoring is followed by a closed-door evaluation, in which an applicant's political background, as well as that of his or her parents and other important kin, is examined. If the candidate passes the evaluation, he or she will become a 'probationary Communist Party member', who will be under closer monitoring by the Party branch for another year before finally being accepted as a formal member.[26]

'I have no interest in politics at all, but being a Party member is so useful,' Makang explained. The Communist Party membership is viewed as a scarce political resource that in practice can be turned into economic benefits.[27] The situation is more obvious in villages, since in China direct democratic elections only take place at village level.[28] In villages local Communist Party members enjoy more political rights than ordinary villagers, meaning they enjoy not only higher social status, but also better welfare and some 'grey' income. For instance, if a village wants to sell collectively owned farmland to developers, only local Communist Party members have the right to vote on the decision. As mentioned previously, naturally those who can vote become the target of developers to make *guanxi*. To join the Party has become extremely difficult in villages. Current Party members always try to keep the balance of political power among various big families in a village, thus the allocation of the Party membership is in most cases pre-decided. For most villagers, like Makang, who do not come from a big family with political influence, one of the alternative ways to join the Party was through the factory outside the village.

Now it is not difficult to understand why Makang decided to make such a huge effort to join the Party. For him, such an active and direct political participation was perceived as nothing to do with politics. The pursuit of Party membership was more like purchasing an insurance to provide some of the security that he had not yet experienced in 'floating' life.

None of the topics discussed above had ever appeared on Makang's Qzone. Here there are very few reference to politics; over a whole year, there are only five postings about politics out of 59. The five postings consist of two 'anti-Japan' posts, one 'anti-corruption', one about the social inequality suffered by rural migrants and one about the rise of China as an economic and political power.[29] Posts were consistently on the national or even international level; even though some specific local events did appear, all of them referred to events in other parts of China. The pattern of MaKang's political postings on social media is typical among rural migrants: local political matters, which have most immediate concerns to people, have hardly any visibility on social media.

Furthermore, on rural migrants' social media, postings about the leadership of China were usually very positive. The positive image of Chinese leadership on public internet arena is the result of political propaganda,[30] but the equally positive impressions on personal social media indicate the fact that many people appear to believe it. For example Yan Mei, a migrant worker, commented 'In China the high officials (*da guan*) of the leadership are very good; only local officials (*xiao guan*) are not good'. She also gave a well-known anecdote of the previous premier Wen Jiabao as an example: in 2003, Premier Wen pledged to help migrant workers expedite payment of unpaid wages during his surprise inspection tour after an ordinary rural migrant woman had made a complaint to him about the the wages owed to her husband by a local construction company.[31] The extensive administrative and fiscal decentralisation that China has experienced since 1980 benefited economic development remarkably. However, such decentralisation also led to the situation in which regional bureaucrats are supposed to take full responsibility when problems occur, and so become the target of complaints.[32]

However, such complaints about regional officials are rarely vented on social media. The same Yan Mei who said that 'only local officials are not good' was involved in a demolition dispute. Her family spent three months discreetly approaching various individuals who may have some *guanxi* (social relations) in the local government to help them to remedy their situation, rather than airing their grievances publicly on social media. People are clearly aware of the negative consequences that online exposure of local issues could potentially provoke. A family member of Yan Mei described the position, which also accounts for the political apathy of most rural migrants who see themselves as insignificant individuals in political life:

> You want to solve the problem, rather than make it into a bigger one. Online is for those who want to make big news, or those who

had no other choice left...for our powerless ordinary people, to 'play politics' (*wan zhengzhi*) is meaningless and dangerous: you have no chance of winning unless you are super lucky.

For most workers joining the Communist Party is not really a likely option. Indeed, their relationship to politics of any kind is fairly tenuous. This is partly because as a 'floating' population that does not expect to remain in this particular area indefinitely, they assume they have little at stake in relation to local politics itself – even though political decisions may in effect have a considerable impact upon them.[33] They also assume that no one of any importance would have any real interest in what they think or say. But equally, much as they might wish to be engaged in anything political, they would not have considered social media as an appropriate place for such activities – the very idea of social media is for them so closely related to everyday communication, and also to everyday fantasy, that it would not occur to them that politics should feature there.

Not everybody took an indifferent attitude towards politics, however, and a few did appear politically active. 'Phoenix man' Da Fei, discussed below, represents this minority group.

The 'phoenix man' and his political life

'Around 99 per cent of the people who work on the assembly lines are rural migrants, and only one per cent of the people who sit in the offices are rural migrants.' The seemingly exaggerated situation described by a senior factory manager actually seemed to be consistent with ethnographic observation. The situation arises partly from the fact that local people do not want to take on heavy labour on assembly lines, while the poor educational qualifications of most rural migrants prevent them from gaining more advanced office jobs. But it is also partly due to the management model of local factories, in which factory owners tend to hire relatives and local people, rather than rural migrants, as officials and managers.[34] Given such a rigid rural–urban divide at the workplace, Da Fei, a young man from a rural background with a university education, almost achieved a miracle by becoming a senior manager. The term 'phoenix man' (*fenghuang nan*), from the traditional saying 'a phoenix soars out of a chicken coop' (*jiwo li feichu fenghuang*), is used to refer to this type of rural male – one who came from a humble beginning, but made his way through school and managed to rise to an urban life.[35]

'Phoenix man' Da Fei was also one of the few who constantly showed his strong dissatisfaction with politics, both online and offline. In the factory his main job was to increase efficiency by reducing cost – a task that proved almost impossible in the face of pervasive nepotism. Firstly, most of the senior managers were relatives of the factory owner, and all tended to protect their own interests rather than work with Da Fei to cut costs. Moreover, nepotism existed from top to bottom: everybody tried to put their relatives or fellow villagers into 'juicy' positions, expecting that this would be reciprocated in the future. Da Fei was turned down when he tried to get real information concerning scrap rates from the assembly line, for example, because the worker in charge of reporting the scrap rate was the son-in-law of a section manager; the section manager's family in turn was dealing with the steel recycling business, which benefits from a suspect scrap rate for steel products in the factory. As a result, after a year all Da Fei's efforts proved to be in vain: his only achievement had been to offend all the managers and their relatives in the factory. As a result he became the most unwanted person everywhere, offline and online.

When Da Fei joined the factory, he was added to the WeChat group of all the senior managers. Initially Da Fei was welcomed as he brought interesting news to the group. Gradually he felt the collective hostility against him, as nobody responded to his messages in a group chat at all. The tension became white-hot when a senior manager (a relative of the factory owner) wrote on the WeChat group: 'Why do we need an "outsider" to sort out the family business?' Two days later Da Fei found that he had been removed from the chat group. This WeChat event was the last straw: it made Da Fei quit. Two weeks later he also left GoodPath.

Da Fei's frustrating political struggle offline extended to his Qzone. Here political postings account for the majority. 'The internet is the only weapon we have to push for democracy; online the people's voice will be heard by the world!' he once said proudly. A typical political posting on his Qzone read:

> Those at the top of the power hierarchy always stand high above, enjoying their privileges and welfare, never affected by the situations of economic development. However, ordinary people have to live a tough life. For those who live at the bottom of society, except being submissive to oppression, what else can they do? What a pathetic country.

Like this one, most criticism about corruption, nepotism or the political system on his QQ expressed strong negative personal opinions. However, none of them were censored, which seems to reinforce the argument that the Chinese censorship system does in fact allow people to release very negative emotions and criticism online as long as there is no possibility of these causing collective action.

The reason for highlighting Da Fei's story in this section is not just that he was one of the very few political activists in GoodPath who continued to fight nepotism and to criticise all sorts of social problems online: more importantly, Da Fei's story throws light on a key finding – that in the political lives of ordinary people, the really crucial and effective censorship does not come from the far-reaching party-state, but from one's personal relationships. Internet censorship did not prevent Da Fei from expressing himself online; it was the entire management team that struck the fatal blow by removing him from the WeChat group. This suggests that from an ethnographic perspective we gain little from using highly generalised terms and concepts such as democracy. Instead we need to understand the particular arenas of power and control that operate mainly through social consensus locally in places such as GoodPath. In effect the mass population voted against Da Fei. The issue was not one of democracy, however, but of local and personal feelings and local hierarchies and groups. So overall the abstraction of political discourse is far less important than the everyday practice of local culture.

Furthermore, Da Fei's claim that 'on social media the people's voice will be heard by the world' seems to be over-optimistic. Certainly he was absolutely right about the possibilities allowed by social media, which theoretically empower everybody to make their content available to the world. However in the age of Web 2.0, the information flow works differently – 'the power is no longer in the hands of those who control the channels of distribution; the power is now in the hands of those who control the limited resource of attention'.[36] Social media studies on public-facing social media platforms, such as blogs, Twitter and Chinese Weibo (microblog), have pointed out that in practice only a tiny percentage of social media users have influence in terms of information diffusion. The spreadability of the majority of social media profiles is very limited.[37] The deficiency of information spreadability is even more pronounced on relatively closed social media platforms such as QQ and WeChat.

Furthermore, we might expect that with social media people would share information beyond their previous groups. However, a

comparison of the sharing of 145 social media profiles of factory workers and 55 profiles of middle-class Chinese in Shanghai produces evidence to suggest that they do not. Over a period of four months only
one out of 6,000 articles (0.03 per cent) was found to have been shared
in both groups, though 5.1 per cent of articles are shared within the
factory workers group and 1.6 per cent within the Shanghai group.
In the case of rural migrants, the possibility of the same information
being shared within the social group with similar social economic status is 170 times higher than the possibility of it being shared across
groups with different socio-economic statuses. So while most academic debates are concerned with the problems of sharing information
from the West into China, for all intents and purposes one also has to
acknowledge the limitations of information flow between two different social groups within China.

Conclusion

In terms of the technological functions of Chinese social media there
is simply no reason why Chinese social media cannot work as BBM did
in the London riots (2011) or as Facebook and Twitter did in the Arab
Spring (2011). The degree to which social media assumes a political
function is totally determined by the people who use it, rather than by
the affordance of the technology. The key point is that the majority of
Chinese people use social media differently – or to be precise, they use it
in ways that make sense within a Chinese context.

The main finding has been the wide diversity in the way that the
various meanings of 'politics' are interwoven with social media across
the four different social groups used here to represented the population of this ordinary factory town. The case studies started from the
co-operating and pragmatic political attitude held by most local factory owners and concluded with the critical attitude displayed by a few
'phoenix men'. In between are local, middle-class residents, especially
men, who view politics as a form of entertainment, and ordinary rural
migrates who either appear totally indifferent to political participation, regarding themselves as insignificant people who are unable to
change anything, or see coping with politics as a survival skill. What
they view as real politics can be totally unseen, and the 'seen' politics can have nothing to do with real politics. The ethnography also
shows that formal government internet censorship does not influence

the online political expression of ordinary Chinese; the way Chinese people do *guanxi* does.

In a way all of this conclusion is pre-empted if we are sufficiently sensitive to the key Chinese term, which in this case is *guanxi*. Because although we translate *guanxi* as a practice of social relations, as noted in Chapter 1, it is equally regarded as integral to political relations in China. From their perspective, ordinary Chinese people join 'politics' through *guanxi,* rather than through any direct relationship to a political institution. Even in the case of factory owners, we have seen how they deal with local government issues mainly through developing and maintaining personal relationships with local officials. For ordinary people, not in any case likely to engage with formal politics, 'politics' is perceived and practised almost entirely as *guanxi*.[38] The key point of this regarding the book as a whole, however, is that instead of looking to see where people post politics on social media, we need to recognise that social media is now integral to *guanxi*. It almost therefore makes no sense to ask what is, or is not, political on social media.

It has probably not escaped notice that every example in this section was male. As mentioned above, in some ways more overtly political expression may be regarded as masculine, in the same way that a keen interest in football might be. Yet that also tells us something important about the politics of gender, to which we now turn.[39]

Part B: The impact of social media on gender

For anthropologists, gender is never just a biological given. It refers to the social norms pertaining to gender identities as men and women, and the types of relations that exist between them – largely social and cultural constructs.[40] These expectations and social relations are aligned in turn with people's other relationships. So when we think of social media and its attendant technologies, for example, we recognise that these also have gendered associations familiar from stereotypes, such as the concept of the nerd or the geek.

In GoodPath an integral part of social media was deeply involved in many aspects of gender relations. People gossiped on social media, where they spent a lot of time patrolling and speculating there, and they shared and commented upon memes or articles online. Both women and men, young and old, joined the 'debate' about what makes a good woman or a good man.

The good women of China[41]

After dinner, a group of women in their forties sat in a circle, chatting. They were gossiping about a young woman, the girlfriend of one of the women's sons.

> She is definitely pretty ... but the problem is she is not *anfen* at all. I saw her mingling with different guys several times; you'd better warn your son to look out...

'*Anfen*' refers to the ideal situation of a well-behaved woman who knows (and adheres to) what she should and should not do in a family situation and in public. In Chinese the word '*an*' means to be content, while '*fen*' refers to one's social role and fate. Thus together *anfen* means to be content with one's given lot, to know its boundaries and never to go beyond them or even think about it.[42] Based on Confucianism, the traditional Chinese family was organised around a rigid hierarchy of age, generation and gender, where elder men held the say within a family and young women were the least significant.[43] In such a context to be a good young women is not only to accept an inferior social status, but also to feel content about it. Any challenge to such a situation would be regarded as *bu anfen* (not *anfen*) – a very negative description of a young woman, indicating her failure to meet the requirement of submission and to perform an appropriate social role.

In GoodPath flirting with the opposite sex in public was considered damaging to a young woman's reputation, whereas it was acceptable if men did so. Also young women were not supposed to take the initiative (*zhudong*) in romantic relationships, as courting was seen as a man's job. Nowadays, even though virginity is no longer regarded as the most important virtue of young women,[44] and premarital sex no longer regarded as a very shameful thing for women, a frequent change of partners still provokes raised eyebrows. Young women in a romantic relationship for more than a year are supposed to get married – having a public relationship without getting married is considered strange. Young people are 'supposed' to get married and have their first child no later than the age of 25. A married couple without a child was also regarded as strange, inviting speculation that there was 'something wrong' and subjecting them to gossip. It is very common to see older people ask young couples whether they are married or whether they have any plans for having a child. To conclude, the mainstream ideas of gender in GoodPath are in many ways still conservative.

Fig. 5.2 A typical anti-*anfen* meme posted by young factory workers

However, the situation is not the same on social media. Partly because the older generation, who holds the idea that *anfen* is essential to be a good woman, have not yet become active users of social media, young people have enjoyed a greater say online. On social media the association of *anfen* is something totally different. Fig. 5.2 shows a popular meme among young factory workers, both female and male. The text embedded on the image reads: 'Youth: a heart which is not *anfen*.'

As discussed in Chapter 3, some anti-mainstream (*FZL*)[45] memes demonstrated rebellious gestures and were very popular among young people. On this meme, *anfen* equates with the non-adventurous – something to be disregarded by young people, who should do something modern and cool instead. More importantly, when young people embrace the general urban idea of being adventurous, they also accept a gender claim that young women should not be *anfen*. Other postings on social media also demonstrated a trend that the pursuit of gender equality has become 'mainstream' among young women online:

> I feel regret that I got married before reading these wise suggestions ['chicken soup for the soul' articles about love and relationships].[46] When my family arranged things [marriage] for me, I was too young to understand what love is.

So declared Yueling Hu, a 21-year-old factory worker, who got married when she was only 19 (Fig. 5.3). Her husband is also a factory migrant worker from the same village. What made Yueling feel regret was the following: compared to those ideal husbands depicted on the posts she shared on Qzone, her husband appeared to know nothing about romantic love. At the end of the field work, Yueling 'disappeared'. Her husband confirmed that she had been arguing for a divorce for a while, and when she was turned down by him, she ran away from home, leaving her three-year-old son (Fig. 5.3). For many young female rural migrants those posts were the first time ideas of marriage and romantic relationships were publicly discussed, along with a focus on gender equality and the pursuit of happiness. Some young female migrants even reported that they felt very shocked when for the first time they read from friends sharing on QQ about what a marriage should be, and the proper way that a man should treat his wife.

During the 15 months of field work, as far as the researcher knows, six migrant young women left their husbands or had an affair, mainly because they finally realised their marriages were not what they wanted. Even though married men secretly had some affairs, or in most cases purchased sex,[47] none of them divorced their wives for the same reasons as the women mentioned. Among the six women, five, including Yueling, were married to fellow villagers at a very early age, before they experienced rural-to-urban migration; four[48] of them also shared a large number of postings about romantic love and ideal marriages on their Qzones.[49]

However, to put things into perspective, the number of women who make a significant change in their gender relations remains small. In practice, the situation is more mixed and complicated. It is always difficult to determine whether social media is merely a place that is reflecting wider changes in society or if it is in and by itself a liberating and empowering tool for young women seeking to escape from the oppressive gender norms of the offline world. The argument that digital media provide opportunities for people to be able to perform and create identities freely online has also been emphasised by feminist internet scholars.[50] Also, as Chapter 4 has already shown, public displays of intimacy are more acceptable on social media than offline, and many young people see social media as the only place where they can be romantic. Thus from this perspective social media, as a relatively liberating place, strikes a balance with the offline situation where mainstream social norms remain conservative. For these reasons it seems clear that social media is not merely a reflection of other changes, but has emerged as a factor and a force within them.

On the other hand, it is difficult to ignore the strong continuity of gender images of femininity between offline and online. For example, as mentioned in Chapter 3, cute and sweet images were very popular on social media, especially among young women. Among such images the gesture of *sajiao* is an important strategy.[51] In Chinese to be *jiao* is to be delicate, dependent and vulnerable; to *sajiao* means 'to deliberately act like a spoiled child in front of someone because of the awareness of the other person's affection'.[52] Unlike what is often the case in the West, a Chinese woman who deliberately presents herself as dependent and vulnerable, emphasising her weakness and helplessness in order to get her way, is not criticised, since this has no negative connotations. In a way *sajiao* is actually a highly manipulative way in which young women can survive and succeed in a patriarchal society; to some extent it reflects an indirect shift of power in the dominant gender power structure.[53] The common gestures of *sajiao* involve pouting with big puppy eyes or covering half of one's face to show shyness and vulnerability. The images of *sajiao* on social media visually connect the expressions from a small animal to little girls and then to young women (Fig. 5.4).

Such behaviour can seem to pay dividends in the offline world, as Xiao Ying, a 19-year-old factory worker, observed. 'People always say that a woman who knows how to *sajiao* will enjoy a good life . . . I agree, men take that . . . those who *sajiao* in front of the section manager even gets a smaller workload.' On Xiao Ying's Qzone there are many photos of little girls and young women, as well as some selfies of herself, all in *sajiao* poses. Like Xiao Ying, many young women smartly spot the fact that gender differences are not only a source of women's oppression, but also a source of power if applied well. For this reason the traditional gender norms of a woman, in which she appears vulnerable and inferior, were actually strengthened and reinforced on social media.

When young women became mothers, their social media profiles witnessed a clear image shift, manifested in a great many beautiful food images shared from the internet (Fig. 5.5). In many societies, including China, married women are stereotyped as the primary care-givers.[54] Cooking seems in addition to be universally associated with motherhood,[55] and in China it is believed that one of the core criteria of being a 'good mother' is to cook well.[56]

Furthermore, among all the food images, photographs of soup seem to be dominant. The emphasis on images of soup among young mothers online is not a coincidence. In Chinese cuisine soup is valued as one of the most nutritious dishes.[57] The cooking of soup usually takes a long period of time, patience, delicate heat control and a fair knowledge of ingredients. As such it makes a natural analogy to caring for children, also always considered time-consuming and requiring a good deal of patience, understanding and an ability to control the 'heat' in the

Fig. 5.3 Portrait of Yueling and her son. (A partial image of a traditional Chinese painting 'Marriage Battle', 145 × 75 cm; painter: Xinyuan Wang)

relationship. Thus the frequent sharing of soup photos, the way in which young mothers craft an ideal motherhood online, actually reinforces pre-existing dominant ideals of femininity.

Men: From opposition to feminisation

On the other hand, men appeared less keen on the fact that more and more women were beginning to seek a more equal pattern of gender relations, especially when they found their girlfriends or wives to be

Fig. 5.4 Typical images of *sajiao* on social media

among them. Some became nostalgic like Fuqiang, a 31-year-old factory worker:

> Things have changed a lot nowadays; it's impossible to have a woman who is happy to cook for you and wash clothes for you without nagging you to buy expensive items for her. Women are much more demanding these days.

Fuqiang witnessed how his once *anfen* wife had become more and more difficult to control.

He always advised his fellow workers to be careful about their partners' use of QQ, as in his eyes QQ was largely responsible for the bad

Fig. 5.5 Typical images of food on social media.

The text reads: 'How do you keep your children healthy? Young women, when you are 25, or just older than 22, you will be "upgraded" to being a mother. As a young mother, there are so many things to learn...However, there is nothing more important than taking care of your children and making sure that they are healthy. An experienced mother shares several recipes with you here...'

influence on women. Dong Jing was one of Fuqiang's colleagues who was getting worried because of this advice.

In 2013 Chinese lunar New Year, 23-year-old Dong Jing went back to his home village in the mountain area of the province of Guizhou[58] to undergo several blind dates arranged by his family. Fortunately for him, one girl's family selected him.[59] Given that Dong Jing only had two weeks' leave in the village before he went back to the factory, the engagement ceremony took place immediately after the two families made a deal. Three months later Dong Jing went back to his village to get married after having seen his bride only twice. According to Dong Jing, the main job he did is to 'sow human seeds'.

On Dong Jing's Qzone there were some very early postings (memes) about love, indicating how much he was looking for romantic love. Since he got engaged those postings have disappeared, seeming to bring a close to his previous fantasy about a girl he had met two years ago in a factory where he once worked. Just before he wanted to take a further step, however, he discovered that a section manager in the same factory was his rival. Unlike Dong Jing, the section manager had his own office room with an air conditioner. Furthermore, he had a local *hukou* (household registration). To cap it all, the section manager was a Communist Party member, which entitled him to enjoy better social benefits (*fuli*) than non party members...Compared to all that, Dong Jing had nothing to offer. It was after that frustrating experience of having to give up this girl that Dong Jing finally accepted the idea of an arranged marriage, encouraged by his parents' nagging to get married as soon as possible.

Like Dong Jing, more than half of the rural migrant young people in GoodPath ended up with marriages arranged by their families,[60] even though some of them had various experiences of romantic love before. Marriage indicates a re-allocation of resource between the two families united by the marriage.[61] It has long been recorded in anthropology that in traditional societies marriage is not a personal affair between two individuals; it rather involves two kin groups and thus constitutes a community event.[62] People tend to regard arranged marriages as more 'reliable' than free love in terms of compatible family background, financial capability and lifestyle. For young rural migrants it is not very easy to have a long-term relationship in their 'floating' lives, and even more difficult to find a partner who also meets the family's expectations. For young men the family's approval and support is essential, since the bride price (*cai li*)[63] required by the bride's side is normally way beyond an individual's financial capability. In Dong Jing's case his family had to borrow from a number of relatives to provide at least 80,000 RMB (around US $13,300) in advance. This amount of money was only the average according to the local standard, even though it represented about 8–10 years' worth of savings for the young couple, both of whom worked in a factory.[64]

Dong Jing's new wife was shy, nice and four years younger than him; she had never been outside her village and had dropped out of school in order to help with housework at home. All those features made her an obedient (*anfen*) and virtuous (*xian hui*) woman – a good woman and a perfect wife in fellow villagers' eyes. After they got married Dong Jing gave his wife a brand-new iPhone4, which cost him two months wages. At that time nobody owned such a high-end (*gao dang*) smartphone in their village. The first-ever iPhone arrived as if it had a halo, and won a lot of 'face' (*mianzi*) for the bride and her family. Nowadays the couple mainly keep contact on QQ via smartphones, which cost nothing after pre-paid data packages.

However, one thing had been bothering Dong Jing, especially after his colleague Fuqiang's warning of the bad influence that QQ exerts on women. One day his newly married wife shared an article with beautiful photographs of 'top honeymoon destinations worldwide' on her QQ profile with a comment that read:

> My husband has never taken me anywhere, let alone to those honeymoon places. What I have is *zuo yuezi* ['sitting the month', meaning confinement in childbirth] . . .[65]

When he read this Dong Jing's first reaction was 'From where did she get all this urbanite nonsense of honeymoons?' To express his disapproval and dissatisfaction he intentionally ignored the posting by not commenting on it. Making no response is quite unusual, since he always commented on his new wife's QQ postings – not only because such action showed his affection for her in public, but also because it marked his position as 'the husband', and so hopefully warned off other male contacts on his wife's QQ:

> I hope she will get the message . . . I mean a honeymoon is something for foreigners or rich urban people. If she is not *anfen*, and always dreams about something I can't give her, she won't be happy.

Dong Jing's case was typical among rural migrant men whose attitude towards gender relations seemed to be ambivalent. On the one hand young men, just like young women, appear to show a great passion for Western-style romantic love, which unfortunately often has to compromise with traditional expectations in the end. However, once they entered married life men expected their wives to behave in accordance with the traditional social norms of *anfen* which they had both previously opposed. The reason for this contradiction is that even though traditional social norms constrain romantic love, they are in favour of a superior male position in a marriage. Dong Jing's story also indicates a situation encountered by many rural migrant women once they have entered married life. Many are placed under huge social pressure to revert to a conservative gender role, even though before marriage they may have defied convention and been women who are not *anfen*. In practice, different couples had various problems and solutions, but most lived in continual tension between modern and traditional ideas of gender relations in a marriage.

Also, as Dong Jing's story shows, there is a great pressure and urgency for rural young men to get married.[66] There are several reasons for this. First, China has the highest male to female sex ratio at birth (SRB) in the world, particularly at (140:100) in poor rural areas, where most rural migrants come from.[67] Second, as was mentioned in Chapter 1, household registration (*hukou*) has always been one of the greatest obstacles to rural migrants settling down in cities. There are two ways for a rural resident to obtain urban *hukou,* one through property investment and the other through marriage. Given the financial capability of rural migrants, the latter is the only viable choice. However, that choice in practice is only available to women. Marriage is a strategy by which rural women in disadvantaged positions achieve social and economic mobility.[68]

In GoodPath all the local marriages between people with rural and urban *hukou* were between rural women and urban men. In Chinese society, like many other societies, the tendency of the marriage market is for women to marry men of higher socio-economic status, especially when there is a shortage of women.[69] All of this reinforces the evidence that getting married at all has become very difficult for rural migrant men. On the other hand, in traditional Chinese society getting married and becoming a parent is crucial to a sense of identity for men.[70] Single rural migrant men all felt the crisis of their situations, and a remarkable number of them felt a profound sense of failure.[71] Meanwhile the social status of rural women, especially young, unmarried rural women, has been enhanced by such a skewed gender imbalance.

Chinese rural migrants as a whole are a disadvantaged group at the bottom of Chinese social stratification. Most gender studies of Chinese rural migrants seem to focus only on females, assuming that females are the disadvantaged of the disadvantaged.[72] It is true that gender inequality is prevalent in Chinese society, and that in rural areas the situation is more severe. However, what some rural migrant men posted on their QQ suggested that the position is not the same as people assumed when we scrutinise the in-group gender discrepancy among Chinese rural migrants.

The previous section has showcased the way in which *sajiao* (vulnerable and cute*)* images on social media offered a means for young women to strengthen their traditional gender roles. However, on social media *sajiao* is not the exclusive privilege of young women. It has been

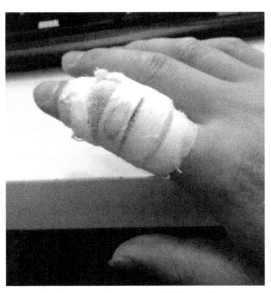

Fig. 5.6   A typical *sajiao* posting by a middle-aged male rural migrant

very common to see men apply *sajiao* too. For example, a middle-aged rural migrant man posted a photo of his wound online (Fig. 5.6), saying: 'I cut myself accidentally; I need someone to comfort me and bring me some fruit!'

Such anti-masculine behaviour can be explained by ethnography. First, rural migrant men as a whole have lost the advantage in the marriage market as described above. Second, Chinese men are supposed to take the main, if not full, responsibility for supporting the family. However, such traditional expectations conflicted with the financial situations and personal capabilities of rural migrant men. As a result, in many cases male rural migrants are actually under much greater pressure in daily life, and feel permanently frustrated by the fact it is impossible to meet social expectations. To summarise, it is no exaggeration to say that male rural migrants actually constitute an equally, if not more, disadvantaged group. Compared to offline situations where men are supposed to respect masculine norms that do not include romanticism, weakness and sensitivity, social media provides the relatively free place where rural migrant men can experiment with what they cannot be in their offline lives – for example, as adopting the strategies of a young woman and playing *sajiao* to get their way in society. This is a remarkable turnaround for a society that has always been known as an example of entirely different gender asymmetries.

Conclusion

This chapter has dealt with two key topics where there is considerable debate regarding the possible impact of social media. Does social media reinforce conservatism, facilitating criticism and subsequent change, or is it a vicarious arena in which things are performed that appear to be consequential but – precisely because they are only online – have no significant impact offline? In both cases this chapter has tried to present concrete evidence that allows us to assess these different possibilities. With regard to politics, for example, the evidence supports the point made in the introduction: rather than empowering or encouraging political participation, the use of social media tends to diminish any motivation for turning discontented thoughts into actual political action. In many ways social media rather helps to monitor and channel public opinion (*yulun daoxiang*) and so further legitimate the Chinese party-state.

The focus on gender is in turn important in helping us to reassess social media's role. From the images of soup posted by young mothers to anti-*anfen* memes shared by young women and those seemingly confusing *sajiao* photographs on the profiles of middle-aged men, social media has served to reinforce, disrupt or simply shift gender roles in different situations.

As we have just seen, a significant break with the social norms of femininity and masculinity occurred in GoodPath when people publicly performed unconventional gendered selves on social media. This was complex to analyse, as the same person can behave differently on social media in different phases of life. For example, when young women retreated from anti-*anfen* public life into the private institution of motherhood, their gendered images on social media changed accordingly. So social media in and of itself is a powerful tool, but not necessarily the key transformative factor. In addition, we need to reflect on some of the underlying factors that have had an impact on peoples' conceptions of gender. These include financial capability, the shifting marriage market and the job market. However, it is the overall migration, with its search for an engagement with modernity, that explains most fully why there is also some acceptance of this modern conceptualisation of gender.

This becomes clearer if we compare what happened in GoodPath to the ethnography of our rural China field site.[73] There QQ, the very same social media platform, has been used in a quite different way in terms of gender relations, although the situation with regard to politics is more similar. In that town men and women mainly shared material which portrayed what they see as traditional family relationships according to Confucianism, including a large number of pictures of children, parents or happy spouses.[74] The way in which people in our two Chinese field sites use social media to express their different ideals of gender relations is the best evidence for showing that social media is *neither* traditional *nor* liberating in and of itself. At the same time this chapter has also shown that we should not take the opposite route and see social media as merely a passive reflection of offline changes. Our evidence points to a middle ground between these two.

This conclusion follows also for politics, where people do use social media to make critical, sometimes angry[75] points about their lives in general, without turning these into specific attacks on local politicians. Yet this is also where we see a difference between the spheres of gender and politics, since social media has not become a significant terrain for imagining an alternative life within an alternative political regime. When it comes to gender and people's more personal lives, however, that is exactly what social media is becoming important for. Already we have seen how in issues of gender both men and women are starting to imagine worlds that were unprecedented in their prior offline lives. But since this refers to a field of relationships that is certainly undergoing change, it is not simply an alternative fantasy world – indeed what emerges quite clearly is that we cannot reduce this to a dualism of online 'fantasy' opposed to offline 'reality'. One of the reasons for this is that creativity, imagination and transcendent other worlds have always been part of everyday life, reflected for instance in realms such as religion. So the conclusions of this chapter with regard to gender will become clearer as we progress to the next chapter, which focuses on precisely these questions.

With respect to this final point, in many ways the evidence and conclusions of this chapter are only completed by the extension represented by Chapter 7. These discussions of gender open up certain key questions about the place of online images within peoples' lives. Do romantic images or images that reflect greater gender equality online drive or merely represent developments offline? To what extent is social media in and of itself a force for change? These are complex issues, and to some extent online images are bound to be involved in all such processes rather than any one of them.

6
The wider world: Beyond social relationships

Chapter 4 mapped out a whole range of social relationships from the perspective of social media use, while Chapter 5 focused upon the topics related to 'power'. By the end of Chapter 5 we could also appreciate that when we talk about 'relationships' in everyday lives, these include both offline and online contexts. The latter continues the work of our individual imaginations and our social beliefs and practices. In this chapter we extend the discussion to encompass even more significant ties. Perceived relationships between a person and the universe, his or her ancestors and the place where he or she came from, as well as with 'oneself', all significantly shape how people live through and make sense of their daily lives. Here we explore these other significant relationships, as expressed through or transformed by social media. These range from the apparently metaphysical to the intensely personal.

The atheist, folk religion and death

Lao Zhang died at the age of 81 without a struggle; he simply passed peacefully away. Local people believed that this was a 'good death' (*hao si*), something only achieved by those who are blessed (*you fu qi*). On the day of Lao Zhang's funeral a 'master' (*da shi*) led the way, chanting spells aloud in a flat tone which, from time to time, was overwhelmed by the fireworks.

A middle-aged man who worked as a driver for a local Party official brought me down to earth by commenting that, 'You know what? Because he [Lao Zhang] was a senior Party member, the Party paid not only the regular funeral expenses, but also the fee for the master (*dashi*).' This seemed confusing to me, so I pressed further:

> 'Really?! . . . but . . . why does a Communist Party member need a folk religion master to perform the funeral ritual?'
>
> 'Why not? The Party leadership thought he deserved a proper funeral.'
>
> 'No, no, no . . . I mean, isn't the Communist Party atheist?'
>
> 'Hey look, he worked for the Party when he was alive, but the problem is the Party can't take care of him after his death, right? So now everything is taken over by the deities (*shen ming*)!'

As the man jerked his head forward, clearly punctuating his statement with an exclamation mark, our conversation was interrupted by shouting from the front of the procession. 'Dad, run! Run fast!' someone exclaimed. 'There will be a big fire!' A chorus of voices shouted 'Run!', 'Run!', 'Run!', 'Run!' – warning the spirit (*hun*) that the body was going to be carried into the incinerator.

After an hour the procession moved on to inter the ashes, led by the master. Before the sealing of the stone cave where the ashes were placed, he re-arranged the display of offerings for better 'Feng Shui',[1] then toasted a cup of spirit (*shao jiu*) to the god of the Earth (*tu di gong*). The toast was a rhetorical negotiation with the deity, which basically ran along these lines: descendants of Lao Zhang will visit here every year and make offerings; therefore, in turn, the god of the Earth shall take care of Lao Zhang under the ground and bless his descendants. After the toast, Lao Zhang's relatives started to burn piles of 'spirit money' – the funeral banknotes (Fig. 6.1) that, according to tradition, would be 'transferred' to Lao Zhang's account underneath the ground, to be used by deities and himself. As we noted in Chapter 2, money is always regarded as a proper expression of family feelings; it is also used in Chinese folk religion to maintain a good relationship with the gods. As a folk saying declares, 'the god of the Earth runs a bank; money opens the way to the gods' (*tu di ye kai yin hang, qian tong shen lu*), reflecting a common belief that 'money' was used widely as 'capital by the gods themselves in transactions with human beings'.[2]

The 'underground' banknote, with a face value of 1 billion, is issued by 'the bank of Earth and heaven' (*tian di yin hang*). It appears to be very international: the layout and signatures are those of the US dollar, while on the side two Chinese characters read 'pounds sterling'. In the middle is an image of Jade Emperor (*yu huang da di*), the supreme

Fig. 6.1 'Spirit money', the funeral banknotes

God in Chinese Taoism. The face value has nothing to do with inflation, but simply suggests that one has an unlimited supply of money – literally, money to burn.

On the way back, the driver took an extremely strange detour, basically turning right and left randomly at each intersection we passed. He explained:

> We need to confuse the sprit. It remembers the way we came here and will follow us, so I need to make a lot of detours to get rid of it. Otherwise we will both suffer from disaster (*zai*) in the following days.

The next day an image of *GuanYin* (Avalokitesvara) was shared on this driver's Qzone (Fig. 6.2). *GuanYin* is a mother Buddha[3] who is also worshipped in Taoist temples. The posting commented:

> If you see this image please share it on your Qzone and WeChat; it will help you to avoid bad luck in the coming seven days. If you don't share, you will have a disaster (*zai*) soon.

Lao Zhang's daughter also posted the image of *GuanYin* on her WeChat and wrote, 'A safe trip, my father'.

People in GoodPath would never use terms such as 'religion' or 'cosmology'. To them, what happens in daily life is a reflection of their beliefs and fears about the universe, deities, bad luck and death.

Fig. 6.2 An image of *GuanYin*, a mother buddha figure, shared on social media

The Communist Party's official doctrine would describe what the driver did both offline and online as 'feudal superstition' (*fengjian mixin*).[4] In practice, however, such folk beliefs, including Feng Shui, have become so deeply rooted that in many cases the Party, or the Party officials actually appear to endorse it.[5] From here we see that, despite the huge effort made by the Communist Party for more than half a century to reshape the 'superstructure' of Chinese society,[6] it has failed to change the essential beliefs held by much of the population. Such beliefs have been practised in folk rituals and handed down from one generation to the next, reinforced by a myriad of folk tales, over hundreds or even thousands of years. 'Say one thing and do another', (*shou yi tao, zuo yi tao*) as people say, and it appears that they do. In the survey I conducted, an overwhelming majority of people (86 per cent) wrote down 'nil' to the inquiry about religion (*zongjiao xinyang*).[7] However, when it comes to immediate personal interests and welfare, such as trying to ensure the best 'after-death life' for a loved one, people have no problem in abandoning the 'politically correct' doctrine and following their own systems of belief. Social media, the platforms on which people feel freer to express themselves, has become one of the major places where people can practise folk religions. The situation is especially true for rural migrants, whose 'floating' lives make practising such folk religion more difficult.

Chinese folk religion: Some background

In brief, Chinese folk religion involves three main categories of supernatural beings: gods, ghosts and ancestors.[8] The latter two both rely heavily on offerings made by living people. Ancestors have a permanent abode within an individual household or an ancestral hall, where they receive offerings of food, incense and flowers.[9] Ghosts however are 'unwanted beings' – usually people who have died a premature, accidental or other 'unnatural' death,[10] after which they wander around as lonely spectres. However, the terms 'ancestor' and 'ghost' are relative. Someone's ancestor can be another person's ghost, because ancestor sprits, unlike a deity, will only bless their own descendants and may be harmful to someone not related to them.[11] That explains why the driver at Lao Zhang's funeral perceived the spirit possibly to be an evil ghost who might bring him bad luck.

Polytheism, meaning belief in more than one god, is a striking concept. In practice Chinese people have no problem in worshipping deities from Buddhism or Taoism or saints from Confucianism all together. As one observed: 'All the deities out there are friends; they just speak different languages.' Most people are tolerant of this diversity in religion and see no reason for bothering about the distinctions.[12]

Orientation towards the secular is another striking feature of Chinese folk religions. The word *ling* (efficacy) is frequently used to describe whether supernatural beings can or would be willing to address the desires and claims from the secular world, whether these concern wealth, health or other specific wishes such as having a baby.[13] Gods are ranked according to efficacy, but such a rank is flexible according to different situations – all suggesting a clear correspondence between Chinese folk cosmology and the structure of secular bureaucracy.[14] In GoodPath people would discuss which temple is the most efficacious one, and a similar rank of deities can be also seen on social media postings.

Deities on social media

GuanYin and *GuanGong* are probably the two deities ranked most highly by rural migrants. It's not the first time *GuanYin*,[15] the mother Buddha, has been mentioned in this volume. In Chapter 1 the young factory worker Dong posted the image of *GuanYin* as he wished for his grandfather to recover from a stroke. In this chapter we also saw how people posted images of *GuanYin* after Lao Zhang's funeral, for various reasons. Traditionally *GuanYin,* is regarded as a mighty goddess who blesses fertility, safety and health; she is worshipped most widely across Chinese society.[16]

Unlike *GuanYin*, whose image was posted and shared by both men and women, images of the male deity *GuanGong* are mainly shared among men on social media. In history *GuanGong* was a great general and minister during the Han Dynasty (in the third century AD); after his death he was worshipped as the deity of the martial virtues.[17] Kai, a factory worker, shared the image of *GuanGong* on his Qzone (Fig. 6.3) when one of his closest colleagues was leaving. On that post Kai wishes that their brotherhood would be like 'The Oath of the Peach Garden' (*Tao yuan jie yi*). The story, recorded in a famous historical novel *Three Kingdoms*,[18] describes how *GuanGong and* two other men took an oath and became sworn brothers in a ceremony in the Peach Garden. The legend is based on historical fact: these three sworn brothers established the state of Chu Han during the Three Kingdoms period.

The popularity of *GuanGong* posts on social media among male rural migrants reflects the widespread ideal of brotherhood they share. Loyalty is always regarded as the most important virtue of such a brotherhood. *GuanGong* was a royal general who had never disobeyed the orders of his sworn elder brother, the emperor Liu Bei. Here brotherhood, in many cases, aligns with China's hierarchical social system, serving as one of the dominant channels of social mobility and networking for men.[19] For young male rural migrants,[20] who have very limited social resources and have to rely on the protection and security of such brotherhoods, this is now even more true. In many cases

Fig. 6.3 An image of the deity *GuanGong* shared on social media

such brotherhoods assumed forms of patronage, mentoring and 'discipleship'.[21] Unfortunately, however, as happened in history,[22] the brotherhood among young male migrant workers can be very fragile and easily quashed. Feige's story in Chapter 4 provides a typical example of a once-valued brotherhood that was actually very short-lived – partly because it was formed under the pressure of survival in a specific situation, and was not strong enough to endure the test of 'floating' life in the longer term.

The image of *GuanGong* on Kai's post,[23] therefore, does not only portray a supernatural being with magical powers to be used for blessing and protecting his brotherhood. As *GuanGong* himself had a secular life and became a deity after death, he can also represent this ultimate ideal brotherhood[24] – something that rural migrants desperately long for, but can hardly ever achieve. The very figure of *GuanGong* resonated with ordinary people, and enabled them to project their own lives on to it. The folk tales of *GuanGong* give the ground and material for people to imagine what brotherhood should be in a secular world. In this sense, traditional folk beliefs have never been separated from the daily practice of social relationships.

In some cases, posts related to folk religion are also a means of making relationships with deities more practical. A typical meme on QQ read:

> From 11 p.m. to 9 a.m. tomorrow morning, *GunYin* Bodhisattva will open the heaven treasury. If you shared this amulet image (*ping an fu*) for people who were born in the year of the cockerel (the years 1969, 1981, 1993 and 2005) they will have good fortune and be healthy and wealthy forever. Share it, and bring good luck to your friends who were born in the year of the cockerel!

There are several similar posts featuring different zodiac animals[25] and offering good luck to people who were born in the year of the rabbit, the goat, the tiger, the dragon and so forth.

'Luck' is probably a universal concept. However, the 'luck' in Chinese folk belief represents a more specific emphasis on human endeavours and efforts. In contrast to 'fate' (*ming*), which refers to one's life-long, immutable fortune, luck (*yun*) refers to a something that people can change or 'shift' (*zhuan*) through their own efforts (such as providing offerings to deities or consulting fortune-tellers).[26] The Chinese character 转 (*zhuan*) is used in both the phrases meaning 'to change one's luck' (*zhuan yun*) and 'to share something on social media' (*zhuan fa*). Thus these two phrases with the same head vowel formed a catchy expression, as people said: 'share it (on social media), so you can have a change of your luck (*zhuan fa jiu zhuan yun*).'

Guang, a factory worker in her thirties, frequently shared images of various deities on her QQ profiles. Her reasons seem to be instinctive rather than carefully considered:

> Well, I don't know exactly why...Anyway...it's a good thing to do. At least...I think the deities (*shen ming*) will be pleased if you show respect to them, and in return you will be blessed (*bao you*), which is very important.

Guang was not alone, Even the majority of people who had shared similar posts failed to give a clear answer to why and how those postings would bring them good luck; they all believed that the very act of sharing the images of deities is, in its own right, a way to please them.[27] As one said, 'It's always safer to believe that they exist rather than not (*ning ke xin qi you, bu ke xin qi wu*). Who knows whom you will offend?' To put it in another way, given the fact that there are so many deities, some of whom are benevolent and some not, people had learned to show respect to all of them so that they will not offend (*de zui*) any by mistake.

Whether the issue was one of pleasing or offending these deities, people assume that these gods were just like human beings, capable of being pleased and offended in the same way on social media. It is thereby evident that Chinese deities are philosophically 'down to earth' in contrast to deities in other religions who are believed to be entirely transcendent, above and beyond humankind.[28] In Chinese folk religion, therefore, people are in a better position to negotiate with deities for their own benefits. Building relationships with various deities is a very similar process to the practice of *guanxi* (social relations); social networking is pragmatically applied on the principle of reciprocity and it seems that deities are rather similar to secular bureaucrats who can be bribed. In addition, the practice of folk religion has been deeply and tightly integrated into people's everyday lives: managing relationships with various deities has always been a part of life for ordinary Chinese rural migrants. Viewing the images of deities that people post on social media, it can be easy to focus on the sharp contrast between the 'digital' and the 'deities', while forgetting that the latter were part of daily life way before the digital age. As a result, when people began to embrace the digital in their lives, they naturally included the deities.

Other kinds of deities are worshipped only by respective kinship groups. As previously noted, in Chinese folk beliefs all people become deities after death; ancestors are then dependent upon regular worship and offerings from their descendants, since without offerings those ancestor spirits will become unwanted ghosts. In return, ancestors will reward filial descendants by protecting and blessing them. There is thus a mutual dependence between the living and the dead.[29] Moreover, a common practice to ensure an efficient approach to higher ranked deities is to go through one's ancestor deities, perceived to be the nearest to the living; the idea of a direct leap from the human world to the metaphysical sphere seems not to be convincing enough.[30] Thus the strategy underlying *guanxi* (social relations), widely applied in human relationships, is also applied in those between humans and deities.

It is not the only one, however, as the traditional respect for ancestors and spirits can also be mediated by relationship to the places associated with them. Such associations of lineage and burial sites was indeed a major theme in the early anthropology of China.[31] Relationships with one's ancestors provide essential intermediaries within the greater human–deity relationship. On social media we can also find the representation of such relationships in the photographs of people's places of origin. However, in several respects this was not as might have been predicted.

The homeland on social media

As mentioned in Chapter 1, this research started with an assumption that social media would play a key role in enabling a displaced migrant population to re-connect with their homelands. However, the accumulated evidence from the ethnography suggests that the degree of diminished contact with their villages of origin was not because of the lack of technological support, but mainly from choice. Furthermore, as discussed in Chapter 4, rural migrants seemed to show more interest in exploring new kinds of social relationships on social media than maintaining contact with those left behind in their villages. The experience of 'seeing the modern world' has made young migrants unwilling to return to a backward and boring rural life: many regard themselves as no longer sharing the same values as those who remained behind.[32] In addition for the majority of migrant workers, as surplus labour, there is nothing left for them to do within the agriculture system: as soon as they return to the villages they risk losing financial independence, or even the chance to earn a living. On top of this, their social networks, built on reciprocity between fellow villagers, largely collapsed when the migrants no longer made any contribution to the local communities. For many, returning to their home villages has become a myth.

For many rural migrants in GoodPath, the feeling towards 'homeland' has become ambivalent. On the one hand, people want to get rid of the rural background and become modern; on the other hand, as the folk saying goes, 'no ancestors, no identity':[33] the home village is the only place to which they can link, and ancestors left behind in their homeland are the most reliable deities to whom they can turn. Moreover, as increasing numbers of the migrant population are born into, and grow up in, such 'floating' lives, many young migrant workers have no real-life connection to the villages where their parents or grandparents came from and their ancestors are buried. Thus for them the homeland, in a way, is not lost – it never existed in the first place. In situations where the physical homeland has atrophied and one can no longer present offerings to ancestors direct, people choose not to return to their homelands physically, but rather to move the homeland where their ancestors live on to their social media profiles.

For Hua, the factory worker in her late thirties, Chinese New Year is a crucial opportunity to win good luck (*hao yun*) for the whole following whole year. Ideally she should go back to her home village for a family reunion and worship of her ancestors, but the length of the trip, plus other expenses and concerns, have prevented her from doing this for many years. However, she has always made sure that some relatives who had remained behind provided offerings to the ancestral grave on her behalf:

> People like us [rural migrants] depend heavily on our luck (*yun qi*) while working outside (*chu lai da gong*); you don't know what will happen, and everything can happen to you. My ancestors can protect me and my family from bad luck…My life has nothing great, well, you know, you can't really change your fate (*ming*), but nothing went terribly wrong…which is good enough.

Besides posts of deities, Hua's Qzone features an album called 'homeland' (*jia xiang*) where she uploaded large numbers of photographs of the mountain behind her native village (Fig. 6.4). The homeland album on social media is commonplace among rural migrants. Around

Fig. 6.4 A typical 'homeland album' on social media

15 per cent of rural migrants' Qzones have a specific online album called 'homeland' or 'home village'. In her homeland album Hua wrote, in an almost nostalgic tone, that she has a strong emotional attachment to the beautiful mountain behind the village where her ancestors have their eternal sleep. Curiously, however, when I asked Hua whether she had thought about moving back to her home village, her answer was a definite 'no'.

'My home village is a place you always miss, but not really a place you want to return to,' she explained. On those homeland photos all the bad memories and negative associations of village life and homeland had been expunged, leaving only the ideal, purified images to symbolise her homeland and ancestors. Her birthplace has thus become a symbol – but one that exists on people's social media and helps to ground daily existence within one's 'floating' life.[34]

'History is always ambiguous, always messy, and people remember, and therefore construct the past in ways that reflect their present need for meaning.'[35] If the popularity of posting deities on social media reveals the continuity of the practice of folk religion, offline and online, then the homeland album takes a step further: through these albums, millions of rural migrants who have been uprooted from their homeland rebuilt their past on social media. In this sense social media, once a symbol of modernity,[36] has reversed the trajectory of Chinese rural migrants' movement from 'tradition' to 'modernity', effectively serving as an 'ancestral temple' where ancestors and other deities are worshipped and folk tales are related.

Nevertheless, to put things into perspective, just as political eradication and crackdowns on folk religions under the rule of the Chinese Communist Party did not change the essential beliefs held by large parts of the population, nor does the mechanism of social media make people 'become' more traditional or religious. Both political regulation and technological methods are outside forces which either restrain or facilitate people's activities in their daily lives. The real reason that social media has come to serve as a 'clan temple' is not because of the technological affordances of QQ or WeChat. It is because Chinese rural migrants strongly believe in the magical power of the deities, and the practice of traditional folk religion has always been part of their daily lives.

Folk tales on social media

Kai's post of the deity image *GuanGong* was associated with a whole range of associated folk tales. Such stories are not only an essential part of Chinese folk beliefs. They also comprise the main body of folk literature – far more persistently and pervasively in history than the 'aristocratic literature' of more 'cultured' groups because they were more readily accepted by the majority of the people.[37] On social media, besides posts of deities and homeland, storytelling also represents a major genre. Almost half of rural migrants have shared at least one story on their social media in their last 20 social media posts.[38] Here are two examples of popular stories widely shared by rural migrants.

Story 1 (in brief)

A very good-looking village woman followed her husband to work outside the village. The couple worked together in a large factory, owned by a very rich man. The woman's beauty soon caught the attention of the factory owner, who seduced her secretly through money and fine promises. Soon the woman betrayed her husband and became the factory owner's secret mistress. Her husband discovered the affair, but was then threatened by the factory owner. Even though he was heartbroken, he decided to let his wife go since he loved her so much and wished her a better life than he could afford. He quit the factory job and came back to the village to take care of the couple's only son. The 10-year-old boy refused to accept that his mother would never come back, and secretly set off alone on a trip to find her. After a very tough, long journey the little boy finally arrived in the city where his parents had worked together. There, at the factory entrance, he had the shock of seeing his mother walking out with a strange man, hand in hand. Before she could recognise him, the little boy dashed away, but unfortunately he was run over by a speeding car. The whole village was outraged and everybody, including the mother's family, cursed her at the boy's funeral. However, the man said nothing. The mother felt so guilty that she committed suicide after the funeral. Hearing of his wife's death, the man still said nothing and disappeared. Two days later he appeared at the factory, where he stabbed the factory owner to death and then committed suicide. The whole village mourned for him and everybody worshipped him as a hero from then on.

The story ends up with a warning that people who live for money, and women who betray their husbands for money, will never come to a good end. Nor will the rich come to a good end if they do not treat the poor as human beings.

For Wei, a 28-year-old factory worker, whether the story is true or not does not really matter. He believed it because of his own experience:

> I have seen a woman like that. The wife of a workmate of mine left him without saying anything. He actually treated her very well; he had never beaten her, always gave her money to buy new clothes...but she still ran away, somebody said she had run away with a businessman. Poor man – now he has to raise two kids all by himself. Alas, there seems to be no way to prevent it; you know, nowadays most women, I bet, are much more realistic...I agree with the story: if you betray your husband for money, you don't deserve a happy ending, and the man had guts. So I shared it.

As noted in Chapter 5, young rural migrant women can improve their socio-economic status via marriage and other relationships, whereas young rural migrant men may risk being jettisoned. Wei's sense of justice has been expressed perfectly through the dramatic tension of the story he shared.

Story 2 (in brief)

When Qiang was a child, he spent the whole day idling around in the village where he lived. His parents became very worried about him, thinking he would end up achieving nothing. On the other hand his neighbour Ming studied very hard, and all the villagers believed that he would become somebody one day.

When Qiang and Ming were both 19 years old, Qiang, not surprisingly, failed the university entrance examination. He then followed other villagers to work outside the village on a highway construction site, earning monthly wages of 3,000 RMB (US $500). Ming by contrast received an offer from a top Chinese university to study road and bridge engineering, with a tuition fee of 5,000 RMB (US $850) per year. When they were both 23 years old, Qiang's parents arranged a marriage for him. The bride was a very capable and virtuous village girl. Meanwhile, Ming had fallen in love with a girl from the city. The following year Qiang brought his new wife to the construction site to look after him. Meanwhile Ming finally graduated and got a job in a construction company.

For Qiang, as a worker, life was not too bad. After work he had plenty of time to enjoy playing cards and watching television. Ming's life as an engineer was much more stressful. During the daytime he had to visit various construction sites, and in the evening he had to work extra hours. Since he was too busy, his girlfriend finally broke up with him. When they were both 28 years old, Qiang had already saved up 200,000 RMB (US $35,000) and had become the father of two children. He went back to his village, where he built a new house and opened a pig farm. Meanwhile Ming finally gained his intermediate engineer qualification certificate, but was still single. So finally he accepted an arranged marriage. For his new family Ming bought an apartment in the city on a mortgage; each month he had to pay the majority of his salary to the bank.

By the time Qiang and Ming were both 35 years old, Qiang had made a fortune from his pig farm. Ming was actually in debt, however, because of his monthly mortgage and the high cost of his son's education. When they were both 50 years old, Qiang had become the grandfather of three grandsons. He enjoyed the sunshine in the village every day. Meanwhile Ming finally got his senior engineering qualification certificate – but he still had to work very hard every day.

When both men were in their seventies Qiang fell ill. He held his wife's hand, saying: 'I have lived for almost 70 years. I have sons and grandsons. I am so satisfied with my life.' Ming also held his wife's hands, saying: 'I was always busy, never at home. I know you have suffered a lot for decades. I feel so sorry.' Soon Qiang recovered, thanks to the clear air of the countryside and fresh vegetables and meat from his own farm. However, Ming was not so fortunate: years of intense work and stress, plus a poor quality of life under the busy pace of the city, finally took their toll. He soon passed away. The story concludes with the scene of Qiang in his eighties, standing in front of Ming's tomb and sighing with emotion as he reflects: 'we only live only once, and how different we are'.

It seems as though the life of rural migrants has been dramatically romanticised in this story. Some Chinese experts[39] have suggested that urban white-collar workers may very well be its original target audience. There certainly is a rather dark sense of humour in the recognition that 'after all the struggles to succeed, a senior engineer's life may end up even worse than a rural migrant's'.[40] Having said that, the story also became popular among rural migrants with a different interpretation. Bobo, a 19-year-old factory worker, dropped out of school two years ago. She shared this story on her Qzone with the comment 'so true':

> Well, I know you would say knowledge can change one's life, but actually education is not that useful for us...Education just isn't my thing, and I don't want to waste money or time on it.

Half a century ago in China, university education almost always ensured a 'job for life' and a secure urban identity.[41] However, this is no longer axiomatic in the context of a market economy with no job guarantees: the massive expansion of university enrolment in China[42] also means that graduates are no longer regarded as the 'elite'. Moreover in China, where top universities are state-owned, the tuition fee for the first tier university is the cheapest or may even be free. By contrast private universities charge a far higher tuition fee to students unable to get into state universities. This means that students pay more for less qualified universities. For rural students, who grow up with relatively poor educational resources and limited family guidance, it has become very difficult to get into first tier universities. As a result many perceive higher education to be a waste of time: years are spent pursuing an expensive but useless university certificate that could have been spent earning money in factories. Faced with such pragmatic concerns, many young people from rural backgrounds choose to drop out of school and work in factories from a very early age. Such decisions are generally supported, or at least not opposed, by their families. This story exactly reflects the attitude towards education among rural migrants, one surprisingly different from the well-known high valuation of education to many Chinese.

There are several common points between the two stories. First, both took place within the setting of ordinary rural migrants' daily lives, settings to which people can easily relate. Second, both contain quite a bit of drama, which both purifies and spices up everday life into a legend, and through which strong and distinct thoughts and attitudes unfolded. Third, they both safeguard and reinforce values and morals shared by the specific rural migrant group.

All these features remind us of the folk tales, which also serve as a pedagogic device, reinforcing morals and values 'particularly, but not exclusively, in non-literate societies'.[43] In those stories we watch the heroes and traitors, the perceived justice and unfairness, the doomed fate and the up-and-down rollercoaster of everyday life. Stories on social media, the folk tales of a digital age, play an important role in recording and shaping the world view of Chinese rural migrants. Compared to other text-based publications, stories on social media have the lowest threshold in terms of getting stories published, and thus the most accessible outlet for less-educated people who may otherwise struggle to get their voices heard. Folk tales were traditionally spread by oral transmission, making them products of an entire community rather than a particular writer.[44] Similarly on social media stories are spread and reproduced by sharing – and in the 'charmed circle' of sharing people contribute their personal experiences and different interpretation. It has been said that 'each of us comes to know who he or she is by creating a heroic story of the self'.[45] By arranging the episodes of their daily lives into stories, Chinese rural migrants seek to invest a fragmented and confusing experience of living with a sense of coherence, and so to discover the truth about what is right and what is meaningful in their on-going 'floating' lives. These new folk tales on social media help people think through changes in their current lives.[46] All of this suggests that there is a clear trajectory of applying social media to deal with one's past and current life, from deity images and homeland albums to the relating of contemporary 'folk tales' on social media. To complement this, the next section explores the ways in which people use social media to create a vision of their future lives.

Future life on social media

In GoodPath there is a popular saying that helps people to deal with the tough life they lead at present: 'bitterness first and sweetness will follow' (*xian ku hou tian*). It is a belief that one day, when enough money is saved and everybody has settled down, one will finally lead a happy, urban-style life without any worries. Before that, however, one has to endure bitterness (*ku*) in life. Such a philosophy of life was mentioned again and again by many migrants, ranging in age from their early twenties to their late fifties, although none of them managed to say when exactly the 'sweetness' (*tian*) would arrive – 'one day', as people always said (Fig. 6.5). The belief that things will be better 'one day' gives meaning for the current struggle to keep going, but what exactly does the future look like in peoples' minds?

As we have seen both in folk religion and on social media, making something visual, or sometimes even making it immaterial,[47] is a form of efficacy in and of itself. Transitions between the tangible, physical world and the intangible world of the deities help people to reflect upon the relationship between the two, which may be what makes these manifestations efficacious. So if you can no longer actually visit the temple in your place of origin, you can equally well make a visual trip online without losing the efficacy. Moreover, such visibility on social media not only ensures the efficacy of deities; it also enables people to conceive a new understanding of themselves, and of what they want to be in the future.

Talking of visibility on social media, Liping, a 22-year-old factory worker, has her own understanding of the word. She once complained

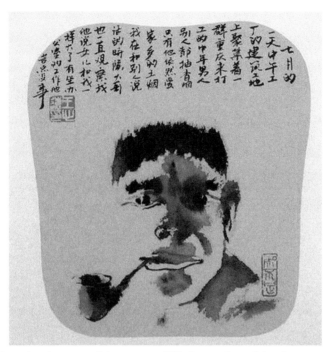

Fig. 6.5 'Eating some bitterness of life for me is nothing.' So says Lao Qin, a middle-aged factory worker who loves smoking his pipe and works hard to support his family. (Traditional Chinese painting 34 × 34 cm; painter: Xinyuan Wang)

that I was always 'invisible' (in terms of my QQ status) online, which is true. The 'invisible' status means that people cannot tell whether the user is online or not. There are six online statuses on QQ: 'I am online'; 'Q me' (chat with me); 'Away'; 'Busy'; 'Do not disturb'; and 'Invisible'. However, there are other 'hidden' options in the advanced setting. Right click any QQ contact's avatar, in the drop down box, and you will see a few more options, including one meaning 'visible to him/her in invisible status' (*yin shen dui qi ke jian*). This enables the selected contact always to 'see' you, even when you are 'invisible' to others. For Liping, such a tailored 'visibility' has some significance in a relationship – 'It is like I am always there waiting for you, you know, very close and exclusive,' Liping explained.

'*To see*' is different from '*to look*': the latter happens all the time in social life, but does not necessarily lead to the former. A factory manager once remarked that the logic of the assembly line lies in perceiving humankind to be part of the machine. When asked whether he knew any of the factory workers personally, given that he spends most of his time in factory workshops, the answer was 'no, it's not necessary'. In vast factory workshops, monotony on a daily basis is the grand narrative, eclipsing individuality. Most of the time migrant factory workers are 'invisible' as people. In the age when the availability of information has exploded, the scarcity of attention is always palpable to everybody; it has indeed been argued that attention has become the real 'currency' of business for an individual.[48] Migrant workers such as Liping are in general all deep in 'attention deficit'; they are always the attention givers, but rarely become attention gainers. In this sense social media is the only place where these workers can enhance their social visibility and see themselves as they want to be perceived.

JiaDa is a 23-year-old forklift driver in a factory. He sees himself as a 'wolf' – an animal that is always 'cool, alone and very masculine' – and he named his QQ group in similar vein as 'the youth who are like wolves and tigers' (*ru lang si hu de qing nian*). This QQ group includes JiaDa's 168 online friends, all of whom are also rural migrants. The group's profile includes 'group album' (*qun xiangce*), and 'group notification' (*qun gonggao*). The group notification reads: 'I hope everybody may be a person with *suzhi*.' *Suzhi* means 'human quality' and is a concept that has been constantly discussed in many academic studies of Chinese society, since the word is associated with the Chinese urban–rural divide.[49] People living in cities use expressions such as 'low *suzhi*' or 'without *suzhi*' to refer to rural people whom they regard as intrinsically inferior. The clear message is that within social media people can effectively create a world of self-respect that accords with the dominant ideals of modern China. Photographs displayed in the group album were collected from online, the most important criteria are again 'being cool' and 'being modern' according to JiaDa (Fig. 6.6). Images such as 'modern city landscape', 'consumer culture' (luxury cars and other goods), 'sex', smoking, large sunglasses, denim and some audacious gestures from the West such as the 'f**k' gesture are regarded as 'modern' and 'cool'.

One day JiaDa came to me and claimed: 'You know what, our factory owner's wife has a similar car (the brown luxury car in the photo) parked just outside the factory plant – isn't that cool?' He said this as proudly as if he owned the Porsche Panamera himself. In a way JiaDa is right: he does own a luxury car somewhere else. YY is another social media platform that he uses specifically for playing massive multi-player online games. This is where he keeps his luxury car: online, not offline.

On YY, there are not only fast cars, but also 'noble titles' which bring users privileges. The titles include 'baron', 'earl', 'duke' and 'king',

Fig. 6.6 Images about modern life shared on rural migrants' social media

all depending on how much you pay. For example, the lowest 'baron' costs 250 RMB (US $42) per month, while to be able to use the title 'king' online the user has to pay 120,000 RMB (US $20,000) per month. As shown on the screenshot (Fig. 6.7), section 1 is the photograph of the live show broadcaster of this channel; section 2 is a list of top monthly contributors (people are encouraged to buy gifts for the broadcaster); section 5 is a list of gifts one can purchase; section 6 is a virtual avenue for nobles who come in their luxury cars (a baron's car is a Smart car, and a king's is a Rolls-Royce Phantom). Here on section 6 the news feed reads: 'Let's welcome Viscount so and so to this show in his Mercedes Benz SLR!'

JiaDa bought himself a 'baron' title that cost him 250RMB per month – almost one-tenth of his monthly salary and more than the monthly rent of his small room. 'Well, maybe I can never afford a real

Fig. 6.7   The screenshot of YY

car, but here I can,' he said half-jokingly. Now it's easy to think how silly it is to spend the equivalent of a month's rent on buying a useless virtual car just to feel good. However, when this is compared to people who splash out millions and millions on real luxury cars or yachts, and consider what that amount of money could do in building rows of dwellings for homeless refugees, what JiaDa did to make himself 'feel good'[50] actually seems rather less ridiculous.

Like JiaDa, many factory workers talked of the luxury cars belonging to factory owners with a trace of pride. People took photographs of the cars, or even photographs of themselves with the cars. The fact that they could not afford such a fast car did not seem to bother people, as far as one can tell. On the contrary: they seemed to celebrate the moments in their offline lives when they encounter the glamorous things that they have been collecting online. Ownership of images of such luxury cars, either by collecting photographs of cars or purchasing virtual cars online, or even just taking photographs of a car, is viewed as a way of engaging with the modern world that they hope one day to inhabit.

Through JiaDa's wide online collection of luxury cars, alluring ladies and all the other 'cool' and 'modern' things, we also come to acknowledge the consumer culture among low income rural migrants. In such 'floating' lives, an imaginary existence built around an urban, luxurious lifestyle can provide an alternative 'reality'.[51] One can sense rural migrants' acute desire for these luxury goods, especially for the foreign ones. However, the use of photography to create a new reality is not unique to the digital age. The definition of a fancy car may have changed, but the technique of archiving a 'modern' self remains the same. A century ago people went to a photographer's studio to have a portrait photograph taken with a foreign backdrop. An elaborate 'paper' car, for example, might be integrated as a prop in such a portrait.[52]

In addition, slide shows were very popular among Chinese peasants in the 1860s. People from the countryside, who had never had the opportunity to travel, learned about foreign places through such slide shows, discovering the world that existed beyond their villages.[53] The images people view on smartphone screens must be different from those that their relatives saw through a little hole of a peepshow half a century ago. However, it seems that the motivations behind the two viewings are in fact very similar.

Today a photography studio is located at the digital centre in GoodPath. All the young women in the town seem to dream of taking a nice set of 'art photos' (*yishu zhao*). Lily, a 19-year-old factory worker from a Chinese inland village, was delighted when the chance arose to create her own art photos:

> I always wanted to, but I didn't save up enough money for that. Last week they launched a sale, and with 50 Likes on WeChat[54] I was able to have a basic set of art photos for half the price.

It took the stylist two and half hours to make up Lily's face. Large amounts of foundation were applied to her skin and 'fake eyelashes' were glued to her eyelids, while meticulous hairstyling sculpted her straight hair into perfectly shaped curls. Finally, when all was complete, Lily was helped into an evening dress with padding at the breast and folds that exaggerated her hips. In just a few hours the stylist had transformed a factory girl into a generic look-alike film star, no longer recognisable to her parents or closest friends (Fig. 6.8). She explained why:

> I wanted to record my youth, the most beautiful phase in my whole life. One day I will get married, and no longer be young.

Yet such a perspective made her decision of taking 'art photos' seem even more bizarre. Why would she consider such a 'once-in-a-life-time' look to be the 'record of her youth'? According to the stylist all the young women attending the studio are satisfied by the evening dress on offer; none of them had ever worn one before. As the judge of fashion and

Fig. 6.8 An 'art photo' of Lily

beauty, his job seemed more like a punching machine in a factory, producing identical beauties from factory workers:

> My job is to make them fashionable and beautiful, no matter how plain they may be; after the styling and Photoshop everybody looks equally fashionable and beautiful. They don't need to have a clue as I know how to deal with everything.

In this sense, what Lily wanted is not to record her youth, but to have a beautiful youth created in the studio and preserved in an image. Such youth should be as beautiful as the photographs she collected on QQ (Fig. 6.9).

Lily updated her Qzone at least once a day. It is neat and clean, using the colours of light blue and white. Online Lily is surrounded by a group of admirers, and talks as if she was a princess who is waiting for true love. In GoodPath she is not alone at all; she lives with her parents,

我一生渴望，被人收藏好，妥善保存，细心安放，免我惊，免我苦，免我颠沛流离，免我无枝可依，但我知，我一直都知，那人永不会回来。

Fig. 6.9 Princess images on Lily's social media profile.
The text with the photos reads: 'In my life I have always dreamt about my true love; he will treat me very well, protect me from all the uncertainties, instability, sadness and loneliness. However, I have always known that such a person will never turn up.'

younger brother and sister, while almost 40 other members of her large family live nearby. Lily's parents work in the same factory. The five members of her family inhabit two small rooms and share a toilet with two other rural migrant families. In summer the family wash themselves in the shared bathroom, which is without a shower: a plastic bucket and a plastic washbasin serve as a shower set. There is used toilet paper and dirty water on the floor, and the wall is stained. However, the toilet at home is still much better than the one at the factory plant, which people usually forget to flush after using it, attracting swarms of flies. In winter, when temperatures fall below 0°C (32°F) roughly once a week, the family go to a public bath to shower because there is no heating or hot water at home.

At home Lily shares the bed with her 11-year-old sister in the upstairs room, also used as a storage room of the small grocery downstairs run by the landlord (Fig. 6.10). In summer, during the day, the indoor temperature can exceed 38°C (100°F) and there is no air conditioning. One day after work Lily was 'working with' her smartphone, a

Fig. 6.10 The room Lily shares with her sister

Huawei smartphone, which she had bought for 1,850 RMB (US $308). She was captivated by the 'online world', as if she had completely forgotten where she was. After a while she looked up to see me. I was still sitting there, sweating like a pig. 'Life outside the mobile phone is unbearable, huh?' she smiled.

Lily's remark leads to the question 'where do people live?'. In GoodPath there are very many young factory workers such as Lily, who actually live simultaneously offline and online. We need to understand where people live, without assuming that the offline is necessarily more real or more material. In research on Javanese modernisation in Kampung, a dreadful residential town, the anthropologist James L. Peacock argued that the local theatre show, Ludruk, played an important role in the daily lives of working-class people there.[55] One Ludruk story is that of a young woman from a humble background who managed to gain higher social status through marriage and personal development, thereby becoming able to enjoy modern city life. Peacock argued that the reason for the show's huge popularity was that it enabled the working-class audience to participate in a purified and modern life. He observed that the show 'provides its participants with a series of symbolic actions which lead them to repudiate elements of Kampung society and vicariously move out of that environment into extra-Kampung realms of sexual and social happiness'.[56]

There are some striking parallels between Chinese rural migrants' use of social media and Javanese workers' engagement with Ludruk shows. For many rural migrants, what they post on social media reflects the far more interesting and modern world in which they want to live in the future. In a way, therefore, they already live in a future visualised and conceived in advance on social media. We are actually witnessing a dual migration: one from villages to factories, and the other from offline to online.

Conclusion

This chapter aimed to present the typical ways in which Chinese rural migrants use social media in their daily lives, encompassing a wide variety of relationships in addition to core social ties. The chapter started by examining links with traditional spiritual realms, reflected in folk beliefs and ancestor worship. All of these existed before social media, but are highly significant today: they emerge as structural factors that deeply influence the use of social media among Chinese rural migrants.

Each section of this chapter focused upon a specific instance of this transformation in social media use. In the first section the presence of folk religion on social media illustrated how and why the efficacy of social media postings has become recognised. It showed how such efficacy has been widely accepted by people who view this as an integral aspect of the relationship between the secular world and the deities' realm. The point being made is more complex than simply suggesting that folk religion is expressed on social media. Such a sense of religious efficacy has a profound effect upon what people think a social media posting is, and what they believe it might achieve.

The chapter then considered the discrepancy between my own expectations of how social media might be used reconnecting with the homeland and what the ethnography actually encountered. Such discrepancy provided the basis for explaining a possible shift from offline homeland visiting to the creation of online homeland albums, in effect relocating the effective homeland for these rural migrants. In this way we saw how social media has been used as the agency for people to achieve this re-connection with their pasts and the places where they came from, but in an entirely different manner to that anticipated.

The third section revealed the way in which posts of folk tale-like narratives illustrate a key moment when social media became a centre for a whole set of world views. Attitudes towards marriage, justice and education gradually emerged in the context of the current rural-to-urban migration. All the stories shared on the social media profiles implicitly, and often explicitly, constitute a moral judgement, reflecting the views of ordinary people about the dichotomy of right and wrong or good and evil within the given context of their 'floating' lives. Thus these new stories on social media provide moral guidance just as folk tales traditionally did, helping people to make sense of, and to think through, transformations of 'the current'.

The final section turned to the role of social media in creating 'the future', both as an imagined concept and a conceived, visualised place. Yet to appreciate this we need to return to the example of folk religion. In a way Chinese folk religion can confuse us, as it is highly pragmatic and materialistic – quite distinct from a Western perspective of religion in a transcendent heavenly sphere contrasting with life in the physical realm below. However, it is only by understanding such 'practical actions', through which folk religion is used as a 'technology' in everyday life, that we appreciate the role social media plays in creating an imaginary prospect set within everyday life.

Once again, however, social media is the means but not the cause. Before social media existed people already lived with an imaginary connection to their ancestors and other deities as well as a vision of an anticipated happy future – both ways of dealing with the trials of everyday life. Now, however, thanks to the visualisations of social media, one's future life arrives earlier, on and through social media. Considering all these sections together, we can see how social media constitutes an integration of one's remembered past, perceived present and anticipated future. As such, life on social media is not separated from 'real' life; it is rather an essential and integral part of rural migrants' everyday lives.

7
Conclusion: The dual migration

This book started with a series of claims. The first was that, in effect, this is a study of two simultaneous migrations, both taking place on a vast scale: one from rural to urban, the other from offline to online.[1]

At first this may appear to be simply a 'neat' attention-seeking analogy. It might seem glib to try to equate the vast upheaval represented by a population leaving its ancestral home for the alienating environment of a huge factory system to the increasing use of smartphones and social media. Now, however, having reached the end of the book, it should be clear that this was never intended as a mere analogy. It is rather entirely possible that the study of social media has revealed a migration as profound and as consequential as the physical movement with which it coincided.

The deep rupture offline

The process of the rural-to-urban migration is first of all a deep rupture. It began with the fragmentation of the rural collective community and then took shape as a turbulent 'floating life' leading to severe social exclusion. At the start of the book we saw the example of Dong, the young factory worker who dropped out of school when he was 16, trying to escape the boring and depressing life of a child left behind by his parents to embrace the modern life that he had dreamt of instead. For many young Chinese factory workers, unlike their parents, the decision to break with that rural life was not determined purely by the pressure of poverty. Many were willing and determined to take what they saw as the first step towards a better life. However, what they were not prepared for was the frustrating gap between the dream of becoming modern and the reality of being denied, excluded and even ignored as mere cogs in massive factory machines.

In GoodPath we have witnessed the estrangement between locals and migrants – a situation already evident in the local primary school, where children from local and migrant families were strictly segregated in different classes. We have also seen how anxiety about *guanxi* (social relations) has become pervasive, to the extent that it has become common practice among rural migrants to check whether one has been deleted from others' WeChat contacts lists. What was happening in GoodPath was also taking place in hundreds of other similar 'transitional towns' across industrial China, places in which hundreds of millions of migrant workers were striving for a better life. However, rather than being a 'good path', the route they followed was a narrow, winding and uneven one.

The term migration can refer to a simple process by which people start from a fixed location A and end up in a new settled location of B. But the migration of Chinese people from villages to factories has always led to them been termed a 'floating' population since the regulations of household registration (*hukou*) did not really allow them to settle down as local residents in urban areas.[2] One of the direct consequences of such a floating life is passivity.[3] Many migrants seem apparently content with the status quo and less motivated for change, since efforts to improve either living and working conditions or to establish local networking are frustrated and begin to feel pointless. Therefore, as noted in Chapter 3, the concept of a 'passing traveller' (*guoke*) resonated among migrant workers, becoming a popular term on the memes they posted and shared on Qzone. The mindset of being a 'passing traveller' coats the 'floating' life with a protective layer consisting of an attitude of pretended indifference. People appear less interested, or even entirely uninterested, in their current job, their place of residence and those they meet in their daily lives. This was considered further in Chapter 5, which revealed how this 'passing traveller' mindset also partly explains the extremely low political participation rate among rural migrants, both online and offline. All in all, the absence of feelings of belonging and the rupture experienced within the urban/industrial space was fully expressed by Guo Biao, a factory worker, in Chapter 1: 'It [GoodPath] is just where I work...of course it's not a home. Home is where you go back once a year to celebrate Chinese New Year.'

Even though many migrant workers, like Guo Biao, tended to see their home villages as their real 'home', this book has revealed how the new reality is not that straightforward. In Chapter 6, Hua, the factory woman in her

Fig. 7.1   A migrant worker uses his mobile phone during lunch break on the construction site of a factory. (Traditional Chinese painting 45 × 68.5 cm; painter: Xinyuan Wang)

late thirties whose youth had been spent as a rural migrant, commented that 'homeland is the place you always miss, but will never return to'. Most migrant workers who had spent large parts of their lives 'floating' from one factory town to another experienced at some point a poignant moment of recognition: that their 'floating' journeys had led them to cross a point-of-no-return. As discussed in Chapter 6, one may visit one's home village once a year, but returning to live there is almost impossible. Three decades ago Chinese peasants finally gained the freedom to leave their homes.[4] Three decades later they have realised that, along the way, they have somehow lost the 'freedom' to go back.

Confronting rural migrants' sense of alienation from both agricultural and industrial communities, a natural question then takes shape: where do (or can) these people really live? No more illuminating answer can be given to this question than the emic[5] view of Lily, an ordinary young factory worker. I met up with her one summer evening in the small, run-down bedroom that she shared with her younger sister. It was hot and humid, and Lily's sigh acknowledged this with a helpless smile: 'Life outside the smartphone is unbearable!' What she was claiming was that the place she most enjoyed living in, and where she felt most alive, was on her Qzone, inside the online world. The online has become the real home for most migrant workers who feel they do not belong in either villages or factory towns.

The profound reconstruction online

Lily's remark leads us to the other side of the story – the profound reconstruction in forms of individualisation and modernisation now taking place alongside this profound break. In fact, thanks to the vast empty space left by the rupture caused by migration, the personal pursuit of individual value and modernity has gained legitimacy and become more radical. Once affordable budget smartphones provided the material wherewithal, the perceived gap between aspiration and reality pushed young migrants to embrace to their utmost the new possibilities of social media. In such an environment young people from rural backgrounds find their post-school education and coming of age on social media. Here they discover and explore not only friendship, but also a new understanding and practice of various social relationships, including encounters with strangers online. They gain awareness of privacy, and often their first living experience of it, on social media, and all their diverse personal aspirations about a modern life and a modern identity find their fullest expression on social media rather than in offline life.

For anthropologists it is important to set this discussion alongside the kinds of material presented in the first half of Chapter 6. Chinese folk religion, popular among rural migrants, is very different from religions such as Christianity and other systems of belief. It follows a set of pragmatic principles, related not to a transcendent world, but rather what might be called 'magical practices', intended to gain luck and prevent misfortune. Understanding the magical quality of those religious beliefs helps us to appreciate that social media may itself be invested with 'magical' properties. Even as erecting a physical temple constructs a particular kind of sacred place, so does creating a particular online space in which we can now circulate images of deities and other ideal images.

Such an awareness led on to the subsequent developments explored in Chapter 6. These revealed the ways in which people use social media to align themselves with what they perceive as the new styles of 'cool' and 'modern' – for example by purchasing a virtual fast car or noble title. As far as social media users are concerned, migrating to online has brought them closer to the cool, stylish world of modern China with its images of wealth and successful pop stars to whom they want to get closer. Knowing how folk religion works among migrant workers, we should at least not dismiss the real power of such 'magic' on social media. In Chapter 4 the widely held philosophy of 'bitterness first and sweetness will follow' (*xian ku hou tian*) further reflected the fact that the 'floating' life itself is future-oriented – namely the imagination of a guaranteed, sweet future that helps people to survive today's bitterness and stress. In other words, millions of Chinese rural migrants are always living in an anticipated future, rather than in the problematic present. In this sense the magic they experience on social media is no more 'virtual' than the role of magic in their pre-digital lives. It works, and is perceived as an intrinsic part of actual life. Real life is not where rural migrants live offline, which is constantly insecure and in flux. Instead they rely upon their ability to engage in the imaginative construction online of what they might one day become. That is where millions of people now live.

At this point the focus moves to Chapter 4, which provides the core evidence of what it is now like to live inside social media. The chapter describes a key expression for this experience: 'hot and noisy' (*renao*), which is exactly what people want this space to be like. It is not just a person who has to spend boring and exhausting hours in a factory who wants to spend their leisure time in this online world. Such space also attracts those who are shy or lonely; a person who constantly feels the pressure of living up to the social standards of being a good man or a good woman; a person who no longer feels connected to the village from which he or she once came; a person who does not bother with offline friendships in this factory town, since tomorrow he or she may be living elsewhere. All of these people turn to the online for their sociality or self-expression. Here they seek the familiar 'hot and noisy' experience that so many now miss in offline settings.

The claims made concerning the reality of dual migration are thus based on evidence presented over several chapters of this book. We can thus say that the images discussed both in Chapter 3 and at the end of Chapter 6 are not just fantasy. They are in effect solid visual technologies that give people a better sense of where they live and where they belong.

Most studies of social media in China have focused on the use of social media among urban populations, who have easy access to a whole range of digital technologies and are supposedly social media savvy. This book argues that it may actually be Chinese rural migrants – a relatively digital have-less population, still in the process of becoming 'modern' – who provide a more appropriate subject for such research. This is because China's rural migrants may in certain respects represent a more radical population, notably in how they fully embrace the possibilities that online can offer. In the global project of which this study is one part,[6] it has been found that the online world of people in various countries (for instance the English,[7] Italian,[8] Indian[9] or traditional Chinese[10]) corresponds more closely to their offline world. Yet in the case of Chinese rural migrants we have encountered an unprecedented rupture, severing the constraints of traditional social expectations ('what they should be') and shifting the focus on to potential and aspiration ('what they could be'), given expression through the advent of social media. In this sense Chinese rural migrants epitomise a genuine 'social media population' that provides an unusually clear guide to the new possibilities represented by social media.

We need to put this discovery in perspective. The frustrations of their offline lives are certainly important, but poverty is not the only reason why Chinese factory workers embrace social media to this extent. After all, many people who do not live in conditions of poverty are also migrating part of their lives to online. Most people in most places are experiencing some variant of this offline to online migration, though generally less extreme in form and more integrated into their offline lives. Moreover, social media was not the first – and is not the only – 'place' where 'magic' takes place. Films such as *Muriel's Wedding* which predate the digital era portray the imagining and pursuit of a glamorous wedding as more important than the wedding itself – a fantasy that dominates the daily life of a middle-class Australian girl. An even greater claim could be made about the precedent represented by religion. For much of human history, and for most societies, religion has been a major, if not the single most important, component of many peoples' lives. Both our comparative book and the other volumes that make up this series consistently refuse to regard online life as something virtual, inextricably opposed to another world of 'real' life.

What this book has in common with other comparative studies, therefore, is an insistence upon the integration of online life as a substantive part of peoples' real lives. However, it is still possible to argue that the situation of these Chinese factory workers is exceptional, as the consequences of such an immersion in online life are both more radical and profound. The ruptures experienced by migrants more generally in their lives have opened them up more fully to the possibilities of this new online life. This explains the basic narrative of this volume. In China a vast population has embarked upon an offline journey from their villages to factories. Yet it is the parallel migration online that has so far allowed them to journey beyond the factory, to engage with an experience of the modern life that inspired this journey in the first place.

Notes

Chapter 1

1. See Chan, K. 2013. 'China, internal migration'. Ness, I. ed. *The Encyclopedia of Global Migration*. Oxford: Wiley-Blackwell.
2. National Bureau of Statistics of the People's Republic of China. 2016. 'China's economy realized a moderate but stable and sound growth in 2015'. http://www.stats.gov.cn/english/PressRelease/201601/t20160119_1306072.html
3. For the past 35 years China has instituted a policy of one child per family to keep its booming population in check. At the time of writing (October 2015), the Chinese government had recently announced that the one child policy will be revised into a two child policy. Anthropologists have conducted thorough research of the Chinese one child policy and its consequences, for example see Fong, V.L. 2004. *Only Hope: Coming of age under China's one-child policy.* Stanford, CA: Stanford University Press. For a less academic read see Xue, X. 2015. *Buy Me the Sky: The remarkable truth of China's one-child generations.* London: Ebury Publishing.
4. The Chinese 'tiger mother' may be a typical example of how Chinese parents emphasise their children's education in modern China. See Chua, A. 2011. *Battle Hymn of the Tiger Mother.* London, Berlin, New York, Sydney: Bloomsbury Publishing. For a comprehensive academic inquiry into Chinese education see Kipnis, A.B. 2011. *Governing Educational Desire: Culture, politics, and schooling in China.* Chicago, Il: University of Chicago Press.
5. As rightly pointed out by Murphy, R. 2009. *Labour Migration and Social Development in Contemporary China.* London and New York: Routledge.
6. For a further discussion of the motivation of the first wave of migration see Zhao, Y. 2014. 'Leaving the countryside: Rural-to-urban migration decisions in China.' *The American Economic Review* 89 (2): 281–66.
7. Also see Zhu, Y. et al. 2012. 'Do migrants really save more? Understanding the impact of remittances on savings in rural China.' *Journal of Development Studies* 48 (5): 654–72.
8. Also see a similar analysis of the motivation of the new generation at Fan, C.C. and Chen, C. 2014. 'The new-generation migrant workers in China.' *Rural Migration in Urban China, Enclaves and Transient Urbanism.* Wu, F. et al., eds. London and New York: Routledge. 17–35.
9. The situation of rural young people fighting for autonomy from their families is also observed and analysed in the study of Yan, Y. 1999. 'Rural youth and youth culture in North China.' *Culture, Medicine, and Psychiatry* 23: 75–97.
10. Murphy, R. 2009.
11. See the full case study in Chapter 6 of this volume.
12. This is a direct quote from a young male factory worker who set up a social media group with the hope that a higher human quality (*suzhi*) will be gained online; see the full case study in Chapter 6 of this volume.
13. For example Fan, C. 2003. 'Rural–urban migration and gender division of labor in transitional China.' *International Journal of Urban and Regional Research* 27 (1): 24–47. Davin, D. 1997. 'Migration, women and gender issues in contemporary China.' Sharping, T., ed. *Floating Population and Migration in China.* Hamburg: Institut fur Asienkunde. 297–314.
14. See further discussion in Chapter 3 of this volume.
15. 'Little match children: Children bear a disproportionate share of the hidden cost of China's growth.' *The Economist.* 17 October 2015.

16 Also see Démurger, S. and Xu, H. 2015. 'Left-behind children and return migration in China.' *IZA Journal of Migration.* http://www.izajom.com/content/pdf/s40176-015-0035-x.pdf

17 It is found that children left behind by parents usually find learning difficult and boring, as a result of the parents' absence. See detailed analysis in Zhou, M. et al. 2014. 'Effects of parents' migration on the education of children left behind in rural China.' *Population and Development Review* 40 (2): 273–92.

18 For example Qiu, J. L. 2009. *Working-Class Network Society: Communication Technology and the Information Have-Less in Urban China.* Cambridge, MA: MIT Press; Wallis, C. 2013. *Technomobility in China: Young Migrant Women and Mobile Phones.* New York, London: New York University Press. Wu, F. et al, eds. 2014. *Rural Migration in Urban China: Enclaves and transient urbanism.* London and New York: Routledge.

19 2013 Report of Chinese floating population development (2013 *zhongguo liudong renkou fazhan baogao*). http://www.moh.gov.cn/ldrks/s7847/201309/12e8cf0459de42c981c59e-827b87a27c.shtml

20 Data collected from two local clinics and primary school by the author in 2013. Also this seems to remain in line with a 2011 survey of migrant workers conducted by All-China Women's Federation (ACWF 2011). This survey reveals that 78.1 per cent of married new generation migrants work in the same city as their spouses, and 58.2 per cent of the married new generation migrants have brought their children to the city.

21 As Wang and Cai argue, even though the economic advantage of rural-to-urban migration is no longer significant, migrant workers are nonetheless exposed to considerable risks and vulnerabilities given the social exclusion and labour market discrimination that still exists in cities. See Wang, D. and Cai, F. 2015. 'Migration and poverty alleviation in China.' *Labour Migration and Social Development in Contemporary China.* Murphy, R., ed. London and New York: Routledge. 17–46.

22 It is also found that the new generation of migrant workers feel more strongly than the older generation about rural–urban inequality. See Li, P. and Tian, F. 2010. 'The new generation migrant workers: Social attitudes and behavioral choices.' *Chinese Journal of Sociology* 31(3): 1–23.

23 Also see Lan, P, 2014. 'Segmented incorporation: The second generation of rural migrants in Shanghai.' *The China Quarterly* 217: 243–65.

24 Chapter 3 is devoted to a detailed analysis of actual postings by rural migrants on their social media profiles.

25 See further discussion in Chapter 4.

26 The very concept of 'friendship' is a cultural construct. See a solid anthropological discussion of 'friendship' at Bell, S. and Coleman, S. 1999. *The Anthropology of Friendship.* London: Bloomsbury Academic.

27 For example Lee, N. 2014. *Facebook Nation: Total information awareness.* New York: Springer. boyd, D. 2008. 'Facebook's privacy trainwreck: Exposure, invasion, and social convergence.' *The International Journal of Research into New Media Technologies* 14 (1): 13–20.

28 For example Shriky, C. 2008. *Here Comes Everybody: The power of organizing without organizations.* New York: Penguin.

29 See also Kluver, R. and Chen, Y. 2005. 'The internet in China: A meta-review of research.' *The Information Society* 21 (4): 301–8.

30 See Freeman, M., ed. 1970. *Family and Kinship in Chinese Society.* Stanford, CA: Stanford University Press.

31 Here 'family' is used for ease of reference, as a term embracing all kinship-related concepts (lineage, clan, surname group). However, it is worthwhile noting that in the traditional anthropology of China the definition of different kinship concepts *per se* has attracted a lot of academic debate. See Watson, J. L. 1982. 'Chinese kinship reconsidered: Anthropological perspectives on historical research.' *The China Quarterly* 92: 589–622.

32 For example Esherick, J. and Rankin, M. 1990. *Chinese Local Elites and Patterns of Dominance.* Berkeley, Los Angeles, Oxford: University of California Press.

33 For example Sung, L. 1981. 'Property and family division'. Ahern, E. and Gates, H., eds. *Anthropology of Taiwanese Society.* Stanford, CA: Stanford University Press. Cohen, M. 1976. *House United, House Divided: The Chinese family in Taiwan.* New York: Columbia University Press.

34 See Freeman, M. 1967. 'Ancestor worship: Two aspects of the Chinese case.' Freeman, M., ed. *Social Organization: Essays presented to Raymond Firth*. Chicago, Il: Aldine. Ahern, E. 1973. *The Cult of the Dead in a Chinese Village*. Stanford, CA: Stanford University Press.

35 See Cohen, M. 1969. 'Agnatic kinship in south Taiwan.' *Ethnology* 15: 237–92. Baker, H. 1979. *Chinese Family and Kinship*. New York: Columbia University Press.

36 See Freedman, M. 1957. *Lineage Organization in Southeastern China*. London: Athlone Press.

37 See Baker, H. 1979.

38 Yan, Y. 1997. 'The triumph of conjugality, structural transformation of family relations in a Chinese village.' *Ethnology* 36 (3): 204.

39 Such structure of social life was described as 'differential mode of association' (*cha-xu-ge-ju*) by anthropologist Fei. See Fei, X. 1939. *Peasant Life in China: A field study of country life in the Yangtze Valley*. London: Routlege and Kegan Paul.

40 See Hwang, K. 2005. *Confucian Relationalism: Reflections on culture and the reconstruction of paradigm*. Taipei: National Taiwan University.

41 See Kim, U. et al., eds. 1994. *Individualism and Collectivism: Theory, method and applications*. Newbury Park, CA: Sage.

42 In Chinese society individuals are valued by their ability to live harmoniously with others and how they perceived themselves in a multiple-tier *guanxi* network. *Guanxi* is not only widely used in daily life, but also in the political and economic sphere. See Gold, T. et al. 2002. *Social Connections in China*. Cambridge: Cambridge University Press.

43 Like *guanxi*, *mianzi* does not have an exact equivalent in English. See a detailed discussion of face at Hu, H. 1944. 'The Chinese concept of "face".' *American Anthropologist* 46 (1): 45–64.

44 'China's floating migrants' LSE. 2007. Migration Studies Unit, Working Papers at http://www.lse.ac.uk/government/research/resgroups/MSU/documents/workingPapers/WP_2011_07.pdf (accessed 17 October 2015)

45 See detailed discussion of *hukou* at Cheng, T. and Sedlen, M. 1994. 'The origins and social consequences of China's *Hukou* system.' *The China Quarterly* 139: 329–50.

46 Chan, K. and Zhang, L. 1999. 'The *hukou* system and rural–urban migration: processes and changes.' *The China Quarterly* 160: 818–55.

47 See a detailed introduction of the 'floating population' at Fan C. 2008. *China on the Move: Migration, the state, and the household*. Abingdon: Routledge.

48 See discussion of motivations behind the migration of the floating population at Li, B. 2006. 'Floating population or urban citizens? Status, social provision and circumstances of rural–urban migrants in China.' *Social Policy & Administration* 40 (20), II: 174–95.

49 The first wave of migration started in the mid-1980s. See Zhao, Y. 1999. 'Leaving the countryside: Rural-to-urban migration decisions in China.' *The American Economic Review* 89 (2): 281–86.

50 In 2012 the average age of Chinese rural migrants was 28 years old. More than half of today's migrant population were born after the 1980s and around 75 per cent had started to work outside their home villages before reaching 20 years of age. See 2013 Report of Chinese floating population development (2013 *zhongguo liudong renkou fazhan baogao*) http://www.moh.gov.cn/ldrks/s7847/201309/12e8cf0459de42c981c59e827b87a27c.shtml

51 See also Saunders, D. 2010. *Arrival City: How the largest migration in history is reshaping our world*. London: Heinemann.

52 Data from the local statistical bureau (accessed June 2013).

53 Ibid.

54 The 2013 Chinese national census of domestic migration. http://www.moh.gov.cn/zhuzhan/xwfbh/201309/12e8cf0459de42c981c59e827b87a27c.shtml (accessed 7 October 2015).

55 See also Hao, P. et al. 2013. 'Spatial analyses of the urban village development process in Shenzhen, China.' *International Journal of Urban and Regional Research*. 37 (6): 2177–97.

56 A similarly disordered situation was also observed in cities such as Beijing. See Zhang, L. 2001. 'Contesting crime, order and migrant spaces in Beijing.' Nancy N. et al., eds. *China Urban: Ethnographies of contemporary culture*. Durham, NC: Duke University Press: 201–27.

57 Data from a survey of 238 rural migrants and 75 local people conducted in GoodPath in June 2014. The survey was conducted via social media and all the informants were the researcher's social media contacts.

58 Data collected by researcher by counting several hundred passers-by at various times (8 a.m., 11 a.m., 5 p.m., 9 p.m.) on the high street in May 2014.

59 See further discussion of China's one-child policy at Greenhalgh, S. 2003. 'Planned births, unplanned persons: "Population" in the making of Chinese modernity'. *American Ethnologist* 30 (2): 196–215.

60 The penalty varies in line with the economic development of different regions. Usually it is more than a couple's annual income, sometimes a few multiples of this.

61 These kinds of mobile phone shops are privately-owned agencies of *China mobile*, the biggest telecom company in China. Shops of this kind are usually named after the owner.

62 The concept of front-stage behaviour was first suggested by sociologist Erving Goffman in his 'Dramaturgical model of social life'. According to Goffman, social interaction is like a theatre and people are like actors on a stage, each playing a variety of roles. In social interaction, as in a theatrical performance, front-stage behaviour is what actors do when they know they are being watched. Thus front-stage behaviour depends on the audience and is open to judgement by those who observe it. See detailed discussion of front-stage behaviour in Goffman, E. 1990. *The Presentation of Self in Everyday Life*. London: Penguin.

63 See detailed discussion of *mianzi* in Hwang, K. 1987. 'Face and favor: The Chinese power game.' *The American Journal of Sociology* 92 (4): 944–74.

64 Also see Hu, X. 2012. 'China's "New Generation" rural–urban migrants: Migration motivation and migration patterns.' *Migration Information Source*. http://papers.ssrn.com/sol3/papers.cfm?abstract_id=1978546

65 Also see Fan, C. and Chen, C. 2014.

66 You can also view a film in which I used my paintings and calligraphy to try and give some sense of the experience, as well as film footage from the town. See https://youtu.be/4XZ0WJrvE_M

67 A detailed explanation of 'participant observation' is given in the comparative title of the Why We Post series. See Miller, D. et. al. 2016. *How the World Changed Social Media*. London: UCL Press.

68 Many real stories in this book were collected in such a way. However, it is highly unlikely that the person involved could be recognised, given the high degree of anonymity.

69 During the field work nine different surveys were conducted. The scale of various questionnaires ranges from approximately 100 to 250 persons.

70 The average educational attainment level is below middle school.

71 In Shanghai 39 in-depth interviews were conducted. Access was gained to the personal social media profiles of 109 people in Shanghai for the purpose of analysing social media behaviour.

Chapter 2

1 For those who want to grasp a quick impression of the Chinese social media landscape, please watch the video clip of 'What does Chinese social media look like?' by McDonald, T. and Wang, X. at https://www.youtube.com/watch?v=5qROXrmyMbQ

2 FlorCruz, J.A. and Seu, L. 2014. 'From snail mail to 4G, China celebrates 20 years of Internet connectivity', CNN news report, http://edition.cnn.com/2014/04/23/world/asia/china-internet-20th-anniversary/ (accessed October 2015).

3 See discussion of the Great FireWall at Clayton, R., Steven J. et al. 2006. 'Ignoring the Great Firewall of China.' *Privacy Enhancing Technologies*. 4258: 20–5; Deibert, R.J. 2002. 'Dark guests and great firewalls: The internet and Chinese security policy.' *The Society for the Psychological Study of Social Issues* 58 (1): 143–59.

4 The 35th CNNIC statistical report on Internet Development in China. 2015. http://www1.cnnic.cn/AU/MediaC/rdxw/2015n/201502/t20150204_51650.htm (accessed October 2015).

5 Chiu, C. et al. 2012. 'Understanding social media in China' *McKinsey Quarterly*. http://asia.udp.cl/Informes/2012/chinamedia.pdf

6   ICTs: abbreviation of Information and Communication Technology.

7   Qiang, C.Z. 2007. *China's Information Revolution: Managing the economic and social transformation*. Washington, DC: World Bank Publications.

8   Dai, X. 2003. 'ICTs in China's development strategy.' Hughes, C. and Wacker, G., eds. *China and the Internet: Politics of the digital leap forward*. London: RoutledgeCurzon.

9   Hughes, C.R. and Wacker, G. eds. 2003. *China and the Internet: Politics of the digital leap forward*. London: RoutledgeCurzon.

10 See Lieberthal, K. and Burns, J.P. 1995. *Governing China: From revolution through reform*. New York: Norton.

11 See Zhang, X. and Zheng, Y., eds. 2009. *China's Information and Communications Technology Revolution: Social changes and state responses*. London: Routledge.

12 See Li, R. and Shiu, A. 2012. 'Internet diffusion in China: A dynamic panel data analysis.' *Telecommunications Policy* 36: 872–87.

13 Figure of MAU of QQ and Qzone: http://www.chinainternetwatch.com/10928/renren-q3-2014/; WeChat: https://www.techinasia.com/wechat-650-million-monthly-active-users/; SinaWeibo: http://www.chinainternetwatch.com/14371/weibo-q2-2015/; Renren: http://www.chinainternetwatch.com/10928/renren-q3-2014/; Facebook: http://www.statista.com/statistics/264810/number-of-monthly-active-facebook-users-worldwide/; WhatsApp: http://www.statista.com/statistics/260819/number-of-monthly-active-whatsapp-users/; Twitter: http://www.statista.com/statistics/282087/number-of-monthly-active-twitter-users/

14 See Xinhua news, 'Chinese government online', http://news.xinhuanet.com/politics/2010-06/08/c_12195450.htm (accessed on Oct 2015)

15 The name 'QQ' actually arrived two years later. When Tencent company first released the IM software its original name was 'OICQ', which was soon accused of infringement by ICQ, the first instant messaging program for personal computers developed in the mid-1990s.

16 In the second quarter of 2015, the number of active monthly users of Qzone was 659 million. http://www.chinainternetwatch.com/14304/wechat-maus-reached-600-million-in-q2-2015/ (accessed October 2015)

17 The renamed QQ number on contacts lists does not change, even if the contact changes his or her QQ name.

18 Data collected from 49 people in Shanghai and 205 rural migrants in GoodPath.

19 Q-coin, issued by Tencent, is the payment tool for paid digital services on QQ. As a virtual currency, Q-coin has become increasingly accepted by online stores and gaming sites.

20 See Jenkins, H. 2006. *Convergence Culture: Where old and new media collide*. New York: New York University Press.

21 See Hjorth, L. 2005. 'Odours of mobility: Mobile phones and Japanese cute culture in the Asia Pacific.' *Journal of Intercultural Studies* 26 (1–2): 39–55.

22 See a detailed discussion of the difference between Chinese and Western website design at http://www.slideshare.net/cxpartners/chinese-web-design-patterns-how-and-why-theyre-different (accessed October 2015)

23 See http://www.smashingmagazine.com/2010/03/showcase-of-web-design-in-china-from-imitation-to-innovation-and-user-centered-design/ (accessed October 2015)

24 http://www.szlh.gov.cn/main/xwzx/bkzy/21281.shtml (accessed October 2015)

25 http://blog.imqq.com/how-to-calculate-qq-membership-level/ (accessed February 2015)

26 Communicative technology has long being regarded as playing an essential role in the formation of modern societies. See Thompson, J.B. 1995. *Media and Modernity: A social theory of the media*. Stanford, CA: Stanford University Press.

27 See Li, R. and Shiu, A. 2012. 'Internet diffusion in China: A dynamic panel data analysis.' *Telecommunications Policy* 36: 872–87.

28 See Harwit, E. and Clark, D. 2008. 'Government policy and political control over China's Internet.' Damm, J. and Thomas, S., eds. 2008. *Chinese Cyberspace: Technological changes and political effects*. London and New York: Routledge. 11–37.

29 See Tai, Z. 2006. *The Internet in China: Cyberspace and civil society*. New York and Abingdon: Routledge.

30 CNNIC, 2015. 'Statistical Report on Internet Development in China'. http://www1.cnnic.cn/IDR/ReportDownloads/201507/P020150720486421654597.pdf

31 See Potter, S. H. 1983. 'The position of peasants in modern China.' *Modern China* 9 (4): 465–99.

32 See Yan, Y. 1999. 'Rural youth and youth culture in north China.' *Culture, Medicine, and Psychiatry*. 23: 75–97.

33 In the social media age, we are the first people in history to create vast online records of our lives. The digital legacy is the sum of our relationship, interests and belief that people record on social media. See Paul-Choudhury, S. 2011. 'Digital legacy: The fate of your online soul.' *New Scientist* 210. 2809: 41–3. Carroll, E. and Romano, J. 2010. *Your Digital Afterlife: When Facebook, Flickr and Twitter are your estate, what's your legacy?* Berkeley, CA: New Riders.

34 '2015 WeChat impact report' http://www.199it.com/archives/398617.html (accessed October 2015)

35 See http://www.chinainternetwatch.com/15287/wechat-users-insights-2015/ (accessed October 2015)

36 A survey conducted by the author during in-depth interviews with 49 people in Shanghai in July 2014.

37 Even though it was very common to use QQ for work purposes in Shanghai since QQ works very well for transferring files.

38 A survey conducted by the author in June 2013, among 205 rural migrants in GoodPath.

39 'Active users' refers to users who use WeChat or QQ more than three times per day.

40 A survey conducted by the author in August 2014, among 119 rural migrants in GoodPath.

41 See Chart 2.1

42 http://www.chinainternetwatch.com/10939/wechat-dominates-apac-mobile-messaging-q3-2014/ (accessed October 2015)

43 http://a16z.com/2015/08/06/wechat-china-mobile-first/ (accessed December 2015)

44 http://www.chinainternetwatch.com/11765/wechat-users-reading-habits/ (accessed October 2015)

45 http://gbtimes.com/china/chinese-people-reading-much-less-east-asian-neighbours (accessed October 2015)

46 The WeChat web version only offers far more limited functions.

47 See Burmark, L. 2002. *Visual Literacy: Learn to see, see to learn*. Alexandria, VA: Association for Supervision and Curriculum Development.

48 See a further analysis of WeChat's impact on emotional wellbeing at Wu, J. 2014. 'How WeChat, the most popular social network in China, cultivates wellbeing.' Master of Applied Psychology, Philadelphia, PA: UPENN.

49 See Bryant, F.B. 2003. 'Savoring beliefs inventory (SBI): A scale for measuring beliefs about savoring.' *Journal of Mental Health* 12 (2): 175–96.

50 See Bryant, F.B. and Veroff, J. 2007. *Savoring: A new model of positive experience*. Mahwah, NJ: Lawrence Erlbaum Associates Publishers.

51 'Media richness' refers to the capacity to carry complex information through multiple communication channels. There are several dimensions of media richness, for example the abilities to handle multiple information cues simultaneously, to facilitate rapid feedback, to establish a personal focus and to utilise natural language. See Daft, R.L. and Lengel, R.H. 1986. 'Organizational information requirements, media richness and structural design.' *Management Science* 32 (5): 554–71.

52 See http://www.emarketer.com/Article.aspx?R=1011578

53 See http://www.chinainternetwatch.com/15287/wechat-users-insights-2015/

54 Pinyin is the phonetic transcription system for writing Chinese characters in the roman alphabet that is widely used in text message input. It was only introduced to schools in 1958 and therefore not in widespread use until much later, thus older generations find it less easy to use.

55 See Sun, H. 2012. *Cross-Culture Technology Design: Creating culture-sensitive technology for local users*. Oxford: Oxford University Press. 92.

56 '2015 WeChat Impact Report' (*weixin yingxiangli baogao*). http://www.199it.com/archives/398617.html

57 Data from a survey of 111 residents of GoodPath and 46 residents of Shanghai undertaken in August 2014. The survey was conducted via social media and all the informants were social media contacts of the researcher.

58 As note 57 above.

59 Miller, D. and Sinanan, J. 2014. *Webcam*. Cambridge: Polity Press.

60 http://www.pri.org/stories/2014-08-10/if-you-use-wechat-china-wants-know-your-real-name

61 For a detailed introduction to adding WeChat contacts see http://advicesacademy.com/how-to/ways-to-add-friends-on-wechat/

62 Each WeChat account has a QR code.

63 Since QQ and WeChat are owned by the same company, Tencent, QQ users can register WeChat with their QQ numbers.

64 In addition to being scanned directly from the contact's smartphone screen, a QR code can also be obtained from an image file. However, in most cases the QR code method is only applied in face to face situations, partly because it works most conveniently in these.

65 '2015 WeChat Impact Report' (*weixin yingxiangli baogao*). http://www.199it.com/archives/398617.html

66 Data collected from 49 residents of Shanghai and 200 rural migrants in GoodPath from July to August 2014.

67 One of the 'privileges' that users can pay for on QQ is the ability 'to visit other's Qzone without leaving a footprint' (*yin shen fang wen*).

68 See Lindner, K.A. 2008. 'The effects of Facebook "stalking" on romantic partners' satisfaction, jealousy, and insecurity'. http://indigo.uic.edu/bitstream/handle/10027/9569/Lindner_Katherine.pdf?sequence=1

69 See a detailed comparison between the privacy settings of Facebook and WeChat at Wu, J. 2014.

70 Oetzel, J.G., and Ting-Toomey, S. 2003. 'Face concerns in interpersonal conflict: A cross-cultural empirical test of the face negotiation theory.'*Communication Research* 30 (6): 599–624.

71 Other research also shows that Chinese QQ users tend to make friends enthusiastically and communicate with strangers on QQ. See Tice, W. et al. 1995. 'When modesty prevails: Different favorability of self-presentation to friends and strangers.' *Journal of Personality and Social Psychology* 69: 1120–38.

72 http://thenextweb.com/asia/2014/02/05/messaging-app-wechat-brings-chinese-new-year-traditions-into-the-mobile-era/

73 You can receive a red envelope on WeChat without having to link it to your bank card. However, actually to use the money in the red envelope requires you to link your bank account to WeChat.

74 WeChat payment service was officially launched on 4 March 2014.

75 See http://a16z.com/2015/08/06/wechat-china-mobile-first/

76 See detailed analysis of this new business move at http://techcrunch.com/2015/04/24/why-wechat-city-services-is-a-game-changing-move-for-smartphone-adoption/

77 WeChat has played a key role as a driver of e-commerce in China. See 'E-commerce in China: Driving a new consumer culture.' January 2014. KPMG Global China Practice report.

78 http:////www.demandware.com/blog/2014/08/27/social-commerce-in-china/

79 Data from a survey of 213 people conducted in GoodPath in June 2014.

80 To meet Dee, and to gain a vivid impression of people's daily engagement with WeChat business, you can watch a three-minute short film 'WeChat and Small Business', taken during field work. https://www.youtube.com/watch?v=WGuyM9eu9X4&index=4&list=PLVwGSavjGgEzPCcXI4txF2gY9pibWeO4F

81 See 'Understanding social media in China.', *McKinsey Quarterly*. April 2012. http://www.mckinsey.com/insights/marketing_sales/understanding_social_media_in_china

82 Also see Luo, Y. 1997. '*Guanxi*: Principle, philosophies, and implications.' *Human System Management* 16 (1): 43–51.

83 As the anthropologist Marcel Mauss pointed out, gift exchange serves as a mean of establishing and maintaining social relationships by creating social obligations between individuals that in the long-term bind people together. Though such gifts are apparently voluntary, there is no 'free gift' in a real sense as they are always given with the expectation of return. See Mauss, M. 1950. *The Gift: The form and reason for exchange in archaic societies*. New York: Norton.

84 See Mullis, E. 2008. 'Toward a Confucian ethic of the gift,' *Dao* 7 (2): 175–94.

85 See Yan, Y. 1996. *The Flow of Gifts: Reciprocity and social networks in a Chinese village*. Stanford, CA: Stanford University Press. Yang, M. 1989. 'The gift economy and state power in China.' *Comparative Studies in Society and History* 31 (1): 25–54.

86 See Yang, M. 1994. *Gifts, Favors and Banquets: The art of social relationships in China.* Ithaca: Cornell University Press.

87 Qian, W. et. al. 2007. 'Chinese cultural values and gift-giving behaviour.' *Journal of Consumer Marketing* 24 (4): 214–28.

88 Hu, W. and Grove, C.L. 1999. *Encountering the Chinese: A guide for Americans.* Yarmouth, MA: Intercultural Press. 64.

89 For example, it is found on Facebook that word-of-mouth marketing is less successful than traditional word-of-mouth marketing in face to face situations. See Eisingerich, A.B. et al. 2015. 'Why recommend a brand face-to-face but not on Facebook? How word-of-mouth on online social sites differs from traditional word-of-mouth.' *Journal of Consumer Psychology* 25 (1): 120–8.

90 Cited in Zelier, V.A. 1997. *The Social Meaning of Money.* Princeton, NJ: Princeton University Press. 82.

91 Mukai, C. P. 1999. 'Chinese perspectives.' *Geriatric Nursing* 20 (1): 18–22.

92 To put it in a simple way, the term 'technology affordances' refers to the perceived and actual use of specific technologies, or the possible uses that humans can make use of specific technologies. The term has been defined differently in literature, with some scholars putting emphasis on the interactions between users and technologies. For example, Wijekumar, K.J. et. al. 2006. 'Technology affordances: The "real story" in research with K-12 and undergraduate learners.' *British Journal of Educational Technology* 37 (2): 191–209. Meanwhile some used the term as a middle ground between technology determinist and social constructivist perspectives. For example, Graves, L. 2009. 'The affordances of blogging: A case study in culture and technological effects.' *Journal of Communication Inquiry,* 31: 331–46. http://dx.doi.org/10.1177/0196859907305446.

93 http://www.chinainternetwatch.com/14371/weibo-q2-2015/

94 See a detailed comparative study of use of Sina Weibo and Twitter. For instance, Weibo users are more likely to disclose personal information and their interests change more frequently. Gao, Q. et al. 2012. 'A comparative study of users' microblogging behavior on Sina Weibo and Twitter.' Mastiff, J. et al., eds. *User Modeling, Adaptation and Personalization.* Heidelberg: Springer-Verlag. LNCS 7379: 88–101.

95 Data based on 203 rural migrants in GoodPath in September 2013.

96 See http://chinamarketingtips.com/weibo-marketing-strategic-direction/

97 Among 49 people from Shanghai, more than half of Weibo users admit they used Weibo less in 2014. Date collected in July 2014.

98 http://www.pewinternet.org/files/2013/05/PIP_TeensSocialMediaandPrivacy_PDF.pdf

99 Paid followers, those paid to post comments online to influence public opinion on Sina, Weibo can be bought and sold online for as little as 4 yuan (US $0.63) per thousand. http://news.xinhuanet.com/english2010/indepth/2011-11/22/c_131261763.htm

100 https://advocacy.globalvoicesonline.org/2013/07/09/targeting-rumors-on-chinas-sina-weibo/

101 http://www.theguardian.com/world/2013/sep/10/china-social-media-jail-rumours

102 http://www.economist.com/news/china/21594296-after-crackdown-microblogs-sensitive-online-discussion-has-shifted-weibo-wechat

103 See note 103 above.

104 The 34th China Internet Network Information Center (CNNIC) Statistical Report on Internet Development in China. July 2014.

105 The combination of higher cost and less portability means that personal computers are not affordable or practical. This is particularly important given the 'floating life' that rural migrants have.

106 For a detailed introduction to *shanzai* mobile phones, see Tse, E. et. al. 2009. 'Shan Zhai: A Chinese phenomenon.' *Strategy* http://www.strategyand.pwc.com/media/file/Shan_Zhai_AChinese_Phenomenon.pdf

107 For a detailed analysis of the XiaoMi budget smartphone market strategy see Gupta, S. and Dhillon, I. 2014. 'Can Xiaomi shake the global smartphone industry with an innovative "services-based business model"?' *AIMA Journal of Management & Research* 8 (3/4). https://apps.aima.in/ejournal_new/articlesPDF/338-Sonam%20Gupta.pdf

108 For example: http://www.goodchinabrand.com/8323200070en.html

109 Data based on 200 rural migrants in GoodPath in August 2014.

110 Wallis, C. 2013. *Techonomobility in China*. New York: New York University Press.
111 The term 'information have-less' was used to refer to Chinese migrants and unemployed workers who populate the vast zone on the other side of China's digital divide. See Qiu, J. 2008. 'Working-class ICTs, migrants, and empowerment in South China.' *Asian Journal of Communication* 18 (4): 333–47.

Chapter 3

1 Data collected from a survey of 427 people, including 350 residents of GoodPath and 77 residents of Shanghai. (July–September 2014).
2 Rose, G. 2012. *Visual Methodologies: An introduction to research with visual materials*. London: Sage. 3.
3 See Miller et al. 2016 *How the World Changed Social Media*. London: UCL Press. Chapter 11 'Visual images'.
4 The visual analysis based on 8,540 visual postings (the last 20 visual postings of each participant) by 461 participants (377 in GoodPath, 84 in Shanghai) on WeChat or QQ (data collected from July–September 2014)
5 See Foster, H., ed. 1988. *Vision and Visuality*. Seattle, WA: Bay Press.
6 In this chapter all the statistical results related to visual genres are based on 7,540 social media postings of 377 participants in GoodPath, including 90 young women and 135 young men (16–35); 25 middle-aged men and 16 middle-aged women (aged 35–50); 7 older men and 4 older women (aged 50 +). Figures are illustrated in group size order.
7 *Oxford English Dictionary* 2013. See also a history of the 'selfie' at Saltz, J. 2014. 'Art at arm's length: a history of the selfie' available at http://www.vulture.com/2014/01/history-of-the-selfie.html
8 See genre 14, the *feizhuliu* postings.
9 See Hogan, B. and Wellman, B. 2014. 'The relational self-portrait: Selfies meet social networks.' Graham, M. and Dutton, W.H., eds. *Society and the Internet: How networks of information and communication are changing our lives*. Oxford: Oxford University Press. 53–66.
10 It is common to see arguments about the link between self-love and the selfie, for example Barry, C.T. et al. 2015. 'Let me take a selfie: Associations between self-photography, narcissism, and self-esteem.' *Psychology of Popular Media Culture*. Advance online publication. http://dx.doi.org/10.1037/ppm0000089
11 http://www.bbc.co.uk/newsbeat/article/34620535/selfie-of-the-year-sergio-aguero-the-pm-and-chinese-president-xi-jinping
12 'Meme' refers to frequently reposted visual postings consisting of images and embedded text. A meme can be reproduced quickly on social media. On social media memes have become a very popular mode of visual postings.
13 Also see Zhang, X. and Li, G. 2003. 'Does *guanxi* matter to non-farm employment?' *Journal of Comparative Economics* 31 (2): 315–31.
14 The founder of 'Taobao' and 'Alibaba', the first mainland Chinese entrepreneur to appear on the cover of *Forbes Magazine*. Today he ranks as one of the world's billionaires.
15 See also discussion of Chinese 'nouveau riches' at Goodman, David, S.G. 2008. *The New Rich in China: Future rules, present lives*. Abingdon: Routlege.
16 See McDonald, T. 2016. *Social Media in Rural China*. London: UCL Press.
17 Ibid.
18 See Knight, J. and Yueh, L. 2004. 'Job mobility of residents and migrants in urban China.' *Journal of Comparative Economics* 32 (4): 637–60.
19 See Kwek, A. and Lee, Y. 2013. 'Consuming tourism experiences.' *Journal of Vacation Marketing* 19 (4): 301–15.
20 Levitt, P. 1998. 'Social remittances: Migration driven local-level forms of cultural diffusion.' *International Migration Review* 32 (4): 926–48.
21 Also the diffusion and appropriation of ICT, such as mobile phones and computers in rural China, have taken a form of 'social remittance' from migrant workers to rural residents. See Oreglia, E. 2013. 'From farm to farmville: Circulation, adoption, and use of ICT between urban and rural China.' PhD thesis, University of California, Berkeley. http://digitalassets.lib.berkeley.edu/etd/ucb/text/Oreglia_berkeley_0028E_13617.pdf

22 Stafford, C. 1995. *The Road of Chinese Childhood: Learning and identification in Angang.* Cambridge: Cambridge University Press.

23 See Zhao, S. 2005. 'China's pragmatic nationalism: Is it manageable?' *The Washington Quarterly* 29 (1): 131–44.

24 See Chang, K.C., ed. 1977. *Food in Chinese Culture: Anthropological and historical perspectives.* London and New York: Yale University Press.

25 Watson, James L. 1987. 'From the common pot: Feasting with equals in Chinese society.' *Anthropos,* 1987 (82): 389–401.

26 Stafford, Charles. 1995. *The Roads of Chinese Childhood: Learning and identification in Angang.* Cambridge: Cambridge University Press. 4.

27 Watson, James L. 1987. 'From the common pot: Feasting with equals in Chinese society.' *Anthropos,* 1987 (82): 389–401.

28 See a detailed discussion of the youth of China's countercultures at Liz, T. 2011. 'I didn't make it for you.' *The World of China* 1 (5): 42–9.

29 See a further analysis of anti-mainstream culture in Shen, Y. 2009. 'The reasons for the popularity of the anti-mainstream culture.' *Journal of Zhangzhou Normal University (Philosophy and Social Science)* 2: 139–142.

30 See a further discussion of images of youth rebels at Zhou, X. L. 2007. *Young Rebels in Contemporary Chinese Cinema.* Hong Kong: Hong Kong University Press.

31 Lester, P. 2006. 'Syntactic theory of visual communication.' Fullerton, CA: California State University at Fullerton. http://paulmartinlester.info/writings/viscomtheory.html (accessed March 2016)

32 Data based on 8,540 visual postings (the last 20 visual postings of each participants) by 461 participants (377 living in GoodPath, 84 in Shanghai) on WeChat or QQ (data collected from July–September 2014).

33 Research on digital photography has suggested that photographs on social media somehow remain similar to the analogue photography as a form of memory in the pre-social media age. For example, see Dijck, J. van. 2007. *Mediated Memories in the Digital Age.* Stanford, CA: Stanford University Press.

34 See Bucholtz M. 2002. 'Youth and cultural practice'. *Annual Review of Anthropology* 525–52.

35 Kjeldgaard D. and Askegaard S. 2006. 'The globalization of youth culture: The global youth segment as structures of common difference.' *Journal of Consumer Research,* 33 (2): 231–47.

36 See Kipnis, A.B. 2001. 'Articulating school countercultures.' *Anthropology & Education Quarterly* 32 (4): 472–92.

37 Yan, Y. 1999. 'Rural youth and youth culture in North China.' *Culture, Medicine and Psychiatry* 23(1): 75–97.

38 See Anita Chan, 2002. 'The culture of survival: Lives of migrant workers through the prism of private letters', in Link, P., Madsen, R.P. and Pickowicz, P.G., eds. *Popular China: Unofficial culture in a globalizing society.* 163–88.

39 See Barthes, R. 1981. *Camera Lucida: Reflections on photography.* New York: Hill and Wang. Benjamin, W. 1970. *Illuminations.* London: Jonathan Cape. Sontag, S. 1978. *On Photography.* London: Allen Lane.

Chapter 4

1 'Sociality' means the way in which people associate with each other to form social relations and societies.

2 See also Skinner, G.W. 1964. 'Marketing and social structure in rural China, Part I.' *The Journal of Asian Studies* 24 (1): 3–43.

3 As mentioned in Chapter 1, a one-month period of research was conducted in Shanghai. For this specific comparison 35 social media profiles of people in Shanghai were examined.

4 See Smart, A. 1999. 'Expression of interest: Friendship and *guanxi* in Chinese society.' *The Anthropology of Friendship,* Bell, S. and Coleman, S., eds. Oxford: Berg. 119–36.

5 See Fried, M. 1969. *Fabric of Chinese Society.* New York: Octagon Books.

6 See the relationship between QQ and Qzone in Chapter 2.

7   See Warden, C. and Chen, F. 2009. 'When hot and noisy is good: Chinese values of *renao* and consumption metaphors.' *Asia Pacific Journal of Marketing and Logistics* 21 (2): 216–31.

8   See Pan, I. 1993. '*Renao*: A socio-psychological phenomenon of Chinese.' *Indigenous Psychological Research*, 1: 330–7.

9   Lan's story has been presented in the painting 'locked albums', as part of the 'visual ethnography' project. See http://www.visualethnographyxy.co.uk/#!big-paintings/c1t44

10 See Jankowiak, W. 2002. 'Proper men and proper women: Parental affection in the Chinese family.' *Chinese Femininities / Chinese Masculinities: A reader.* Browned, S. and Wasserstrom, J., eds. Berkeley, CA: University of California Press. 361–81.

11 On QQ visiting will be recorded and shown. However, one of the paid services of QQ is 'invisible visit', which allows users to view others' profiles without being recorded.

12 See Goffman, E. 1975. *Frame Analysis.* Harmondsworth: Penguin.

13 See Madianou, M. and Miller, D. 2012. *Migration and New Media.* London: Routledge.

14 See Smart, A. 1999.

15 See Ruan, D. 1993. 'Interpersonal networks and workplace controls in urban China.' *Australian Journal of Chinese Affairs* 29: 89–105.

16 See Bell, S. and Coleman, S., eds. 1999. *The Anthropology of Friendship,* Oxford: Berg.

17 For example, Cocking, D. and Matthews, S. 2000. 'Unreal friends.' *Ethics and Information Technology* 2 (4): 223–31. Fröding, B. and Peterson, M. 2012. 'Why virtual friendship is no genuine friendship.' *Ethics and Information Technology* 14 (3): 201–7. Turkle, S. 2011. *Alone Together.* New York: Basic Books.

18 For example, see Vallor, S. 2012. 'Flourishing on Facebook: Virtue friendship and new social media.' *Ethics and Information technology* 14 (3): 185–99. Hartup, W. 1995. 'The three faces of friendship.' *Journal of Social and Personal Relationships* 12 (4): 569–74. Tong, S. et al. 2008. 'Too much of a good thing? The relationship between number of friends and interpersonal impressions on Facebook.' *Journal of Computer-Mediated Communication* 13 (3): 531–49. Elder, A. 2014. 'Excellent online friendships: An Aristotelian defense of social media.' *Ethics and Information Technology* 16 (4): 287–97.

19 See Guan, S. 1995. *Cross-culture Communication and English Learning.* Beijing: Peking University Press. 37–41.

20 See McDougall, B. and Hansson, A., eds. 2002. *Chinese Concepts of Privacy.* Vol. 55. Leiden: Brill.

21 Hirshleifer, J. 1980. 'Privacy: Its origin, function, and future.' *The Journal of Legal Studies* 9 (4): 649–64.

22 James, G. 'Privacy vs. secrecy'. http://www.jamesgrubman.com/sites/default/files/Privacy-v-Secrecy.pdf

23 Yan, Y. 2003. *Private Life under Socialism: Love, intimacy, and family change in a Chinese village, 1949–1999.* Stanford, CA: Stanford University Press. 137.

24 Lü, Y. 2005. 'Privacy and data privacy issues in contemporary China.' *Ethics and Information Technology* 7 (1): 7–15. McDougall, B. 2001. 'Privacy in contemporary China: A survey of student opinion, June 2000.' *China Information* 15 (2): 140–52. Wang, H. 2011. *Protecting Privacy in China: A research on China's privacy standards and the possibility of establishing the right to privacy and the information privacy protection legislation in modern China.* Berlin: Springer.

25 See Yan, Y. 1997. 'The triumph of conjugality: Structural transformation of family relations in a Chinese village.' *Ethnology* 36 (3): 191–217. Yan. Y. 2003.

26 Though the issue of privacy cannot be reduced to the idea that people have some basic need for private space.

27 For a further discussion of the role that 'strangers' play in society see Simmel, G. 1950. *The Sociology of Georg Simmel.* New York, Free Press.

28 See Simmel, G. 1906. 'The sociology of secrecy and secret societies.' *American Journal of Sociology* 11 (4): 441–98.

29 See Tu, W. 1985. *Confucian Thought: Selfhood as a creative transformation.* Albany: State University of New York Press.

30 See Yan, Y. 2013. 'The drive for success and the ethics of the striving individual.' Stafford, C., ed. *Ordinary Ethics in China.* New York, London: Bloomsbury Academic. 263–89.

31 See Prensky, M. 2001. 'Digital natives, digital immigrants.' *On the Horizon* 9 (5): 1–6.

32 See the detailed explanation of 'scalable sociality' at Miller, D. et al. 2016. *How the World Changed Social Media.* London: UCL Press.

Chapter 5

1 For example see Coltrane, S. 1992. 'The micropolitics of gender in nonindustrial societies.' *Gender & Society* 6 (1): 86–107. Morley, L. 2000. 'The micropolitics of gender in the learning society.' *Higher Education in Europe* 25 (2): 229–35.

2 For example Shirky, C. 2008. *Here Comes Everybody: The power of organizing without organizations*. New York: Penguin Press. Shirky, C. 2011. 'The political power of social media.' *Foreign affairs* 90 (1): 28–41. Shirk, S. 2011. *Changing Media, Changing China*. Oxford: Oxford University Press. Yang, G. 2003. 'The co-evolution of the internet and civil society in China'. *Asian Survey* 43 (3): 405–22.

3 For example Zhang, L. 2006. 'Behind the great firewall: Decoding China's internet media policies from the inside.' *International Journal of Research into New Media Technologies* 12 (3): 271–91. Shirk, S. 2011.

4 For example Lagerkvist, J. 2010. *After the Internet before Democracy: Competing norms in Chinese media and society*. Bern: Peter Lang. Herod, D. and Marolt P., eds. 2011. *Online Society in China: Creating, celebrating, and instrumentalising the online carnival*. New York: Routledge. Franceschini, I. and Negro, G. 2014. 'The "jasmine revolution" in China: the limits of the cyber-utopia.' *Postcolonial Studies*. 17 (1): 23–35. Xiao, Q. 2011. 'The battle for the Chinese internet.' *Journal of Democracy*. 22 (2): 47–61. Yang, G. 'The Co-evolution of the internet and civil society in China.' *Asian Survey* 43 (3): 405–22.

5 http://rsf.org/index2014/en-index2014.php

6 Feng, G. and Guo, Z. 2013. 'Tracing the route of China's internet censorship: An empirical study.' *Telematics and Informatics* 30 (4): 335–45.

7 King, G. et al. 2013. 'How censorship in China allows government criticism but silences collective expression.' *American Political Science Review* 107 (2): 326–43.

8 'Wu mao dang' refers to people hired by the government or the Party to post comments in favour of Party policies (each positive post is said to be paid RMB 0.50, around GBP 0.05).

9 Chen, X. and Peng, H. A. 2011. 'Internet police in China: Regulation, scope and myths.' *Online Society in China: Creating, celebrating, and instrumentalising the online carnival*, Herold, D. and Marolt, P., eds. New York: Routledge. 40–52.

10 King, G. et al. 2013.

11 Ibid.

12 'Let some people get rich first' was the famous quote of Deng Xiaoping, the de facto leader of China 1978–92, to which this refers. BBC News. 22/08/2004. 'China celebrates Deng centenary.' http://news.bbc.co.uk/1/hi/world/asia-pacific/3587838.stm

13 See Fan, C. 1997. 'Uneven development and beyond: Regional development theory in post-Mao China.' *International Journal of Urban and Regional Research* 21 (4): 620–39.

14 Yan, Y. 1996. *The Flow of Gifts: Reciprocity and social networks in a Chinese village*. Stanford, CA: Stanford University Press. 14.

15 Smart, A. 1999. 'Friendship and *guanxi* in Chinese societies', in Bell, S. and Coleman, S., eds. *The Anthropology of Friendship*. Oxford: Berg. 130.

16 'China cracks down on GRAFT' *China Daily*, http://www.chinadaily.com.cn/china/2014crackongraft/ (accessed February 2016).

17 See the introduction of WeChat red envelopes in Chapter 2.

18 See Fan, Y. 2002. 'Guanxi's consequences: Personal gains at social cost.' *Journal of Business Ethics* 38 (4): 371–80.

19 Also see Dunfee, T. and Warren, D. 2001. 'Is guanxi ethical? A normative analysis of doing business in China.' *Journal of Business Ethics* 32 (3): 191–204.

20 See Chen, X. 2013. 'The rising cost of stability.' *Journal of Democracy* 24 (1): 57–64.

21 For example Marxists argued that democracy arose because it helped capitalists in pursuit of their economic interests. See Sanderson, S. 2013. *Sociological Worlds: Comparative and historical readings on society*. New York, London: Routledge.

22 See also Chen, J. and Dickson, B.J. 'Allies of the state: Democratic support and regime support among China's private entrepreneurs.' *The China Quarterly* 196 (2008): 780–804.

23 A few accounts also confirm this status quo-oriented attitude among Chinese entrepreneurs. For example, see Pearson, M. 1997. *China's New Business Elite: The political consequence of economic reform*. Berkeley, CA: University of California Press. Dickson, B.J. 2008. *Wealth into Power: The Communist Party's embrace of china's private sector*. New York: Cambridge

University Press. Tsai, K. 2007. *Capitalism without Democracy: The private sector in contemporary China*. Ithaca: Cornell University Press.

24 See Sabo, D. and Panepinto, J. 1990. 'Football ritual and the social reproduction of masculinity.' Messner, M. et al., eds. *Sport, Men, and the Gender Order: Critical feminist perspectives*. Champaign: Human Kinetics Publishers. 115–26.

25 Also see Feng, W. et al. 2002. 'Rural migrants in Shanghai: Living under the shadow of socialism.' *International Migration Review* 36 (2): 520–45.

26 See Bian, Y. et al. 2001. 'Communist Party membership and regime dynamics in China.' *Social Forces* 79 (3): 805–41.

27 Also see Morduch, J. and Sicular, T. 2000. 'Politics, growth, and inequality in rural China: Does it pay to join the Party?' *Journal of Public Economics* 77 (3): 331–56. Lam, K. 2003. *Earnings Advantage of Party Members in Urban China*. Hong Kong: Business Research Centre, School of Business, Hong Kong Baptist University.

28 See O'Brien, K. and Li, L. 2000. 'Accommodating "democracy" in a one-party state: Introducing village elections in China.' *The China Quarterly* 162: 465–89.

29 See the 'political' postings in Chapter 3 of this volume.

30 See Brady, A. 2009. *Marketing Dictatorship: Propaganda and thought work in contemporary China*. Washington DC: Rowman and Littlefield.

31 'Relief for migrant laborers', *China Daily*, 6 December 2013. http://www.chinadaily.com.cn/en/doc/2003–12/06/content_287881.htm

32 See Li, D. 1998. 'Changing incentives of the Chinese bureaucracy.' *The American Economic Review*. 88 (2): 393–7. Jin, H. et al. 2005. 'Regional decentralization and fiscal incentives: Federalism, Chinese style.' *Journal of Public Economics* 89: 1719–42.

33 See also the sub-genre of 'Passing travellers' images on rural migrants' social media profiles in Chapter 3.

34 See the discussion of paternalism and nepotism in family enterprises in south China at Poutziouris, P. et al. 2002. 'Chinese entrepreneurship: The development of small family firms in China.' *Journal of Small Business and Enterprise Development* 9 (4): 383–99.

35 See 'When a "phoenix man" meets a "peacock woman"' *China Daily*, 26 August 2009. http://www.chinadaily.com.cn/china/2009-08/26/content_8617800.htm

36 boyd, D. 2010. 'Streams of content, limited attention: The flow of information through social media.' *Educause Review* 45 (5): 26–36.

37 For example see Meraz, S. 2009. 'Is there an elite hold? Traditional media to social media agenda setting influence in blog networks.' *Journal of Computer-Mediated Communication* 14: 682–707. Romero, D. et al. 2011. 'Influence and passivity in social media.' *Machine Learning and Knowledge Discovery in Databases*. Berlin: Springer. 18–33. Ding, Z. et al. 2013. 'Measuring the spreadability of users in micro-blogs.' *Journal of Zhejiang University SCIENCE*. 14 (9): 701–10.

38 See also Jacobs, J. 1982. 'The concept of *guanxi* and local politics in a rural Chinese cultural setting.' *Social Interaction in Chinese Society*. Greenblatt, S. et al., eds. Westport: Praeger Publishers. 209–36.

39 See Ortner, S. 1997. *Making Gender: The politics and erotics of culture*. Boston: Beacon Press.

40 See Ortner, S. and Whitehead, H., eds. 1981. *Sexual Meanings: The cultural construction of gender and sexuality*. Cambridge: Cambridge University Press.

41 This heading is to show respect for the book *The Good Women of China*, written by Xinran Xue. The book, which features extraordinary true stories of ordinary Chinese women, reveals the real lives of Chinese women in the post-Mao era to the West as never before. See Xue, X. 2003. *The Good Women of China: Hidden voices*. London: Random House.

42 See Rowe, W. 2001. *Saving the World: Chen Hongmou and elite consciousness in eighteenth-century China*. Stanford, CA: Stanford University Press.

43 See Baker, H. 1979. *Chinese Family and Kinship*. New York: Columbia University Press.

44 In traditional Chinese society, sexual purity and sexual loyalty was the essential measure of women's value, reflecting a male-dominated society in which women were considered as equivalent to property. Men pressured female relatives to maintain a good reputation by strictly obeying all the rules of proper behaviour, including the suicides of widows, and bans on widow remarriage. See Chow, K. 1994. *The Rise of Confucian Ritualism in Late Imperial China: Ethics, classics, and lineage discourse*. Stanford, CA: Stanford University Press.

45 See details of the anti-mainstream (*FZL*) genre of visual posting in Chapter 3.

46 See details of the 'chicken soup for the soul' genre postings in Chapter 3.

47 There are approximately around 150 to 250 sex workers in GoodPath, all of them rural migrant women. The market is huge and low-end, with customers, all rural migrant men, paying around RMB 50–100 (US $8–16) per time. The income of a sex worker is usually two to three times that of a female factory worker.

48 The researcher only had access to the social media profiles of four of them.

49 The story of one of the couples has been presented in the painting 'Marriage battle', part of the 'visual ethnography' project at http://www.visualethnographyxy.co.uk

50 For example see Vogt, C. and Chen, P. 2001. 'Feminisms and the internet.' *Peace Review* 13 (3): 371–4. Van Doorn, N. and Van Zoonen, L. 2008. 'Theorizing gender and the internet: Past, present, and future'. *The Routledge Handbook of Internet Politics* (2008): 261–74.

51 See Qiu, Z. 2013. 'Cuteness as a subtle strategy: Urban female youth and the online *feizhuliu* culture in contemporary China.' *Culture Studies* 27 (2): 225–41.

52 Hunt, A. 2011. 'What's that cute and pouty, pretty and bratty face? It's *sajiao*.' http://english. cri.cn/7146/2011/10/09/2702s661875.htm

53 Farris, C. 1995. 'A semiotic analysis of *sajiao* as a gender marked communication style in Chinese.' *Unbound Taiwan: Closes ups from a Distance*. Johnson, M. and Chiu, F., eds. Chicago, Centre for East Asian Studies. 1–29.

54 See McDowell, L. 1999. *Gender, Identity and Place*. Minneapolis: University of Minnesota Press.

55 See Avakian, A. 1998. *Through the Kitchen Window: Women explore the intimate meanings of food and cooking*. Boston, MA: Beacon Press.

56 See Jing, J., ed. 2000. *Feeding China's Little Emperors: Food, children, and social change*. Stanford, CA: Stanford University Press.

57 See Li, J. and Hsieh, Y. 2004. 'Traditional Chinese food technology and cuisine.' *Asia Pacific Journal of Clinical Nutrition* 13 (2): 147–55.

58 The province with the lowest GDP in China.

59 There are a number of accounts of Chinese rural marriage that indicate that the role of parents in marriage decisions is dominant. Today such a situation remains still largely the same in those remote villages, where most rural migrants in GoodPath come from. See Xu, X. and Whyte, M. 1990. 'Love matches and arranged marriage: A Chinese replication.' *Journal of Marriage and the Family*. 52: 709–22. Pasternak, B. 1986. *Marriage and Fertility in Tianjin, China: Fifty years of transition*. Honolulu: East–West Population Institute.

60 Arranged marriage among young people from rural areas still remains the norm among rural migrants, especially those from the poorest areas. See also the news report of blind dates and arranged marriages in Chinese rural areas among migrants who have returned for the Chinese New Year. 'Marriage in rural areas with Chinese characteristics: The busy season of blind dates during the period of Chinese lunar New Year'. *zhongguo shi nongcun hunlian: chunjie qijian pinfan xiangqin*. Xinhua Net, 4 February 2014. http://news.xinhua-net.com/local/2014-02/04/c_119211913.htm

61 As for the purposes of marriage in rural China, the literature is very rich. The main purposes include 'continuance of a family line', 'a way of increasing hands in the field', 'formation of alliances', 'provision of old age support and security', etc. See Wolf, M. 1972. *Women and the Family in Rural Taiwan*. Stanford, CA: Stanford University Press. Potter, S. and Potter, J. 1990. *China's Peasants: The anthropology of a revolution*. Cambridge: Cambridge University Press. Riley, N. 1994. 'Interwoven lives: Parents, marriage, and guanxi in China'. *Journal of Marriage and the Family* 56: 791–803.

62 For example Schlegel, A. and Eloul, R. 1988. 'Marriage transactions: Labor, property, status.' *American Anthropologist* 90: 291–309. Harrell, S. and Dickey, S. 1985. 'Dowry systems in complex societies.' *Ethnology* 34: 105–20.

63 In traditional society, daughters would eventually move out and join the husband's family, adding to its labour resources. 'Bride price' has been seen as a direct compensation for raising a daughter of the bride's natal family, and it is often negotiated between two older generations. To see a detailed discussion of the different practices involving betrothal gifts in China cf. Croll, E. and Croll, E. 1981. *The Politics of Marriage in Contemporary China*. Cambridge: Cambridge University Press. Also see a discussion of the changing norms of betrothal gift, in which individual brides and grooms negotiate with their parents over control of the gift, at Yan, Y. 2005. 'The individual and transformation of bride wealth in rural north China.' *Journal of the Royal Anthropological Institute* 11: 637–58.

64 With the rising income in the countryside, rural China has witnessed a revival of hefty bride prices and extravagant wedding celebrations. See also Min, H. and Eades, J. 1995. 'Brides, bachelors and brokers: The marriage market in rural Anhui in an era of economic reform.' *Modern Asian Studies* 29: 841–69.

65 The phrase 'sitting the month' refers to confinement following childbirth. A Chinese traditional post-natal treatment, it basically requires the woman to remain at home for one whole month after her labour. There are many taboos during the confinement period, which include no body washing, no outside activities, no salty food, etc. See Pillsbury, B. 1978. '"Doing the month": Confinement and convalescence of Chinese women after childbirth.' *Social Science and Medicine. Part B: Medical Anthropology* 12: 11–22.

66 So far a number of gender studies and media attention have focused on the phenomenon of Chinese 'leftover women' (*sheng nv*). However, such phenomena only occur in urban China where highly educated, professional women may have 'failed' to get married or chose not to for reasons such as high expectations of the partner, different choice of lifestyles supported by financial independence and so on. See To, S. 2013. 'Understanding *sheng nu* ("leftover women"): The phenomenon of late marriage among Chinese professional women.' *Symbolic Interaction* 36 (1): 1–20. Gaetano, A. 2014. '"Leftover women": Postponing marriage and renegotiating womanhood in urban China.' *Journal of Research in Gender Studies* 2: 124–49.

67 See Zhu, W. et al. 2009. 'China's excess males, sex selective abortion and one child policy: Analysis of data from 2005 national inter census survey.' *British Medical Journal*, 338 (7700): 920–3.

68 Fan, C. and Huang, Y. 1998. 'Waves of rural brides: Female marriage migraine in China.' *Annals of the Association Geographers* 88 (2): 227–51.

69 The technical term for this 'marrying up' is 'hypergamy'. See Xu, X. et al. 2000. 'Social and political assortative mating in urban China.' *Journal of Family Issues* 21 (1): 47–77.

70 See Pimental, E. 2000. 'Just how do I love thee? Marital relations in urban China.' *Journal of Marriage and the Family* 62 (1): 32–47.

71 See also Zhou, X. et al. 2011. 'The very high sex ratio in rural China: Impact on the psychosocial well-being of unmarried men.' *Social Science & Medicine* 73: 1422–7.

72 For example, Gaetano, A. and Jacka, T. 2013. *On the Move: Women and rural-to-urban migration in contemporary China.* New York: Columbia University Press. Gaetano, A. 2008. 'Sexuality in diasporic space: Rural-to-urban migrant women negotiating gender and marriage in contemporary China.' *Gender, Place and Culture* 15 (6): 629–45.

73 See McDonald, T. 2016. *Social Media in Rural China.* London: UCL Press.

74 See Miller. D. et al. 2016. *How the World Changed Social Media.* London: UCL Press.

75 Tong, J. 2015. 'The formation of an agonistic public sphere: Emotions, the internets and new media in China.' *China Information* 29 (3): 333–51. The article argues that this may be having wider consequences for elite urban populations.

Chapter 6

1 Feng Shui, which explains how the universe is held in harmony by 'yin' and 'yang' forces, is a core philosophic system closely linked to Chinese Taoism. Feng Shui is widely practiced in Sino-Asia (including Hong Kong, Taiwan, Singapore etc.), and its main purpose is to arrange a balance in peoples' lives between humankind and the surrounding environment. Maintaining such a harmonious relationship is regarded as a key element influencing one's welfare and luck. See Lip, E. 1995. *Feng Shui: Environments of power: A study of Chinese architecture.* London: Wiley.

2 There are many other uses of money in the burial rites of Chinese folk religion. In some cases real currency, not only 'spirit money', is involved – for example people will pay a master to communicate with a dead person. See more detailed discussion and analysis of the use and value of money in Chinese folk ideologies at Gate, H. 1987. 'Money for the gods.' *Modern China* 13 (3): 259–77.

3 *Guanyin,* as the one of most popular deities worshipped in Chinese households, is multifaceted. See a detailed analysis of *Guanyin* at Yu, C. 1979. 'Images of Kuan-yin in Chinese folk literature.' *Hanxue yanjiu* 8 (1): 221–86.

4   Feudal superstition, which includes all folk religious activities, has been ruled to be illegal and unworthy of protection. See details at Donald, E.M. 1989. *Religion in China Today: Policy and practice.* Maryknoll, New York: Orbis Books.

5   See Chau, A. 2006. *Miraculous Response: Doing popular religion in contemporary China.* Stanford, CA: Stanford University Press.

6   Yang, F. 2011. *Religion in China: Survival and revival under communist rule.* Oxford: Oxford University Press.

7   A demographic survey conducted among 238 rural migrants and 75 local people in GoodPath in June 2014.

8   Wolf. A.P. 1974. 'Gods, ghosts and ancestors'. A.P. Wolf, ed. *Religion and Ritual in Chinese Society.* Stanford, CA: Stanford University Press. 131–82.

9   See Ahern, E.M. 1982. *Chinese Ritual and Politics.* Cambridge: Cambridge University Press.

10 Wolf, A.P. 1974. 'God, ghosts and ancestors' in A.P. Wolf, ed. *Religion and Ritual in Chinese Society.* Stanford, CA: Stanford University Press. 131–82.

11 Eng, Kuah-Pearce K. 2006. 'Moralising ancestors as social-moral capital: A study of a transnational Chinese lineage.' *Journal of Social Science.* 34 (2): 243–63.

12 See Harrell, S. 1977. 'Modes of belief in Chinese folk religion.' *Journal for the Scientific Study of Religion.* 16 (1): 55–65.

13 See Baity, P.C. 1975. *Religion in a Chinese Town.* Taipai: Orient Cultural Service. 238–69.

14 Sangren, P.S. 1983. 'Female gender in Chinese religious symbols: Kuan yin, ma tsu, and the "eternal mother"'. *Signs* 9 (1): 4–25.

15 For a detailed analysis of the origin of GuanYin as a female deity, see Sangren, P.S. 1983. 'Female gender in Chinese religious symbols: Kuan yin, ma tsu, and the "eternal mother"'. *Signs* 9 (1): 4–25.

16 Ibid.

17 *GuanGong* is not only worshipped in temples, but also in stores and shops. People believe that he has the ability to suppress evil demons, thus he is viewed as a means of protection for people and prosperity for business. In addition, because of his interest in history and literature, he is also regarded by many Chinese scholars as a deity of literature. See Cohen, A. and Jaw, Y. 1977. 'A Chinese temple keeper talks about Chinese folk religion.' *Asian Folklore Studies,* 36 (1): 1–17.

18 See the details of this novel at Roberts, M. 1976. *Three Kingdoms: China's epic drama.* New York: Knopf.

19 See Mann, S. 2000. 'The male bond in Chinese history and culture.' *The American Historical Review* 105 (5): 1600–14.

20 The disadvantaged situation of young male rural migrants discussed in Chapter 3 is nothing new in history. As the most vulnerable group, rootless and homeless people have always according to records been treated harshly and brutally discriminated against. The marriage market traditionally ensured that virtually all the rootless and homeless poor were men. See Kuhn, P. A. 1990. *Soulstealers: The Chinese sorcery scare of 1768.* London, Cambridge: Harvard University Press.

21 See Mann, S. 2000. 'The male bond in Chinese history and culture.' *The American Historical Review* 105 (5): 1600–14.

22 One of the famous events in Chinese history was the failed Boxer Rebellion that occurred during the Qing dynasty. It was a major anti-foreign explosion among Chinese rural males, and the brotherhood claimed by the secret society was especially attractive to unemployed and powerless village men. See Cohen, P.A. 1997. *History in Three Keys: The boxers as event, experience, and myth.* New York: Columbia University Press.

23 For female rural migrants the expression of bonding between females seems to be more straightforward. As we have seen in Chapter 3, people would post group photographs or other images illustrating close relationships between female friends.

24 No specific deity figure represents bonding between women or a non-family tie between men and women in Chinese folk religion. This is mainly because social life in traditional Chinese society is strongly segregated by gender. Girls and women, except for courtesans and prostitutes, were mainly confined to the domestic domain, while men spent most of their leisure time exclusively with other men. Such homo social bonds and male culture gave rise to a special emphasis on male bonding in traditional Chinese society. See Mann, S. 2000. 'The male bond in Chinese history and culture.' *The American Historical Review*

105 (5): 1600–14. Ebrey, P.B. 1993. *The Inner Quarters: Marriages and the lives of Chinese women in the Song period.* Berkeley, CA: University of California Press.

25 The Chinese Zodiac, known as *Sheng Xiao*, is based on a 12-year cycle, with each year in that cycle being related to an animal sign.

26 Harrell, S. 1987. 'The concept of fate in Chinese folk ideology.' *Modern China,* 13 (1): Part I: 90–109, esp. 100.

27 This echoes with another anthropological observation about the practice of folk religion in Taiwan: 'what matters to the practical believers is not whether the offerings they put out are actually eaten in some spiritual way by hungry ghosts, but whether by putting out such offerings they can cure their children's lingering fever. More people are willing to profess belief in the efficacy of such offerings than will state that they believe ghosts exist'. See Harrell, S. 1977. 'Modes of belief in Chinese folk religion.' *Journal for the Scientific Study of Religion.* 16 (1): 55–65.

28 See Holzman, D. 1998. 'The place of filial piety in ancient China.' *Journal of the American Oriental Society* 118 (2): 185–99.

29 Hock, Y. 1997. 'Chinese family religion and world religion.' *Singapore Bahá'í Studies Review* 2: 91–119.

30 See Holzman, D. 1998. 'The place of filial piety in ancient China.' *Journal of the American Oriental Society* 118 (2): 185–99.

31 See Watson, R. 1988. 'Remembering the dead: Graves and politics in southeastern China.' *Death Ritual in Late Imperial and Modern China* 205: 140–3. Cohen, M. 1990. 'Lineage organization in north China.' *The Journal of Asian Studies* 49 (3): 509–34.

32 The same mindset was also recorded in Zheng, T. 2009. *Red Lights: The lives of sex workers in postsocialist China.* Minneapolis and London: University of Minnesota Press.

33 Ang, I. 1993. 'To be or not to be Chinese: Diaspora, culture and postmodern ethnicity.' *Asian Journal of Social Science* 21 (1): 1–17

34 See Safran, W. 1991. 'Diasporas in modern societies: Myths of homeland and return.' *Diaspora: A Journal of Transnational Studies* 1 (1): 83–99.

35 Ang, I. 1993. 'To be or not to be Chinese: Diaspora, culture and postmodern ethnicity.' *Asian Journal of Social Science* 21 (1): 1–17.

36 See Chapter 2.

37 Hung, Chang-tai. 1985. *Going to the People: Chinese intellectuals and folk literature, 1918–1937.* Cambridge, MA: Harvard University Press.

38 Data collected from 377 social media profiles of rural migrants in GoodPath.

39 The researcher consulted two journalists and a university lecturer on literature upon the authorship of the two stories during her one-month period of research in Shanghai, July 2013.

40 Such self-deprecation among the urban population has become an internet phenomenon in China. People intentionally depict themselves as *diaosi* ('losers') in order to vent frustration about society and mock various severe social problems in contemporary China, including high fees for education, the high price of housing, environmental pollution etc. It's worth noting that most people who described themselves as 'losers' online actually possess a decent education and are university students or white-collar workers. It is very rare to see rural migrants describe themselves as 'losers' online, since they have already suffered a lot from being socially stigmatised in this vein. For a detailed analysis of *diaosi* internet culture see Yang, P. et al. 2015. '*Diaosi* as infrapolitics: Scatological tropes, identity-making and cultural intimacy.' *Media, Culture and Society.* 37 (2): 197–214.

41 In terms of education people called it *Du chu lai* (literally meaning 'study it "out"'). This refers to the situation in which rural people become urban residents through receiving higher education in the city, followed by getting white-collar work or a non-manual job in the city.

42 The acceptance rate of colleges is now higher than 70 per cent.

43 Bascom, W. R. 1954. 'Four functions of folklore.' *The Journal of American Folklore* 67 (266): 333–49.

44 See Hung, C. 1985. *Going to the People: Chinese intellectuals and folk literature, 1918–1937.* Cambridge, MA: Harvard University Press.

45 McAdams, D.P. 1993. *The Stories We Live by: Personal myths and the making of the self.* New York, London: The Guilford Press. 12.

46 Compare Peacock, J.L. 1968. *Rites of Modernization: Symbolic and social aspects of Indonesian proletarian drama.* Chicago: University of Chicago Press.

47 For instance burning funeral banknotes.

48 See Davenport, T. and Beck, J. 2001. *The Attention Economy: Understanding the new currency of business.* Boston, MA: Harvard Business School Press.

49 See a detailed discussion of *Suzhi* at Murphy, R. 2004. 'Turning peasants into modern Chinese citizens: "Population quality" discourse, demographic transition and primary education.' *The China Quarterly* 177: 1–20.

50 In the inspiring study of individualisation of rural youth in contemporary China, anthropologist Y. Yan observed the phenomenon in which the previous idea of 'being a good person', with the social expectation of self-sacrifice in a collective society, has gradually given way to an individual pursuit of 'feeling good' with an emphasis on self-development. See Yan, Y. 2009 *The Individualization of Chinese Society.* Vol. 77. Oxford: Berg.

51 See Ngai, P. 2003. 'Subsumption or consumption? The phantom of consumer revolution in "globalizing" China.' *Cultural Anthropology* 18 (4): 469–92.

52 Dikotter, F. 2007. *Things Modern. Material culture and everyday life in China.* New York: Hurst.

53 Ibid.

54 See the explanation of 'collection likes' on WeChat in Chapter 2.

55 Peacock, J.L. 1968.

56 Ibid.

Chapter 7

1 Demarcation of online or offline follows a simple rule: online refers to using the internet or other digital mobile platforms, while offline refers to activities without internet involvement.

2 See Goodkind, D. and West, L.A. 2002. 'China's floating population: Definition, data and recent findings.' *Urban Studies* 39 (12): 2237–50.

3 This is an ironic passivity, though, as it was a very definite decision for action that led rural migrants into the situation.

4 Three decades ago rural-to-urban migration was illegal under the strict household registration regulation (*hukou*).

5 'emic' and 'etic' refer to twin research approaches in anthropology: put simply, 'emic' refers to subjective and insider accounts, while 'etic' refers to objective and outsider accounts.

6 http:////www.ucl.ac.uk/why-we-post

7 See Miller, D. 2016. *Social Media in England.* London: UCL Press.

8 See Nicolescu, R. 2016. *Social Media in Southeast Italy.* London: UCL Press.

9 See Venkatraman, S. 2016. *Social Media in South India.* London: UCL Press.

10 See McDonald, T. 2016. *Social Media in Rural China.* London: UCL Press.

References

Ahern, E. 1973. *The Cult of the Dead in a Chinese Village*. Stanford, CA: Stanford University Press.

Ahern, E. 1982. *Chinese Ritual and Politics*. Cambridge: Cambridge University Press.

Ang, I. 1993. 'To be or not to be Chinese: Diaspora, culture and postmodern ethnicity.' *Asian Journal of Social Science* 21 (1): 1–17.

Avakian, A. 1998. *Through the Kitchen Window: Women explore the intimate meanings of food and cooking*. Boston, MA: Beacon Press.

Baity, P. C. 1975. *Religion in a Chinese Town*. Taipai: Orient Cultural Service.

Baker, H. 1979. *Chinese Family and Kinship*. New York: Columbia University Press.

Barry, C.T. et al. 2015. 'Let me take a selfie: Associations between self-photography, narcissism, and self-esteem.' *Psychology of Popular Media Culture*. Advance online publication. http://dx.doi.org/10.1037/ppm0000089

Barthes, R. 1981. *Camera Lucida: Reflections on photography*. New York: Hill and Wang.

Benjamin, W. 1970. *Illuminations*. London: Jonathan Cape.

Bascom, W. 1954. 'Four functions of folklore.' *The Journal of American Folklore* 67 (266): 333–49.

Bell, S. and Coleman, S., eds. 1999. *The Anthropology of Friendship,* Oxford: Berg.

Bian, Y. et al. 2001. 'Communist Party membership and regime dynamics in China.' *Social Forces* 79(3): 805–41.

boyd, D. 2008. 'Facebook's privacy trainwreck: Exposure, invasion, and social convergence.' *The International Journal of Research into New Media Technologies* 14 (1): 13–20.

boyd, D. 2010. 'Streams of content, limited attention: The flow of information through social media.' *Educause Review* 45 (5): 26–36.

Brady, A. 2009. *Marketing dictatorship: Propaganda and thought work in contemporary China*. Lanham, MD: Rowman & Littlefield.

Bryant, F.B. 2003. 'Savoring beliefs inventory (SBI): A scale for measuring beliefs about savoring.' *Journal of Mental Health* 12 (2): 175–96.

Bryant, F.B. and Veroff, J. 2007. *Savoring: A new model of positive experience*. Mahwah, NJ: Lawrence Erlbaum Associates Publishers.

Bucholtz, M. 2002. 'Youth and cultural practice.' *Annual Review of Anthropology* 31 (1): 525–52.

Burmark, L. 2002. *Visual Literacy: Learn to see, see to learn*. Alexandria, VA: Association for Supervision & Curriculum Development.

Carroll, E. and Romano, J. 2010. *Your Digital Afterlife: When Facebook, Flickr and Twitter are your estate, what's your legacy?* Berkeley, CA: New Riders.

Chan, A, 2002. 'The culture of survival: Lives of migrant workers through the prism of private letters.' Link, Perry, Madsen, R.P. and Pickowicz, P.G., eds. *Popular China: Unofficial culture in a globalizing society*. Lanham, MD: Rowman & Littlefield. 163–88.

Chan, K. 2013. 'China, internal migration.' Ness, I., ed. *The Encyclopedia of Global Migration*. Oxford: Blackwell Publishing Ltd.

Chan, K. and Zhang, L. 1999. 'The *hukou* system and rural–urban migration: Processes and changes.' *The China Quarterly* 160: 818–55.

Chang, K.C., ed. 1977. *Food in Chinese Culture: Anthropological and historical perspective*. London, New York: Yale University Press.

Chau, A. 2006. *Miraculous Response: Doing popular religion in contemporary China*. Stanford, CA: Stanford University Press.

Chen, J. and Dickson, B. J. 2008. 'Allies of the state: Democratic support and regime support among China's private entrepreneurs.' *The China Quarterly* 196: 780–804.

Chen, X. 2013. 'The rising cost of stability.' *Journal of Democracy* 24 (1): 57–64.

Chen, X. and Peng, H. A. 2011. 'Internet police in China: Regulation, scope and myths.' Herold, D. and Marolt, P., eds. *Online Society in China: Creating, celebrating, and instrumentalising the online carnival*. London and New York: Routledge. 40–52.

Cheng, T. and Sedlen, M. 1994. 'The origins and social consequences of China's *hukou* system.' *The China Quarterly* 139: 329–50.

'China's Floating Migrants.' 2007. LSE Migration Studies Unit, Working Papers. http://www.lse.ac.uk/government/research/resgroups/MSU/documents/workingPapers/WP_2011_07.pdf (accessed on 17 October 2015)

Chiu, C. et al. 2012. 'Understanding social media in China.' *McKinsey Quarterly*. http://asia.udp.cl/Informes/2012/chinamedia.pdf

Chow, K. 1994. *The Rise of Confucian Ritualism in Late Imperial China: Ethics, classics, and lineage discourse*. Stanford, CA: Stanford University Press.

Chua, A. 2011. *Battle Hymn of the Tiger Mother*. London, Berlin, New York, Sydney: Bloomsbury Publishing.

Clayton, R., Steven, J. et al. 2006. 'Ignoring the Great Firewall of China.' *Privacy Enhancing Technologies* Lecture Notes in Computer Science 4258: 20–35.

CNNIC, 2015. 'Statistical report on internet development in China.' http://www1.cnnic.cn/IDR/ReportDownloads/201507/P020150720486421654597.pdf

Cocking, D. and Matthews, S. 2000. 'Unreal friends.' *Ethics and Information Technology* 2 (4): 223–31.

Cohen, A. and Jaw, Y. 1977. 'A Chinese temple keeper talks about Chinese folk religion.' *Asian Folklore Studies* 36 (1): 1–17.

Cohen, M. 1969. 'Agnatic kinship in south Taiwan.' *Ethnology* 15: 237–92.

Cohen, M. 1976. *House United, House Divided: The Chinese family in Taiwan* NY: Columbia University Press.

Cohen, M. 1990. 'Lineage organization in north China.' *The Journal of Asian Studies* 49 (3): 509–34.

Cohen, P.A. 1997. *History in Three Keys: The boxers as event, experience, and myth*. New York: Columbia University Press.

Coltrane, S. 1992. 'The micropolitics of gender in nonindustrial societies.' *Gender & Society* 6 (1): 86–107.

Croll, E. and Croll, E. J. 1981. *The Politics of Marriage in Contemporary China*. Cambridge: Cambridge University Press.

Daft, R.L. and Lengel, R.H. 1986. 'Organizational information requirements, media richness and structural design.' *Management Science* 32 (5): 554–71.

Dai, X, 2003. 'ICTs in China's development strategy.' Hughes, C. and Wacker, G., eds. *China and the Internet: Politics of the digital leap forward*. London: Routledge.

Davenport, T. and Beck, J. 2001. *The Attention Economy: Understanding the new currency of business*. Boston, MA: Harvard Business School Press.

Davin, D. 1997. 'Migration, women and gender issues in contemporary China.' *Floating Population and Migration in China*. Sharping, T., ed. Hamburg: Institut fur Asienkunde.

Deibert, R.J. 2002. 'Dark guests and great firewalls: The internet and Chinese security policy.' *The Society for the Psychological Study of Social Issues*. 58 (1): 143–59.

Démurger, S. and Xu, H. 2015. 'Left-behind children and return migration in China.' *IZA Journal of Migration*. http://www.izajom.com/content/pdf/s40176-015-0035-x.pdf

Dickson, B. 2008. *Wealth into Power: The communist party's embrace of China's private sector*. New York: Cambridge University Press.

Dikotter, F. 2007. *Things Modern: Material culture and everyday life in China*. New York: Hurst & Company.

Ding, Z. et al. 2013. 'Measuring the spreadability of users in microblogs.' *Journal of Zhejiang University SCIENCE*. 14 (9): 701–10.

Donald. E.M. 1989. *Religion in China Today: Policy and practice*. Maryknoll, NY: Orbis Books.

Dunfee, T. and Warren, D. 2001. 'Is guanxi ethical? A normative analysis of doing business in China.' *Journal of Business Ethics* 32 (3): 191–204.

Ebrey, P.B. 1993. *The Inner Quarters: Marriages and the lives of Chinese women in the Song period*. Berkeley, CA: University of California Press.

Eisingerich, A.B. et al. 2015. 'Why recommend a brand face-to-face but not on Facebook? How word-of-mouth on online social sites differs from traditional word-of-mouth.' *Journal of Consumer Psychology* 25 (1):120–8.

Elder, A. 2014. 'Excellent online friendships: An Aristotelian defense of social media.' *Ethics and Information Technology* 16 (4): 287–97.

Eng, K. 2006. 'Moralising ancestors as social-moral capital: A study of a transnational Chinese lineage.' *Journal of Social Science* 34 (2): 243–63.

Esherick, J. and Rankin, M. 1990. *Chinese Local Elites and Patterns of Dominance.* Berkeley, CA and Oxford: University of California Press.

Fan C. 2008. *China on the Move: Migration, the state, and the household.* Abingdon: Routledge.

Fan, C. 1997. 'Uneven development and beyond: Regional development theory in post-Mao China.' *International Journal of Urban and Regional Research* 21 (4): 620–39.

Fan, C. 2003. 'Rural–urban migration and gender division of labor in transitional China.' *International Journal of Urban and Regional Research* 27 (1): 24–47.

Fan, C. and Huang, Y. 1998. 'Waves of rural brides: Female marriage migraine in China.' *Annals of the Association Geographers* 88 (2): 227–51.

Fan, C.C. and Chen, C. 2014. 'The new-generation migrant workers in China.' *Rural Migration in Urban China, Enclaves and Transient Urbanism.* Wu, Fulong et al., eds. New York and London: Routledge.

Fan, Y. 2002. 'Guanxi's consequences: Personal gains at social cost.' *Journal of Business Ethics* 38 (4): 371–80.

Farris, C. 1995. 'A semiotic analysis of *sajiao* as a gender marked communication style in Chinese.' *Unbound Taiwan: Close-ups from a distance.* Johnson. M. and Chiu, F., eds. Chicago: Centre for East Asian Studies. 1–29.

Fei, X. 1939. *Peasant Life in China: A field study of country life in the Yangtze valley.* London: Routledge and Kegan Paul.

Feng, G. and Guo, Z. 2013. 'Tracing the route of China's internet censorship: An empirical study.' *Telematics and Informatics* 30 (4): 335–45.

Feng, W. et al. 2002. 'Rural migrants in Shanghai: Living under the shadow of socialism.' *International Migration Review* 36 (2): 520–45.

Fong, V. 2004. *Only Hope: Coming of age under China's one-child policy.* Stanford, CA: Stanford University Press.

Foster, H., ed. 1988. *Vision and Visuality.* Seattle, WA: Bay Press.

Franceschini, I. and Negro, G. 2014. 'The "Jasmine revolution" in China: The limits of the cyber-utopia.' *Postcolonial Studies.* 17 (1): 23–35.

Freeman, M., ed. 1967. 'Ancestor worship: Two aspects of the Chinese case.' *Social Organization: Essays Presented to Raymond Firth.* London: Frank Cass. 85–104.

Freeman, M. 1957. *Lineage Organization in Southeastern China.* London: Athlone Press.

Freeman, M., ed. 1970. *Family and Kinship in Chinese Society.* Stanford, CA: Stanford University Press.

Fried, M, 1969. *Fabric of Chinese Society,* New York: Octagon Books.

Fröding, B. and Peterson, M. 2012. 'Why virtual friendship is no genuine friendship.' *Ethics and Information Technology* 14 (3): 201–7.

Gaetano, A. 2008. 'Sexuality in diasporic space: Rural-to-urban migrant women negotiating gender and marriage in contemporary China.' *Gender, Place and Culture* 15 (6): 629–45.

Gaetano, A. 2014. '"Leftover women": Postponing marriage and renegotiating womanhood in urban China.' *Journal of Research in Gender Studies* 2: 124–49.

Gaetano, A. and Jacka, T. 2013. *On the Move: Women and rural-to-urban migration in contemporary China.* New York: Columbia University Press.

Gao, Q. et. al. 2012. 'A comparative study of users' microblogging behavior on Sina Weibo and Twitter.' Mastiff et al., eds. *User Modeling, Adaptation and Personalization.* Heidelberg: Springer-Verlag. Lecture Notes in Computer Science 7379: 88–101.

Gate, H. 1987. 'Money for the Gods.' *Modern China* 13 (3): 259–77.

Goffman, E. 1975. *Frame Analysis.* Harmondsworth: Penguin.

Goffman, E. 1990. *The Presentation of Self in Everyday Life.* London: Penguin.

Gold, T. et al. 2002. *Social Connections in China.* Cambridge: Cambridge University Press.

Goodkind, D. and West, L. A. 2002. 'China's floating population: Definition, data and recent findings.' *Urban Studies* 39 (12): 2237–50.

Goodman, D. 2008. *The New Rich in China: Future rules, present lives.* Abingdon: Routledge.

Graves, L. 2009. 'The affordances of blogging: A case study in culture and technological effects.' *Journal of Communication Inquiry* 31: 331–46. http://dx.doi.org/10.1177/0196859907305446.

Greenhalgh, S. 2003. 'Planned births, unplanned persons: "Population" in the making of Chinese modernity.' *American Ethnologist*. 30 (2): 196–215.

Guan, S. 1995. *Cross-Culture Communication and English Learning*. Beijing: Beijing University Press. 37–41.

Gupta, S. and Dhillon, I. 2014. 'Can Xiaomi shake the global smartphone industry with an innovative "services-based business model"?' *AIMA Journal of Management & Research* 8 (3/4). https://apps.aima.in/ejournal_new/articlesPDF/338-Sonam%20Gupta.pdf

Hao, P. et al. 2013. 'Spatial analyses of the urban village development process in Shenzhen, China.' *International Journal of Urban and Regional Research* 37 (6): 2177–97.

Harrell, S. 1977. 'Modes of belief in Chinese folk religion.' *Journal for the Scientific Study of Religion*. 16 (1): 55–65.

Harrell, S. 1987. 'The concept of fate in Chinese folk ideology.' *Modern China*. 13 (1): 90–109.

Harrell, S. and Dickey, S. 1985. 'Dowry systems in complex societies.' *Ethnology* 34: 105–20.

Hartup, W. 1995. 'The three faces of friendship.' *Journal of Social and Personal Relationships* 12 (4): 569–74.

Harwit, E. and Clark, D. 2008. 'Government policy and political control over China's Internet.' Damm, J. and Thomas, S., eds. 2008. *Chinese Cyberspace: Technological Changes and Political Effects*. New York and London: Routledge. 11–37.

Herod, D. and Marolt P., eds. 2011. *Online Society in China: Creating, celebrating, and instrumentalising the online carnival*. New York: Routledge.

Hirshleifer, J. 1980. 'Privacy: Its origin, function, and future.' *The Journal of Legal Studies* 9 (4). 649–64.

Hjorth, L. 2005. 'Odours of mobility: Mobile phones and Japanese cute culture in the Asia-Pacific'. *Journal of Intercultural Studies* 26 (1–2): 39–55.

Hock, Y. 1997. 'Chinese family religion and world religion.' *Singapore Bahá'í Studies Review*, 2: 91–119.

Hogan, B. and Wellman, B. 2014. 'The relational self-portrait: Selfies meet social networks.' Graham, M. and Dutton, W. H., eds. *Society and the Internet: How networks of information and communication are changing our lives*. Oxford, United Kingdom: Oxford University Press. 53–66.

Holzman, D. 1998. 'The place of filial piety in ancient China.' *Journal of the American Oriental Society* 118 (2): 185–99.

Hu, H. 1944. 'The Chinese concept of "face".' *American Anthropologist* 46 (1): 45–64.

Hu, W. and Grove, C. L. 1999. *Encountering the Chinese: A guide for Americans*. Yarmouth, MA: Intercultural Press.

Hu, X. 2012. 'China's "new generation" rural–urban migrants: Migration, motivation and migration patterns.' *Migration Information Source*. http://papers.ssrn.com/sol3/papers.cfm?abstract_id=1978546

Hughes, C.R. and Wacker, G. 2003. *China and the Internet: Politics of the digital leap forward*, London: Routledge.

Hung, C. 1985. *Going to the People: Chinese intellectuals and folk literature, 1918–1937*. Harvard, MA: Harvard University Press.

Hunt, A. 2011. 'What's that cute and pouty, pretty and bratty face? It's *sajiao*.' http://english.cri.cn/7146/2011/10/09/2702s661875.htm

Hwang, K. 1987. 'Face and favor: The Chinese power game.' *The American Journal of Sociology* 92 (4): 944–74.

Hwang, K. 2005. *Confucian Relationalism: Reflections on culture and the reconstruction of paradigm*. Taipei: National Taiwan University Press.

Jacobs, J. 1982. 'The concept of *guanxi* and local politics in a rural Chinese cultural setting.' Greenblatt, S. et al., eds. *Social Interaction in Chinese Society*. Westport, CT: Praeger Publishers. 209–36.

Jankowiak, W. 2002. 'Proper man and proper women: Parental affection in the Chinese family.' Browned, S. and Wasserstrom, J., eds. *Chinese Femininities/Chinese Masculinities: A reader*. Berkeley, CA: University of California Press. 361–81.

Jenkins, H. 2006. *Convergence Culture: Where old and new media collide*. NY: New York University Press.

Jin, H. et al. 2005. 'Regional decentralization and fiscal incentives: Federalism, Chinese style.' *Journal of Public Economics* 89: 1719–42.

Jing, J. ed. 2000. *Feeding China's Little Emperors: Food, children, and social change*. Stanford, CA: Stanford University Press.

Kim, U. et al., eds. 1994. *Individualism and Collectivism: Theory, method and applications*. Newbury Park, CA: Sage.

King, G. et al. 2013. 'How censorship in China allows government criticism but silences collective expression.' *American Political Science Review* 107 (2): 326–43.

Kipnis, A.B. 2011. *Governing Educational Desire: Culture, politics, and schooling in China*. Chicago: University of Chicago Press.

Kipnis, A.B. 2001. 'Articulating school countercultures.' *Anthropology & Education Quarterly* 32 (4): 472–92.

Kjeldgaard, D. and Askegaard, S. 2006. 'The globalization of youth culture: The global youth segment as structures of common difference.' *Journal of Consumer Research* 33 (2): 231–47.

Kluver, R. and Chen, Y. 2005. 'The internet in China: A meta-review of research.' *The Information Society* 21 (4): 301–8.

Knight, J. and Yueh, L. 2004. 'Job mobility of residents and migrants in urban China.' *Journal of Comparative Economics* 32 (4): 637–60.

KPMG 2014. 'E-commerce in China: Driving a new consumer culture.' KPMG Global China Practice report. January.

Kuhn, P. 1990. *Soulstealers: The Chinese sorcery scare of 1768*. London, Cambridge, MA: Harvard University Press.

Kwek, A. and Lee, Y. 2013. 'Consuming tourism experiences.' *Journal of Vacation Marketing* 19 (4): 301–15.

Lagerkvist, J. 2010. *After the Internet before Democracy: Competing norms in Chinese media and society*. Bern: Peter Lang.

Lam, K. 2003. *Earnings Advantage of Party Members in Urban China*. Hong Kong: Business Research Centre, School of Business, Hong Kong Baptist University.

Lan, P. 2014. 'Segmented Incorporation: The second generation of rural migrants in Shanghai.' *The China Quarterly* 217: 243–65.

Lee, N. 2014. *Facebook Nation: Total information awareness*. New York: Springer.

Lester, P. 2006. 'Syntactic theory of visual communication'. Fullerton, CA: California State University. http://paulmartinlester.info/writings/viscomtheory.html

Levitt, P. 1998. 'Social remittances: Migration driven local-level forms of cultural diffusion.' *International Migration Review* 32 (4): 926–48.

Li, B. 2006. 'Floating population or urban citizens? Status, social provision and circumstances of rural–urban migrants in China.' *Social Policy & Administration* 40 (20), II: 174–95.

Li, D. 1998. 'Changing incentives of the Chinese bureaucracy.' *The American Economic Review*. 88 (2): 393–7.

Li, J. and Hsieh, Y. 2004. 'Traditional Chinese food technology and cuisine.' *Asia Pacific Journal of Clinical Nutrition* 13 (2): 147–55.

Li, P. and Tian, F. 2010. 'The new generation migrant workers; social attitudes and behavioral choices.' *Chinese Journal of Sociology* 31 (3): 1–23.

Li, R. and Shiu, A. 2012. 'Internet diffusion in China: A dynamic panel data analysis.' *Telecommunications Policy* 36: 872–87.

Lieberthal, K. and Burns, J.P. 1995. *Governing China: From revolution through reform*. New York: Norton.

Lindner, K.A. 2008. 'The effects of Facebook "stalking" on romantic partners' satisfaction, jealousy, and insecurity.' http://indigo.uic.edu/bitstream/handle/10027/9569/Lindner_Katherine.pdf?sequence=1

Lip, E. 1995. *Feng Shui: Environments of power: A study of Chinese architecture*. London: Academy Editions.

Liz, T. 2011. 'I didn't make it for you.' *The World of China* 1 (5): 42–9.

Lü, Y. 2005. 'Privacy and data privacy issues in contemporary China.' *Ethics and Information Technology* 7 (1): 7–15.

Luo, Y. 1997. 'Guanxi: Principle, philosophies, and implications.' *Human System Management* 16 (1): 43–51.

Madianou, M. and Miller, D. 2012. *Migration and New Media*. London: Routledge.

Mann, S. 2000. 'The male bond in Chinese history and culture.' *The American Historical Review* 105 (5): 1600–14.

Mauss, M. 1950. *The Gift: The form and reason for exchange in archaic societies.* New York: Norton.

McAdams, D.P. 1993. *The Stories We Live by: Personal myths and the making of the self.* New York and London: Guilford Press.

McDonald, T. 2016. *Social Media in Rural China.* London: UCL Press.

McDougall, B. 2001. 'Privacy in contemporary China: A survey of student opinion, June 2000.' *China Information* 15 (2): 140–52.

McDougall, B. and Hansson, A., eds. 2002. *Chinese Concepts of Privacy.* Vol. 55. Leiden: Brill Academic Publishers.

McDowell, L. 1999. *Gender, Identity and Place.* Minneapolis: University of Minnesota Press.

Meraz, S. 2009. 'Is there an elite hold? Traditional media to social media agenda setting influence in blog networks.' *Journal of Computer-Mediated Communication* 14: 682–707.

Miller, D. and Sinanan, J. 2014. *Webcam.* Cambridge: Polity.

Miller, D. et. al. 2016. *How the World Changed Social Media.* London: UCL Press.

Min, H. and Eades, J. 1995. 'Brides, bachelors and brokers: The marriage market in rural Anhui in an era of economic reform.' *Modern Asian Studies* 29: 841–69.

Morduch, J. and Sicular, T. 2000. 'Politics, growth, and inequality in rural China: Does it pay to join the Party?' *Journal of Public Economics* 77 (3): 331–56.

Morley, L. 2000. 'The micropolitics of gender in the learning society.' *Higher Education in Europe* 25 (2): 229–35.

Mukai, C. P. 1999. 'Chinese perspectives.' *Geriatric Nursing* 20 (1): 18–22.

Mullis, E. 2008. 'Toward a Confucian ethic of the gift.' *Dao* 7 (2): 175–94.

Murphy, R., ed. 2009. *Labour Migration and Social Development in Contemporary China.* New York and London: Routledge.

Murphy, R. 2004. 'Turning peasants into modern Chinese citizens: "Population quality" discourse, demographic transition and primary education.' *The China Quarterly* 177: 1–20.

Ngai, P. 2003. 'Subsumption or consumption? The phantom of consumer revolution in "globalizing" China.' *Cultural Anthropology* 18 (4): 469–92.

Nicolescu, R. 2016. *Social Media in Southeast Italy.* London: UCL Press.

O'Brien, K. and Li, L. 2000. 'Accommodating "democracy" in a one-party state: Introducing village elections in China.' *The China Quarterly* 162: 465–89.

Oetzel, J. G. and Ting-Toomey, S. 2003. 'Face concerns in interpersonal conflict: A cross-cultural empirical test of the face negotiation theory.' *Communication Research* 30 (6): 599–624.

Oreglia, E. 2013. 'From farm to Farmville: Circulation, adoption, and use of ICT between urban and rural China'. PhD thesis. Berkeley, CA: University of California. http://digitalassets.lib.berkeley.edu/etd/ucb/text/Oreglia_berkeley_0028E_13617.pdf

Ortner, S. 1997. *Making Gender: The politics and erotics of culture.* Boston, MA: Beacon Press.

Ortner, S. and Whitehead, H., eds. 1981. *Sexual Meanings: The cultural construction of gender and sexuality.* Cambridge: Cambridge University Press.

Pan, I. 1993. 'Renao: A socio-psychological phenomenon of Chinese.' *Indigenous Psychological Research* 1: 330–7.

Pasternak, B. 1986. *Marriage and Fertility in Tianjin, China: Fifty years of transition.* Honolulu: East-West Population Institute.

Paul-Choudhury, S. 2011. 'Digital legacy: The fate of your online soul.' *New Scientist* 210.2809: 41–3.

Peacock, J.L. 1968. *Rites of Modernization: Symbolic and social aspects of Indonesian proletarian drama.* Chicago: University of Chicago Press.

Pearson, M. 1997. *China's New Business Elite: The political consequence of economic reform.* Berkeley, CA: University of California Press.

Pillsbury, B. 1978. '"Doing the month": Confinement and convalescence of Chinese women after childbirth.' *Social Science & Medicine. Part B: Medical Anthropology* 12: 11–22.

Pimental, E. 2000. 'Just how do I love thee? Marital relations in urban China.' *Journal of Marriage and the Family* 62 (1): 32–47.

Potter, S. and Potter, J. 1990. *China's Peasants: The anthropology of a revolution.* Cambridge: Cambridge University Press.

Potter, S.H. 1983. 'The position of peasants in modern China.' *Modern China* 9 (4): 465–99.

Poutziouris, P. et al. 2002. 'Chinese entrepreneurship: The development of small family firms in China.' *Journal of Small Business and Enterprise Development* 9 (4): 383–99.

Prensky, M. 2001. 'Digital natives, digital immigrants.' *On the Horizon* 9 (5): 1–6.

Qian, W. et al. 2007. 'Chinese cultural values and gift-giving behaviour.' *Journal of Consumer Marketing* 24 (4): 214–28.

Qiang, C.Z. 2007. *China's Information Revolution: Managing the economic and social transformation.* World Bank Publications.

Qiu, J. L. 2008. 'Working-class ICTs, migrants, and empowerment in South China.' *Asian Journal of Communication* 18 (4): 333–47.

Qiu, J. L. 2009. *Working-Class Network Society: Communication technology and the information have-less in urban China.* Cambridge, MA: MIT Press.

Qiu, Z. 2013. 'Cuteness as a subtle strategy: Urban female youth and the online *feizhuliu* culture in contemporary China.' *Culture Studies* 27 (2): 225–41.

Riley, N. 1994. 'Interwoven lives: Parents, marriage, and guanxi in China.' *Journal of Marriage and the Family* 56: 791–803.

Roberts, M. 1976. *Three Kingdoms: China's epic drama.* New York: Alfred Knopf.

Romero, D. et al. 2011. 'Influence and passivity in social media.' *Machine Learning and Knowledge Discovery in Databases.* Berlin: Springer. 18–33.

Rose, G. 2012. *Visual Methodologies: An introduction to research with visual materials.* London: Sage.

Rowe, W. 2001. *Saving the World: Chen Hongmou and elite consciousness in Eighteenth-Century China.* Stanford, CA: Stanford University Press.

Ruan, D. 1993. 'Interpersonal networks and workplace controls in urban China.' *Australian Journal of Chinese Affairs* 29: 89–105.

Sabo, D. and Panepinto, J. 1990. 'Football ritual and the social reproduction of masculinity.' Messner, M. et al., eds. *Sport, Men, and the Gender Order: Critical feminist perspectives.* Champaign, IL: Human Kinetics Publishers. 115–26.

Safran, W. 1991. 'Diasporas in modern societies: Myths of homeland and return.' *Diaspora: A Journal of Transnational Studies* 1 (1): 83–99.

Saltz, J. 2014. 'Art at arm's length: A history of the selfie.' available at http://www.vulture.com/2014/01/history-of-the-selfie.html

Sanderson, S. 2013. *Sociological Worlds: Comparative and historical readings on society.* New York and London: Routledge.

Sangren, P.S. 1983. 'Female gender in Chinese religious symbols: *Kuan yin, ma tsu,* and the "eternal mother"'. *Signs* 9 (1): 4–25.

Saunders, D. 2010. *Arrival City: How the Largest Migration in History is Reshaping our World.* London: William Heinemann.

Schlegel, A. and Eloul, R. 1988. 'Marriage transactions: Labor, property, status.' *American Anthropologist* 90: 291–309.

Shen, Y. 2009. 'The reasons for the popularity of the anti-mainstream culture.' *Journal of Zhangzhou Normal University (Philosophy and Social Science)* 2: 139–42.

Shirk, S. 2011. *Changing Media, Changing China.* Oxford: Oxford University Press.

Shirky, C. 2008. *Here Comes Everybody: The power of organizing without organizations.* New York: Penguin.

Shirky, C. 2011. 'The political power of social media.' *Foreign affairs* 90 (1): 28–41.

Simmel, G. 1906. 'The sociology of secrecy and secret societies.' *American Journal of Sociology* 11 (4): 441–98.

Simmel, G.1950. *The Sociology of Georg Simmel.* New York, Free Press.

Skinner, G.W. 1964. 'Marketing and social structure in rural China, Part I.' *The Journal of Asian Studies* 24 (1): 3–43.

Smart, A. 1999. 'Expression of interest: Friendship and *guanxi* in Chinese society'. *The Anthropology of Friendship,* Bell, S. and Coleman, S., eds. Oxford: Berg. 119–36.

Sontag, S. 1978. *On Photography.* London: Allen Lane.

Stafford, C. 1995. *The Roads of Chinese Childhood: Learning and identification in Angang.* Cambridge: Cambridge University Press.

Sun, H. 2012. *Cross-Culture Technology Design: Creating culture-sensitive technology for local users.* Oxford: Oxford University Press.

Sung, L. 1981. 'Property and family division.' Ahern, E. and Gates, H., eds. *Anthropology of Taiwanese Society.* Stanford, CA: Stanford University Press.

Tai, Z. 2006. *The Internet in China: Cyberspace and civil society.* New York, Abingdon: Routledge.

The Economist, 2015. 'Little match children: Children bear a disproportionate share of the hidden cost of China's growth.' 17 October.

Thompson, J.B. 1995. *Media and Modernity: A social theory of the media.* Stanford, CA: Stanford University Press.

Tice, W. et al. 1995. 'When modesty prevails: Different favorability of self-presentation to friends and strangers.' *Journal of Personality and Social Psychology* 69: 1120–38.

To, S. 2013. 'Understanding *sheng nu* ('leftover women'): The phenomenon of late marriage among Chinese professional women.' *Symbolic Interaction* 36 (1): 1–20.

Tong, J. 2015. 'The formation of an agonistic public sphere: emotions, the internet and news media in China.' *China Information* 29 (3): 333–51.

Tong, S. et al. 2008. 'Too much of a good thing? The relationship between number of friends and interpersonal impressions on Facebook.' *Journal of Computer-Mediated Communication* 13 (3): 531–49.

Tsai, K. 2007. *Capitalism without Democracy: The private sector in contemporary China.* Ithaca, NY: Cornell University Press.

Tse, E. et al. 2009. '*shan zhai* a Chinese phenomenon.' *Strategy* http://www.strategyand.pwc.com/media/file/Shan_Zhai_AChinese_Phenomenon.pdf

Tu, W. 1985. *Confucian Thought: Selfhood as a creative transformation.* Albany, NY: State University of New York Press.

Turkle, S. 2011. *Alone Together.* New York: Basic Books.

Vallor, S. 2012. 'Flourishing on Facebook: Virtue friendship and new social media.' *Ethics and Information Technology* 14 (3): 185–99.

Van Dijck, J. 2007. *Mediated Memories in the Digital Age.* Stanford, CA: Stanford University Press.

Van Doorn, N. and Van Zoonen, L. 2008. 'Theorizing gender and the Internet: Past, present, and future.' *The Routledge Handbook of Internet Politics* (2008): 261–74.

Venkatraman, S. Forthcoming. *Social Media in South India.* London: UCL Press.

Vogt, C. and Chen, P. 2001. 'Feminisms and the internet.' *Peace Review* 13 (3): 371–74.

Wallis, C. 2013. *Technomobility in China: Young migrant women and mobile phones.* New York and London: New York University Press.

Wang, D. and Cai, F. 2009. 'Migration and poverty alleviation in China.' *Labour Migration and Social Development in Contemporary China.* Murphy, R. ed. New York and London: Routledge. 17–46.

Wang, H. 2011. *Protecting Privacy in China: Research on China's privacy standards and the possibility of establishing the right to privacy and the information privacy protection legislation in modern China.* Berlin: Springer Science & Business Media.

Warden, C. and Chen, F. 2009. 'When hot and noisy is good: Chinese values of renal and consumption metaphors.' *Asia Pacific Journal of Marketing and Logistics* 21 (2): 216–31.

Watson, J. 1982. 'Chinese kinship reconsidered: Anthropological perspectives on historical research.' *The China Quarterly* 92: 589–622.

Watson, J.L. 1987. 'From the common pot: Feasting with equals in Chinese society.' *Anthropos* 1987 (82): 389–401.

Watson, R. 1988. 'Remembering the dead: Graves and politics in southeastern China'. *Death ritual in Late Imperial and Modern China* 205: 140–3.

Wijekumar, K.J. et al. 2006. 'Technology affordances: The "real story" in research with K-12 and undergraduate learners.' *British Journal of Educational Technology* 37 (2): 191–209.

Wolf, M. 1972. *Women and the Family in Rural Taiwan.* Stanford, CA: Stanford University Press.

Wolf. A.P. 1974. 'Gods, ghosts and ancestors.' Wolf, A.P. ed. *Religion and Ritual in Chinese Society.* Stanford, CA: Stanford University Press. 131–82.

Wu, F. et al., eds. 2014. *Rural Migration in Urban China: Enclaves and transient urbanism.* New York and London: Routledge.

Wu, J. 2014. 'How WeChat, the most popular social network in China, cultivates wellbeing.' Master of Applied Psychology, Philadelphia, PA: UPENN.

Xiao, Q. 2011. 'The battle for the Chinese internet.' *Journal of Democracy* 22 (2): 47–61.

Xu, X. and Whyte, M. 1990. 'Love matches and arranged marriage: A Chinese replication.' *Journal of Marriage and the Family* 52: 709–22.

Xu, X. et al. 2000. 'Social and political assortative mating in urban China.' *Journal of Family Issues* 21 (1): 47–77.

Xue, X. 2003. *The Good Women of China: Hidden voices.* London: Random House.

Xue, X. 2015. *Buy Me the Sky: The remarkable truth of China's one-child generations.* London: Ebury Publishing.

Yan, Y. 1996. *The Flow of Gifts: Reciprocity and social networks in a Chinese village.* Stanford, CA: Stanford University Press.

Yan, Y. 1997. 'The triumph of conjugality: Structural transformation of family relations in a Chinese village.' *Ethnology* 36 (3): 191–217.

Yan, Y. 1999. 'Rural youth and youth culture in north China.' *Culture, Medicine, and Psychiatry.* 23: 75–97.

Yan, Y. 2003. *Private Life under Socialism: Love, Intimacy, and Family Change in a Chinese Village, 1949–1999.* Stanford, CA: Stanford University Press.

Yan, Y. 2005. 'The individual and transformation of bridewealth in rural north China.' *Journal of the Royal Anthropological Institute* 11: 637–58.

Yan, Y. 2009 *The Individualization of Chinese Society.* Vol. 77. Oxford: Berg.

Yan, Y. 2013. 'The drive for success and the ethics of the striving individual.' Stafford, C. ed. *Ordinary Ethics in China.* New York and London: Bloomsbury Academic. 263–89.

Yang, F. 2011. *Religion in China: Survival and revival under communist rule.* Oxford: Oxford University Press.

Yang, G. 2003. 'The co-evolution of the internet and civil society in China.' *Asian Survey* 43 (3): 405–22.

Yang, M. 1989. 'The gift economy and state power in China.' *Comparative Studies in Society and History* 31 (1): 25–54.

Yang, M. 1994. *Gifts, Favors and Banquets: The Art of Social Relationships in China.* Ithaca: Cornell University Press.

Yang, P. et al. 2015. '*Diaosi* as infrapolitics: Scatological tropes, identity-making and cultural intimacy.' *Media, Culture & Society* 37 (2): 197–214.

Yu, C. 1979. 'Images of Kuan-yin in Chinese folk literature.' *Hanxue yanjiu* 8 (1): 221–86.

Zelier, V.A. 1997. *The Social Meaning of Money.* Princeton, NJ: Princeton University Press.

Zhang, L. 2001. 'Contesting crime, order and migrant spaces in Beijing.' Nancy N. et al., eds. *China Urban: Ethnographies of contemporary culture.* Durham, NC: Duke University Press. 201–27.

Zhang, L. 2006. 'Behind the great firewall: Decoding China's internet media policies from the inside.' *International Journal of Research into New Media Technologies* 12 (3): 271–91.

Zhang, X. and Zheng, Y., eds. 2009. *China's Information and Communications Technology Revolution: Social changes and state responses.* London: Routledge.

Zhang, X. and Li, G. 2003. 'Does *guanxi* matter to nonfarm employment?' *Journal of Comparative Economics* 31 (2): 315–31.

Zhao, S. 2005. 'China's pragmatic nationalism: Is it manageable?' *The Washington Quarterly* 29 (1): 131–44.

Zhao, Y. 'Leaving the countryside: Rural-to-urban migration decisions in China.' *The American Economic Review* 89 (2): 281–6.

Zheng, T. 2009. *Red lights: The lives of sex workers in postsocialist China.* Minneapolis and London: University of Minnesota Press.

Zhou, M. et al. 2014. 'Effects of parents' migration on the education of children left behind in rural China.' *Population and Development Review* 40 (2): 273–92.

Zhou, X. L. 2007. *Young Rebels in Contemporary Chinese Cinema.* Hong Kong: Hong Kong University Press.

Zhou, X. et al. 2011. 'The very high sex ratio in rural China: Impact on the psychosocial wellbeing of unmarried men.' *Social Science & Medicine* 73: 1422–7.

Zhu, W. et al. 2009. 'China's excess males, sex selective abortion and one child policy: Analysis of data from 2005 national inter census survey.' *British Medical Journal* 338: 920–3.

Zhu, Y. et al. 2012. 'Do migrants really save more? Understanding the impact of remittances on savings in rural China.' *Journal of Development Studies* 48 (5): 654–72.

Internet sources

'China celebrates Deng centenary.' BBC News 22 August 2004. http://news.bbc.co.uk/1/hi/world/asia-pacific/3587838.stm

'China cracks down on GRAFT.' *China Daily.* http://www.chinadaily.com.cn/china/2014crackongraft/

'Relief for migrant laborers.' *China Daily.* 6 December 2013. http://www.chinadaily.com.cn/en/doc/2003–12/06/content_287881.htm

'When a "phoenix man" meets a "peacock woman."' *China Daily*. 26 August 2009. http://www.chinadaily.com.cn/china/2009-08/26/content_8617800.htm

zhongguo shi nongcun hunlian: chunjie qijian pinfan xiangqin. Xinhua Net. 4 February 2014. http://news.xinhuanet.com/local/2014-02/04/c_119211913.htm

National Bureau of Statistics of China. 2016. 'China's economy realized a moderate but stable and sound growth in 2015'. http://www.stats.gov.cn/english/PressRelease/201601/t20160119_1306072.html

The 2013 Report of Chinese floating population development (2013 *zhongguo liudong renkou fazhan baogao*) http://www.moh.gov.cn/ldrks/s7847/201309/12e8cf0459de42c981c59e-827b87a27c.shtml

The 2014 report on China's migrant population development. Beijing: China Population Publishing House.

The 2014 report of World Press Freedom Index. http://rsf.org/index2014/en-index2014.php

The 2015 WeChat Impact Report http://www.199it.com/archives/398617.html

The 35th CNNIC statistical report on Internet Development in China. 2015. http://www1.cnnic.cn/AU/MediaC/rdxw/2015n/201502/t20150204_51650.htm

The 2013 Chinese national census of domestic migration. http://www.moh.gov.cn/zhuzhan/xwfbh/201309/12e8cf0459de42c981c59e827b87a27c.shtml

'The industrial China field site' (video footage of the field site). https://www.youtube.com/watch?v=jGmeWuFX2Sc

'The field work' (video of how the researcher conducted field work in GoodPath town). https://www.youtube.com/watch?v=-i3RDQfCV6g&list=PLVwGSavjGgEzPCcXI4txF2gY9pib-WeO4F&index=6

Visual ethnography website: www.visualethnographyxy.co.uk

James, G. 'Privacy vs. Secrecy.' Available at http://www.jamesgrubman.com/sites/default/files/Privacy-v-Secrecy.pdf

'What does Chinese social media look like?' McDonald, T. and Wang, X. at https://www.youtube.com/watch?v=5qROXrmyMbQ

FlorCruz, J. A. and Seu, L. 2014. 'From snail mail to 4G, China celebrates 20 years of internet connectivity.' CNN news report. http://edition.cnn.com/2014/04/23/world/asia/china-internet-20th-anniversary.

'Chinese government online.' *Xinhua News*. http://news.xinhuanet.com/politics/2010-06/08/c_12195450.htm

http://www.chinainternetwatch.com/14304/wechat-maus-reached-600-million-in-q2-2015/

http://www.slideshare.net/cxpartners/chinese-web-design-patterns-how-and-why-theyre-different

http://www.smashingmagazine.com/2010/03/showcase-of-web-design-in-china-from-imitation-to-innovation-and-user-centered-design/

http://www.szlh.gov.cn/main/xwzx/bkzy/21281.shtml

http://blog.imqq.com/how-to-calculate-qq-membership-level/

http://www.chinainternetwatch.com/15287/wechat-users-insights-2015/

http://www.chinainternetwatch.com/10939/wechat-dominates-apac-mobile-messaging-q3-2014/

http://a16z.com/2015/08/06/wechat-china-mobile-first/

http://www.chinainternetwatch.com/11765/wechat-users-reading-habits/

http://gbtimes.com/china/chinese-people-reading-much-less-east-asian-neighbours

http://www.emarketer.com/Article.aspx?R=1011578

http://www.chinainternetwatch.com/15287/wechat-users-insights-2015/

http://www.pri.org/stories/2014-08-10/if-you-use-wechat-china-wants-know-your-real-name

http://advicesacademy.com/how-to/ways-to-add-friends-on-wechat/

http://thenextweb.com/asia/2014/02/05/messaging-app-wechat-brings-chinese-new-year-traditions-into-the-mobile-era/

http://a16z.com/2015/08/06/wechat-china-mobile-first/

http://techcrunch.com/2015/04/24/why-wechat-city-services-is-a-game-changing-move-for-smartphone-adoption/

http://www.demandware.com/blog/2014/08/27/social-commerce-in-china/

'WeChat and Small Business' video. https://www.youtube.com/watch?v=WGuyM9eu9X4&index=4&list=PLVwGSavjGgEzPCcXI4txF2gY9pibWeO4F

http://chinamarketingtips.com/weibo-marketing-strategic-direction/

http://www.pewinternet.org/files/2013/05/PIP_TeensSocialMediaandPrivacy_PDF.pdf

http://news.xinhuanet.com/english2010/indepth/2011-11/22/c_131261763.htm

https://advocacy.globalvoicesonline.org/2013/07/09/targeting-rumors-on-chinas-sina-weibo/

http://www.theguardian.com/world/2013/sep/10/china-social-media-jail-rumours

http://www.economist.com/news/china/21594296-after-crackdown-microblogs-sensitive-online-discussion-has-shifted-weibo-wechat

http://www.goodchinabrand.com/8323200070en.html

http://www.ucl.ac.uk/why-we-post

Index

Lightning Source UK Ltd.
Milton Keynes UK
UKOW07f0819120916

282623UK00018B/21/P